The United States Merchant Marine in National Perspective

The United States Merchant Marine in National Perspective

James R. Barker
Temple, Barker & Sloane, Inc.

Robert Brandwein
Harbridge House, Inc.

Heath Lexington Books
D.C. Heath and Company
Lexington, Massachusetts

Table of Contents

List of Figures

List of Tables

Foreword

Fortunate is the individual, company, or industry that gets a second chance. The U.S. Merchant Marine is in that happy position. For years, this industry has survived either by eking out a precarious commercial existence or alternatively by serving in national emergencies. Its profits have been marginal. From time to time, it has been held up to ridicule for lackluster management, for feeding at the public trough, for having neglected advanced technology, and for setting its rates through a series of shipping conferences. It has been closely regulated not by one but by two Government agencies, and it is one of the few U.S. industries where most of its members were forced by law to buy their equipment in this country, regardless of cost or design.

In addition, there have been several critics in recent years who questioned whether it was necessary to have a U.S.-flag Merchant Marine at all. At one point the Pentagon indicated that it really did not need it for defense purposes. The build-up in Vietnam demonstrated the contrary, since the Merchant Marine lifted most of the tonnage to that theater; and sea lift, in spite of a considerable airlift, was the dominant form of transport. Other critics claimed that there appeared to be neither economic nor political justification for a U.S. merchant fleet.

If the thrust of the study which follows comes to pass, the industry is about to be rescued. It will be rescued not by some major technological invention or break-through but by a box, the simplest of devices, even when it is described as a container and its introduction as the "container revolution." This revolution also includes the use of ships carrying barges instead of boxes.

The burden of the analysis in the following study indicates that because of two advantages which containers provide—much greater ship utilization and lower cargo-handling costs ashore—the U.S. Merchant Marine will again be competitive along major trade routes, both in cost and service. A further conclusion is that by 1973-75 only full container or barge ships will be competitive on these heavy trade routes, thus making obsolete many breakbulk vessels.

Because of greater ship productivity with containerization—including less port time and the ability to provide equivalent service through fewer ports—the new ships which the study posits can generate far greater annual revenues at about the same wage costs as a comparable fleet of breakbulk vessels. This, in return, reduces the significance of wage costs to a relatively small proportion of total expense, which will allow the U.S.-flag fleet to compete vigorously with foreign-flag vessels and carry a greater share of U.S. foreign trade with greater benefits to the nation at lower subsidy costs.

Surely this is the genius of U.S. industry: that it adopts a system which can absorb the high standard of living it provides to its workers.

Of late this old trick seems not to have worked quite so well in international competition, since foreign countries have found out how to use the device as well or better. Nor will it in shipping if labor insists on increased manning scales or on out-of-line wage or fringe charges. And the past history of maritime labor-management relations does not encourage a belief that reasonable settlements can be made in future. Still it is permissable to hope—especially that union leaders will see that the future of the U.S.-flag Merchant Marine rests largely in producing a competitive product.

The description of the promise which containerization holds is, I believe, the richest part of the study. But there are other sections which economists and students of business will find illuminating, not least of which is an analysis of the structure and basic economics of the general cargo shipping industry. (The economics of tankers and dry bulk vessels appear to be somewhat different.) This study also documents the important past contributions of the U.S. Merchant Marine in such areas as balance of payments and national security. These benefits are compared to the costs incurred to place the role of the U.S. Merchant Marine in a national perspective. The specific quantification of net benefits to the nation over the past decade is an important analytical contribution to the sparse economic literature of the industry.

The study was originally undertaken by Harbridge House, Inc., for the Committee of American Steamship Lines which was merged into the American Institute of Merchant Shipping and became the Liner Council of the new organization. One has a right to be suspicious of commissioned studies as tending to "suppressio veri, suggestio falsi". However, in this case, the authors have presented the bitter with the sweet, and essentially their task has been made much easier by virtue of the promised benefits of containerization.

The U.S. shipping industry is a small one by conventional standards. At the same time, it has received comparatively little academic attention, and most of that has been highly critical. On the threshold of what could be a new era for the industry, this study will perhaps serve to balance the overly bleak pictures that have been painted in the past.

Paul W. Cherington
James J. Hill Professor of Transportation
Graduate School of Business Administration
Harvard University

Preface

This study of the U. S. Merchant Marine originated before the days when containerships were a regular part of international shipping. At the outset, the project was conceived as a traditional cost/benefit analysis of the U.S. Merchant Marine. As containerization began making an impact on the economic structure of the industry, it revealed new perspectives not simply for the future of the maritime industry but, paradoxically, for the analysis of the past.

Two factors became increasingly clear: first that the competitive position of the U. S. Merchant Marine has been misunderstood both by the public and by academic observers, and second, that these misconceptions have bred skepticism about the potential of the U. S.-flag fleet as a national resource. The scope of the study was enlarged therefore to present the Merchant Marine in the context of its commercial and governmental environment in order to clarify its economic structure.

This report is organized into four major parts. Chapter 2 outlines the historical economic environment of the U. S. Merchant Marine and the changes wrought by new technology. Chapter 3 develops the sources and quantifies the past industry contributions to national economic goals. Chapter 4 determines the effect of alternative government programs on the physical size of the fleet and the potential economic benefits of each alternative. Chapter 5 examines the importance of market share to the attainment of both commercial and national goals, the role of intermodalism in attaining the requisite trade levels, and the necessity for a partnership of industry and government to promote a vigorous U.S. Merchant Marine. An introductory summary of the analysis and conclusions precedes the text of the study as Chapter 1. Supporting appendixes, which include preliminary studies and documenting exhibits, are furnished at the close of the report.

While *The United States Merchant Marine in National Perspective* does provide basic insights into the creative possibilities for the maritime industry, it presents these potentials as challenges. Maintenance of present policies and practices by both industry and government cannot be justified by our findings, if the industry is to survive and prosper. Ultimately, this report can only name potentials and catalogue remedies; it must depend for its effect on the concerted actions of individuals who are convinced of the necessity for an effective international transportation system promoted by a powerful U. S. Merchant Marine.

James R. Barker
Robert Brandwein

Acknowledgements

This study was conducted by the professional staff of Harbridge House, Inc. for the American Institute of Merchant Shipping. Those staff members making significant contributions were Ruth L. Kleinfeld, Karen A. Reixach, John B. Schnapp, Lawrence Schwartz, and Robert B. Waldner. Because of the broad scope of our topic and the extended span of the study, our debts for assistance are many and profound.

Members and staff of AIMS were extremely generous in reviewing drafts and providing access to industry data. In particular, Albert E. May was an exceptionally able source of administrative support. A multitude of government agencies and individual personnel have given us access to data; we are particularly grateful to members of the Maritime Administration at all levels, whose assistance in data collection was invaluable.

Our research team has been supplemented and greatly aided by the contributions of individual faculty members at the Harvard Graduate School of Business Administration and the Massachusetts Institute of Technology. Specific recognition and appreciation are also due to the following Harvard Business School faculty members for their analytical contributions and rigorous critiques: Dr. Bertrand Fox, Jacob H. Schiff Professor of Investment Banking; Dr. Lewis M. Schneider; and Mr. Wilbert A. Pinkerton. In addition, Dr. Dwight R. Ladd of the Whittemore School of Economics and Business Administration, University of New Hampshire, and Rose H. Kneznek lent coherence to some of our more muddled passages and provided tireless assistance in reviewing the final drafts of the study.

Particular thanks are also due Suzanne Brouillard, Nancy Le Blanc, and Celia Lees-Low for indefatigable secretarial assistance.

To these, then, belong a measure of any credit this report receives; to ourselves we reserve the blame for any lapses in style, fact, or analysis.

The United States Merchant Marine in National Perspective

1 Introductory Summary of Findings and Conclusion

To survey the current United States Merchant Marine is to analyze two industries, one dying and one being born. The old industry has served its nation well, even in the face of its own physical deterioration and the growing commercial competition from foreign lines. The new industry promises to revive the commercial vigor of the U.S. Merchant Marine and, with it, to magnify the benefits to the nation.

The nurture of the new industry depends upon rebuilding the fleet and institutionalizing its potentials in an economically rational manner. A certain measure of commercial success and concomitant national benefits can be assured by exercising timid options in building, but the greatest national and commercial successes are to be gained by setting high sights in both areas—a large building program and an aggressive pursuit of increased market share by development of an international intermodal transportation system.

Past Benefits

The U.S. Merchant Marine is a significant national resource. In the ten-year period from 1958 to 1967, the U.S. Merchant Marine contributed $11.3 billion in quantifiable benefits to the nation at a cost to the government of $2.7 billion. This represents a net benefit of $8.6 billion, or over $4 in benefits for each dollar of cost. The cost/benefit analysis is summarized in Table 1-1.

The U.S. Merchant Marine has benefited the nation in the following areas:

i) balance of payments
ii) national security

The balance of payments is an accounting summary which is calculated as the amount of loss that would be sustained by the transportation sector of the U.S. balance of payments if the shipping services provided by the U.S. fleet were performed instead by another fleet. In the period from 1958 to 1967, the total balance of payments impact was approximately $7.5 billion. The yearly balance of payments impact is presented in Table 1-2.

National security benefits consist of (1) availability of shipping capacity and (2) cost savings attributable to the U.S. Merchant Marine. Only the latter is quantifiable for cost/benefit purposes.

Response to defense sealift requirements over the decade 1958 to 1968 has been rapid and substantial. The U.S. Merchant Marine increased carriage of

Table 1-1

Benefit/Cost Analysis of the U.S. Merchant Marine: 1958-1967 (Dollars in Millions)

Year	Benefits			Costs*				Net Benefits
	Balance of Payments†	National Security‡	Total	Operating Differential Subsidy	Rate Preference§	Ship Exchange Program§	Total	
1967	$ 999	$ 400	$ 1,399	$ 216	$ 68	$ 64	$ 348	$1,051
1966	912	400	1,312	199	76	44	319	993
1965	632	400	1,032	185	68	38	291	741
1964	680	400	1,080	204	77	52	333	747
1963	631	400	1,031	192	79	47	318	713
1962	659	400	1,059	178	59	32	269	790
1961	551	400	951	169	50	12	231	720
1960	715	400	1,115	163	54	12	229	886
1959	748	400	1,148	159	37	–	196	952
1958	758	400	1,158	141	31	–	172	986
Total	$7,285	$4,000	$11,285	$1,806	$599	$301	$2,706	$8,579

Note: The charts in this introductory section are taken from the body of the text. Full information on sources and computational methods can be found in those versions.

*Since constructional differential subsidy is a subsidy to U. S. shipyards and not to the Merchant Marine, it has not been included in costs.

†Data given in fiscal years.

‡Average per year. Does not reflect the nonquantifiable "availability" factor.

§Indirect subsidies.

Table 1-2

Net Balance of Payments Impact of U.S. Merchant Shipping Operations: FY 1958-1967 (Dollars in Millions)

	1958	1959	1960	1961	1962	1963	1964	1965	1966	1967
Gross Revenue										
Freight Receipts:										
Export	$ 429	$ 359	$ 428	$ 424	$ 479	$ 538	$ 599	$ 519	$ 541	$ 523
Import	336	358	346	290	339	340	380	375	500	378
Between Foreign Countries	130	140	136	155	177	154	158	152	139	161
Passenger Fares:										
Foreign Citizens	24	20	19	9	10	10	11	8	10	8
U.S. Citizens	88	85	84	80	83	102	92	72	68	68
Department of Defense	294	289	249	246	303	314	325	330	647	815
Charter Fees Received	8	7	8	8	10	9	9	9	10	8
Total Revenue	$1,309	$1,258	$1,270	$1,212	$1,401	$1,467	$1,574	$1,465	$1,915	$1,961
Deductions										
Port Charges:										
Abroad (Non-DOD)	$170	$155	$167	$231	$260	$288	$317	$281	$ 294	$282
Domestic (Non-DOD)	414	402	421	325	371	376	402	372	436	378
Foreign and Domestic DOD	68	76	68	67	85	89	92	91	163	204
Total Port Charges	$652	$633	$656	$623	$716	$753	$811	$744	$ 893	$864
Adjustment for Lower Port Charges	136	131	137	—	—	—	—	—	—	—
Net Port Charges	$516	$502	$519	$623	$716	$753	$811	$744	$ 893	$864
Charter Fees Paid	35	8	36	38	26	83	83	89	110	98
Total Deductions	$551	$510	$555	$661	$742	$836	$894	$833	$1,003	$962
Balance of Payments Impact	$758	$748	$715	$551	$659	$631	$680	$632	$ 912	$999

Military Sea Transportation Service (MSTS) cargoes by 100% from 1963 to 1967, jumping from 9.1 million measurement tons to 18.2 million.[a] Capacity increased in all categories—charger (time and voyage), berth term, and shipping contract.

U.S.-flag shipping capacity was made available to the government at favorable rates. Without that capacity during the period the government would have been required to pay foreign-flag carriers an additional $4 billion to ship its military cargo. This sum corresponds to an average savings of over $400 million per year. Moreover, in absolute terms U.S.-flag rates for the carriage of defense cargo did not escalate significantly from fiscal year 1963 to fiscal year 1970.

The Commercial Dilemma

Although the nation has continued to benefit from its Merchant Marine, there has been continuing concern over its physical and economic decline. The size of the fleet in proportion to its foreign competition has varied widely in the past. The U.S. fleet averaged about 10% of the total foreign-flag fleet in 1939, rose to almost 50% in 1946, and dropped to 9% by 1958. The growth was war-induced; the decline is explained by the rapid growth of the foreign-flag fleet in the last decade. During this time, the U.S. fleet has remained virtually the same size, hence the proportional decrease. The U.S.-flag fleet consist is detailed in Table 1-3.

Although in the past decade the fleet has been relatively stable in size, it is now in poor condition and is facing block obsolescence. More than one-half of the ships are of World War II vintage and need replacement.

These physical facts can be translated into economic terms. Commercial performance traditionally has been assessed by type of service (liner, nonliner, or tramp), since this represented the market segments. By this measure, U.S. participation in liner markets declined from 48% to 20% from 1958 to 1967. A more significant drop is revealed when the markets are defined by types of cargo rather than types of service. In the commercial general cargo market, which includes a large proportion of high-revenue goods susceptible to containerization, the U.S. share declined from 25% to 8% in the same ten-year period. This increased competitive pressure has reduced the return on investment (net of subsidy) from 11% to 4% for the subsidized sector of the industry.

The poor performance of the U.S. Merchant Marine can be traced to the past competitive advantage of foreign-flag tramp operators. Primarily because of port congestion, liner operators were unable to offer a service which was noticeably better than tramp services. Because foreign tramps operated at a cost per ton lower than that of liners or of unsubsidized U.S.-flag tramps, they were able to

---

[a]It should be noted that measurement tons are used throughout this report unless otherwise specified. Conversion factors are two measurement tons to one long ton for general cargo and defense; one-to-one for bulk.

Table 1-3

Size of U.S.-Flag Fleet: 1968

Segment	No. of Ships	Annual Lift Capacity*		Total
		Breakbulk†	*Container*	
Subsidized	303	32.1	5.2	37.3
Indirectly Subsidized	146	9.4	7.6	17.0
Tramp/Irregular	132	11.1	0.8	11.9
Total	581	52.6	13.6	66.2

Note: Calculations in this exhibit are based on the number of ships at the end of the year. Excluded are 36 dry-bulk ships with almost 10 million measurement tons of capacity.

*Annual lift capacity is expressed in millions of measurement tons.

†Partial container vessels appear in this category.

offer a service, especially to large shippers, which was equally good and less expensive than that offered by liners and U.S.-flag tramps. Consequently, foreign-flag tramp operators flourished in the late 1950's and early 1960's to the detriment of the U.S.-flag fleet.

The Container Era

The traditional system of cargo movement could not overcome the inherent cost advantages of the foreign-flag fleet or distinguish U.S. service from the rest of the industry. In the breakbulk system the carrier and the shipper faced common problems resulting from the fragmentation of the door-to-door system.

For shippers, routing a package door-to-door was an expensive, time-consuming task. Rail, truck, and ocean shipping operations did not interface smoothly, and each mode optimized its own operations without regard to ease of interface. As a result, the shipper and forwarder had to construct a "system" for every piece of cargo to be shipped. Delays were frequent, and the dependability of the total service fluctuated unpredictably. All these inefficiencies increased direct costs incurred by the shippers.

The vessel operators had a separate problem caused by labor-intensive loading and unloading of small, individual packages of cargo. Pilferage and damage costs soared; and as wages rose faster than productivity, costs per ton increased.

More importantly, unpredictable cargo flows and the slow stevedoring process necessitated long loading and unloading times for vessels. Typically, they spent only half their time moving cargo, the other half waiting in port to be unloaded and loaded. Thus, every breakbulk vessel was inefficiently utilized.

In 1965 new technology was introduced to solve the carriers' problem, and a new service was offered to solve the shippers' troubles. The change in technology was high-productivity container or barge-carrying ships; the new service was intermodalism.

Containerization affects the economic structure of the industry in three ways. It brings economies of scale to the stevedoring process, by making the process capital intensive rather than labor intensive, dramatically increases vessel utilization by reducing port-to-sea ratios from 1:1 to 1:4, and makes possible the development of intermodal services by facilitating the interface between carriers. Because of high fixed capital costs, unit costs decrease dramatically as volume increases. Vessel costs per ton may be lowered to one-half of breakbulk operations assuming volume operations are achieved. More significantly, translating increased capacity into annual revenues, the high-productivity ship may achieve as much as five times the revenue of a breakbulk C-4 type vessel.

Thus, the bleak commercial performance of liner operations in the 1950's and 1960's need not be the pattern for the 1970's. For the first time in many decades, the U.S. Merchant Marine, which is basically a liner fleet, has a viable commercial future as well as a continued potential for contributing to national objectives.

The Future

The first requisite for realizing this potential is a rejuvenated fleet. The optimum fleet size can be estimated experimentally by testing alternative fleet sizes for their commercial viability and their potential contribution to national objectives.

The Coming Fleet

The size of the U.S. Merchant fleet in 1976 depends largely on three factors:

  i) the volume of U.S. foreign trade;
 ii) the aging of the existing fleet;
iii) U.S. government maritime policies.

Market Projections. The foreign-trade market gives an indication of the upper limits of capacity required. Our predictions place the general cargo market at 267 million measurement tons and the total dry cargo market at 484 million measurement tons. Table 1-4 summarizes these projections.

Table 1-4

Summary of U.S. Foreign Trade
Projections: 1976 (Measurement Tons
in Millions)

	1967 (Actual)	1976 (Projected)
Commercial:		
General Cargo	180.3	267.1
Dry Bulk	132.8	188.8
Government-Impelled	21.5	21.0
Department of Defense	18.5	7.5
Dry Cargo Total	353.1	484.4

Aging of the Fleet. By 1976 only one-third of the ships in the fleet in 1968 will be available to carry this trade. If no ships are built between now and 1976, the fleet will have dropped from 617 ships with 76,067 million measurement tons of capacity to 206 ships with 33,184 million measurement tons of capacity. This tonnage represents the minimum capacity of the fleet in 1976.

Alternative Government Policies. Additions to the fleet depend largely upon government policies toward subsidy. Because the fleet is rapidly dwindling, changes in the amount of support and its administration are presently being debated. Our analysis focuses upon four alternatives which are currently being advocated by the Nixon administration, members of the industry, or labor:

As Is. This alternative would retain existing policies and levels of support. Subsidy for construction now equals $80 million.

Increased Funding. This alternative would raise CDS levels to $200 million with corresponding increases in ODS levels for presently subsidized operators. Other policies would not be changed.

Extended Benefits. This alternative would provide CDS and ODS to all fleet segments, with amounts increased to $300 million CDS annually. The trade route concept and other responsibilities of the Merchant Marine Act would remain in force for recipients of ODS; vessels built under this program would be excluded from the cabotage trade.

Build Foreign. This alternative would eliminate CDS. Foreign-built vessels would be permitted to register under the U.S. flag and to carry government-impelled and DOD cargoes as well as commercial cargoes. Presently subsidized and unsubsidized operators could build in foreign shipyards and receive ODS, but total ODS dollars would be limited to $300 million, which is approximately the sum of the current ODS and CDS programs. The trade route concept and other responsibilities of the Merchant Marine Act of 1936 would remain in force for ODS recipients; vessels built under this program would be excluded from cabotage trade.

The fleets produced by these four programs range from 271 to 424 ships with from 78.2 million to 164 million measurement tons of capacity. Table 1-5 displays the fleet sizes associated with the alternative government programs.

Commercial Performance

The economic characteristics of the 1976 U.S. Merchant Marine will depend on the fleet consist with attendant expenses, the share of the market, and the rate structure. Breakbulk vessels with labor-intensive supporting systems will be under profit pressure by 1976. The new high-technology vessels, operated as part of a capital-intensive system, are capable of generating attractive returns on invested capital provided the necessary cargo volumes are generated.

Return on investment, which is the incentive to the industry for maintaining a fleet, varies according to fleet size, rate structure and market share. The critical variable for profitability, given selected fleet size and rates, is *market share.*

The relationship among fleet size, market share, and return on investment is presented in Table 1-6. Larger building programs require raising U.S.-flag market share substantially above present levels, thereby increasing the risks of attaining an adequate return on investment. For example, a 20% share of the general cargo market is required to earn a 10% return on investment for the largest fleet-size ($300 million) government program. This is an almost threefold increase in market share from the present 7% share of general cargo.

Net National Benefits

Net national benefits associated with selected combinations of fleet size and market share are presented in detail in Tables 1-7 and 1-8. The net benefits range from $1.9 billion under the largest combination of fleet size and market

Table 1-5

**Number of Ships and Capacity
Associated with Alternative Construction
Programs**

Construction Alternative	No. of Ships	Annual Lift Capacity*
As-Is	271	78.2
Increased Funding	355	125.3
Extended Benefits	424	164.0
Build Foreign	424	164.0

Note: Investment in ships under the Build Foreign option have been assumed to equal the industry's investment under the Extended Benefits option.

*Annual lift capacity is expressed in millions of measurement tons.

Table 1-6

**Return on Investment and Required
Market Share by Fleet Size: 1976**

No. of Ships	Return on Investment	Required Market Share Commercial General Cargo
271*	Breakeven	3%
	10%	7
355*	Breakeven	7%
	10%	11
424	Breakeven	13%
	10%	20

Note: The size of the fleet in 1967 was 616 ships with an annual capacity of 70,987,000 measurement tons; the market share of commercial general cargo was 7.8% with a return on investment of 3.5%

*ROI and market share calculated for subsidized segment only.

Table 1-7

**Estimated Benefits and Costs of the
U.S.-Flag Fleet at Market Share
Yielding Reasonable Return: 1976**

	Construction Program A*	Construction Program B*	Construction Program C
	As Is	*Increased Funding*	*Extended Benefits*
No. of Ships at End of 1976	271	355	424
Share of Commercial General Cargo Market Required	6.70%	11.09%	19.50%
Benefits (in millions):			
Balance of Payments	$733	$1,075	$1,785
National Security	270	319	400
Subtotal	$1,002	$1,394	$2,185
Costs (in millions):†			
Operating Differential Subsidy (ODS)	$141	$196	$240
Rate Preference Program	3	3	60
Subtotal	$144	$199	$300
Net Benefits (in millions)	$8.59	$1,195	$1,885
Benefit/Cost Ratio	7.0	7.0	7.3

*All items except fleet size are calculated for subsidized liner segment only. It was assumed national security benefits would be proportional to subsidized liner capacity in the respective programs. Subsidized liner participation in rate preference programs was estimated at 5% of the total.

†Construction differential subsidy (CDS) is not considered among the costs because the program is a subsidy solely to U.S. shipyards.

Table 1-8

**Estimated Benefits and Costs of the
U.S.-Flag Fleet at Lowest Profitable
Market Share: 1976**

	Construction Program A*	Construction Program B*	Construction Program C
	As Is	*Increased Funding*	*Extended Benefits*
No. of Ships at End of 1976	271	355	424
Share of Commercial General Cargo Market Required	2.84%	7.22%	13.38%
Benefits (in millions):			
Balance of Payments	$476	$ 825	$1,418
National Security	270	319	400
Subtotal	$746	$1,144	$1,818
Costs (in millions):†			
Operating Differential			
Subsidy (ODS)	141	196	240
Rate Preference Program	3	3	60
Subtotal	$144	$199	$300
Net Benefits (in millions)	$602	$945	$1,510
Benefit/Cost Ratio	5.2	5.7	6.0

*All items except fleet size are calculated for   †CDS is not included.
subsidized liner segment only. Assumptions
are the same as in Table 1-7.

share to $1.0 billion under the smallest, compared with $1.2 billion net benefits in 1967.

In all cases ODS costs decline dramatically from the 1967 level of $6.21 per measurement ton of capacity. The range in 1976 is from $1.46 to $3.72 per measurement ton depending upon the ship construction program.

Opportunities and Risks

If the current annual level of ship construction ($80 million of CDS) is continued, the industry will receive a reasonable return on investment of 11% in 1976 at the present market-share level of 7%. This is a low-risk option for the industry. However, in terms of return to the nation, net benefits amount to $1.3 billion per year by 1976—or $.6 billion less than benefits associated with the alternatives of larger ship construction and share of market.

The administration's stated goal of a 30% market share for the U.S.-flag fleet exceeds the physical capacity that would result from the ship construction programs providing only $80 million or $200 million in CDS per year. The $300 million program or foreign-build would be required to meet the goal of a 30% market share.

A $300 million CDS ship construction support program involves high risk for the U.S. Merchant Marine. Under this construction program, the U.S.-flag fleet will have to double its current share of commercial general cargo simply to break even. Nonetheless, such a ship construction support program brings substantial net benefits to the nation. At a 30% market share, each $1.00 of cost to the government generates more than $5 in benefits to the nation, or net benefits of $2.5 billion per year by 1976.

Attainment of an increased market share depends primarily upon the ability of the U.S. Merchant Marine to exploit the economic advantages provided by the new technology and its supporting systems.

Intermodalism

The new technology has the potential to strengthen more than the maritime industry itself: the U.S. Merchant Marine can make a major contribution to the U.S. international transportation system through the development of intermodal systems. Simple pier-to-pier delivery belongs to the breakbulk era: the emerging concept of intermodalism is one of a door-to-door system with the steamship line providing through routing, liability and other supporting services packaged in a through rate. Intermodalism promises lower through costs and higher levels of service. Specifically, intermodalism can provide faster and more reliable transit, simplified supervision of cargo, and lower through costs from packaging as well as carrier rates.

The estimate of the potential of packaging savings ranges from $344 million to $1.7 billion annually. The estimate of rate savings begins at $1.2 billion annually. The cost and rate savings have a multiplier effect on U.S. foreign trade: as rates and costs are lowered, U.S. products will become more competitive abroad.

Intermodalism will permit liner companies to provide frequent port-to-port service on high-volume trade routes which will—for the first time—be a superior service to those operated by tramps.

Promotion of intermodalism depends upon steamship companies. They have the most at stake, since import-export traffic is not a large incentive to other modes whose major business is domestic traffic. Thus, to thrive, shipping lines will be transformed into transportation companies and will play the vital role in determining the shape of the U.S. international transportation system. The United States cannot rely on foreign fleets supported by foreign governments to develop new technology and improve the U.S. international transportation system. However difficult the task in fulfilling the promise of intermodalism the goal of the U.S. Merchant Marine is clear: **to provide the basis of an integrated international intermodal system with significant benefits in improved services and lower through costs.**

Concluding Statement

The potential of an intermodal system and the future success of the U.S. merchant fleet are related. The Nixon administration's Merchant Marine program indicates that as many as 300 new high-productivity ships will be built over the next ten-year period. These ships will represent a $6 billion investment (shared equally by government and industry) without considering the sums that will be spent on auxilliary equipment and supporting systems. As noted earlier, the U.S.-flag share of the foreign commerce general cargo market must increase from 6% to 20%. If the market-share goals are not achieved, the industry will face severe economic losses, the government will not receive its maximum return in contributions to balance of payments and defense needs, and the U.S. economy will not be served by a more efficient international transportation system.

Accordingly, a coordinated industry-government program must be developed to increase market share simultaneous with any undertaking of a large ship construction program. Elements of this program include:

i) rationalization of the regulatory, modal, labor, and management issues leading to the development of a U.S. international intermodal transportation system;

ii) development of a national marketing program aimed at increasing U.S.-flag share of U.S.-controlled shipments;

iii) exploration of the possibility of bilateral agreements and the impact on "third flag" fleets;

iv) development of data banks which more accurately identify projected cargo volumes, levels of U.S.-flag and foreign-flag service, and emerging shipper preferences;

v) examination of the feasibility of carrying all government-impelled cargo in U.S.-flag ships at market or lower than market rates.

For the first time in decades, the U.S. merchant fleet has the potential to develop an economic and service advantage over its foreign-flag competition, by continuing to lead the way in adopting the new capital-intensive technology and systems. The industry-government partnership, working towards the common goal of developing strong transportation companies, is capable of achieving a profitable industry with significant benefits to national objectives.

2

The U.S.
Merchant Marine:
Past and Future

Introduction

Although previous economic studies of the U.S. Merchant Marine have provided useful, fundamental data and analyses, they have, in the main, been so narrow in focus and objectives that often they have clouded the very issues they sought to clarify.[1] The result has been twofold:

i) Federal executive and legislative bodies are inadequately informed regarding the importance of the U.S. Merchant Marine to the national interest.
ii) The general public is thoroughly confused by the image projected of the Merchant Marine and ill-educated as to its role.

The ultimate consequence has been indecision on how to reform the inadequate and contradictory set of past and current government maritime policies and programs.

The U.S. Merchant Marine in National Perspective was initially conceived as an effort to measure the "costs" and "benefits" of the U.S.-flag fleet engaged in foreign trade in order to clarify the nature of the relationships between the government, the industry, and the public sector. However, in the course of developing these economic measures, it became apparent that the issues critical to an understanding of the U.S.-flag fleet have been obscured in the past by the complex structure of the industry; as a result, the Merchant Marine has been viewed in partial terms and has continually been called upon to justify its existence. In contrast, the new conceptual framework used by the authors for examining the industry as a national resource casts more light on the Merchant Marine's past performance and provides a fuller appreciation of its potential.

The subject of this study is the U.S.-flag fleet, which comprises liners (subsidized and nonsubsidized), tramps, and bulk carriers carrying oceanborne dry cargo in U.S. foreign trade (commercial, government-impelled and DOD cargoes). Tankers, lake carriers and coastal vessels as well as all liquid cargoes are excluded from consideration. The "Flags-of-Convenience/Necessity" (FOC/FON) fleet, the Military Sea Transportation Service (MSTS) nucleus fleet and the National Defense Reserve Fleet (NDRF) are also not considered here as part of the U.S.-flag fleet. [a]

In seeking to identify and evaluate the past and potential contributions of this fleet to national objectives, the authors' approach is based on an

---

[a]Definitions and explanations of these terms and other technical terminology can be found in the Glossary at the end of the book.

overview of the characteristics and relationships of the industry to its environment—the government and the marketplace. The industry is seen in two ways: as a commercial institution and as a mechanism for achieving national objectives. Although commercial vigor ensures the existence of a fleet for the achievement of national objectives, commercial and national benefits are not always compatible. For example, the prescription of fixed trade routes insures regular service to essential ports but involves additional vessel costs for the ship operator and limits scheduling flexibility, both of which serve to lower profitability. Therefore, the major goal of government intervention must be:

i) to ensure that the economic costs associated with the fulfillment of national objectives do not eliminate the fleet;
ii) to enforce industry recognition of the necessity of pursuing national benefits.

Unfortunately, with the exception of some national security benefits, the U.S. government has not fully recognized all of the vital contributions of the U.S.-flag fleet to national economic goals nor all the penalties incurred in the process.

While we present statistical information by fleet segment (i.e., directly-subsidized liner, indirectly-subsidized liner and tramp), the focus in this study is on the market sectors of the dry cargo industry, leading to an analysis of the industry by type of cargo carried rather than by the traditional categories of liner and nonliner service as reported by Marad.[2] These market sectors are:

> Commercial: general cargo and dry bulk
> Government-Impelled: general cargo and dry bulk
> Department of Defense: general cargo

This integrated—yet comprehensive—view of the industry permits us to:

i) explain more clearly the historical economic structure of the industry;
ii) assess past benefits and costs of the Merchant Marine;
iii) determine and evaluate the commercial and national economic consequences associated with alternative government ship construction programs;
iv) measure the impact of technological innovations;
v) project the economic principles and relationships that derive from the new technology; and
vi) identify future problem areas confronting the industry and the nation in utilizing its Merchant Marine resources.

The U.S. Merchant Marine: Two Industries

At present the U.S. Merchant Marine is actually two industries with separate sets of economic configurations. The economics of the breakbulk industry help to

Table 2-1

**Size of U.S.-Flag and Foreign
Flag Fleets: 1939-1958**

Year	U.S.-Flag Fleet (Active)		Foreign-Flag Fleet		U.S.-Flag as % of of Foreign-Flag Fleet	
	No. of Ships*	*Deadweight Tonnage†*	*No. of Ships**	*Deadweight Tonnage†*	*No. of Ships**	*Deadweight Tonnage†*
1939	739	5,394	10,142	56,264	7.3%	9.9%
1946	1,858	18,278	6,517	38,512	28.5	47.5
1951	970	10,041	8,467	52,835	11.5	19.0
1958	659	6,989	11,079	76,791	5.9	9.1

*Freighters and combination vessels, includ-
ing bulk carriers.

†Deadweight tonnage is expressed in thousands of long tons.

Source: Derived from: Ferguson, *Economic
Value,* Table 2-2, p. 26.

explain the past performance of the fleet both in commercial and in national
respects. This type of ship is still in the majority in the current fleet and will
necessarily have a role in maritime shipping operations for some time.

The economics of containerization, on the other hand, are only partially
charted and their ultimate effects on the industry can only be guessed because
containerization is relatively new. The competitive climate at the present time—
when new technology and systems are in the midst of restructuring trade
patterns—may be quite different from the future climate when the consolidation
process has been completed. In any event, containerization is an important
force in current shipping with an even larger role to play in the future.

The remainder of this chapter describes the competitive structure of the
postwar maritime shipping industry as it evolved from a breakbulk system to the
dual system of today. An understanding of the two industries is fundamental to
later evaluations of the performance and potentials of the United States
Merchant Marine.

The U.S.-Flag Fleet: 1939-1958

The size of the U.S. merchant fleet in proportion to the foreign-flag merchant
fleet varied widely during the period 1939-1958. From Table 2-1, it can be

seen that U.S. merchant fleet tonnage averaged about 10% of that of foreign-flag tonnage in 1939, rose to almost one-half (47.5%) in 1946, and dropped again to approximately one-tenth (9.1%) of foreign-flag tonnage in 1958. The cause of the tremendous increase—absolutely and relatively—in the U.S. merchant fleet between 1939 and 1946 is obvious: the wartime destruction of the foreign-flag fleet, with no compensatory rebuilding, is reflected in the decline of 3,625 ships during the period, while the concurrent wartime rebuilding and expansion of the U.S. merchant fleet contributed to its postwar prominence. While the U.S. merchant fleet lost as much tonnage to war destruction as other foreign-flag fleets during World War II, ships destroyed in the U.S. fleet were soon replaced by new construction from U.S. shipyards. Britain and Norway—to name two countries whose fleets were greatly diminished in World War II—did not rebuild their fleets immediately; similarly, the Japanese merchant fleet, which was significant prior to hostilities, was almost totally destroyed during the war. Thus, following World War II, the United States held a competitive advantage in all categories—bulk and general cargo operations.

Following the war, foreign fleets bought some ships from the U.S. reserve fleet, but by the late 1940's, foreign shipyards once again began producing vessels. The U.S.-flag fleet not only lost its size advantage but also was handicapped by the economic structure of its operations. By 1951, the foreign-flag fleet showed the results of a rebuilding program, while the U.S. fleet had declined nearly 50%, from 1,858 ships in 1946 to 970 in 1951. This trend continued into the late 1950's at which time the U.S. merchant fleet had declined below its 1939 position while the foreign-flag fleet was larger than in 1939. Thus it can be seen that the temporary prominence of the U.S. merchant fleet was due only to the circumstances which did not include any incentive for the development of an economically superior fleet.

The Economic Dilemma: 1958-1967

By the 1960's U.S. general cargo operations were under severe economic pressure from foreign competition. The economic dilemma of the U.S.-flag merchant fleet was manifested in two ways: low return on investment for the industry; and declining market share. Return on investment for the subsidized-liner segment declined from 7.3% in 1958 to 3.5% in 1967.[b] (It was as high as 20% in the early 1950's.) The declining market share for the U.S. merchant fleet and the decline of the U.S. merchant fleet are related. During the decade 1958-1967, while the commercial general cargo category (excluding government-impelled cargo and DOD tonnage) of U.S. foreign trade more than doubled—rising from 75 million measurement tons in 1958 to 180 million measurement tons in 1967—the U.S.-flag share of this market dropped from 25% to 8%.[c] The

[b]See Table 3-14 for more extensive documentation.

[c]See Tables 3-10 and 3-12.

U.S. failed not only to expand its capacity to meet demand but also lost commercial opportunities to other operators. The complete answers to the deterioration in the U.S. shipping industry may be found in an analysis of the competitive structure of the worldwide shipping industry.

The Economics of Competition. U.S. shipping operators and the government alike have divided the market into two categories: liner and nonliner.[d] This view reflects a marketing strategy which suggests that liner service is different in quality as well as price from tramp service. Before examining the competitive points of price and strategy, however, it is useful to examine the physical basis for differentiating markets—cargo-handling characteristics.

One type of cargo is called general cargo (generally known as "mark and count" cargo) and is synonymous with package cargo.[e] General cargo is loaded/unloaded into/from breakbulk vessels to/from cargo piers that include cargo sheds for storage. The cargo is moved to shipside on pallets, placed into cargo slings rigged from cargo booms on the vessels, moved into the hold, unloaded from the slings, and stored in the hold of the ship. Since all general cargo ships are basically the same, whether liner or tramp, the process is the same for each segment or type of service. The standard charges for handling general cargo are paid for by the shipping line and are included in the shipping rate as a service to the customer. Until containerization, almost all general cargo moved in breakbulk liner or tramp vessels.

A second type of cargo is bulk cargo which can be distinguished from general cargo because it usually moves by the ton, is not packaged, and is loaded/unloaded into/from the ship to/from bulk-loading terminals. Bulk cargoes usually move in large tonnages, and a 20,000-ton parcel of wheat (or other grains), a 60,000-ton cargo of iron ore, or a 40,000-ton cargo of coal is not unusual. Most of the time, bulk cargoes move in full shiploads; and frequently the ship is a large bulk carrier specializing in carrying these cargoes. Unlike general cargo, stevedoring for these cargoes is usually paid by the shipper. While the general cargo market grew rapidly during the 1958-1967 period, the parcels of bulk suitable to liner or tramp carriage remained fairly stable during this period.[f]

The breakbulk liner and tramp vessels of the U.S.-flag and foreign-flag fleets competed for the rapidly expanding general cargo market (and rather stable bulk market) through cost and service. Traditionally, liners purported to give more complete service to the market but at a higher cost, and the liner share of the market was believed to depend on shippers' needs for service rather than cost considerations. Current research suggests that—at least during the period under study—foreign-flag tramp vessels in many cases gave service at least equal to that of the liners but at lower cost, and thus were the major participants in the

[d]Nonliner includes both tramp and bulk carriers.

[e]See Appendix A for a list of general cargo commodities.

[f]See Table 3-10.

growing general cargo market.ᵍ This reality tends to be obscured by the way in which the competitors are viewed in both the popular mind and government policy.

The general public views the liner as a sleek, new freighter, expressing shipments from one modern terminal to another with little or no delay, and pictures the foreign tramp as an old rust bucket, crawling along at 8 knots and pulling up to an unlighted, congested pier. It follows, in this view, that no one would think of putting valuable cargo aboard a tramp. U.S. government policy defines liner firms as those serving specific ports on a semi-fixed schedule. Although this policy ensures that U.S. shippers will have a guarantee of service to many ports in the world, it does not necessarily solve the problem of an individual shipper. While public observers and government officials believe that shippers should not have much trouble differentiating between the service offered by U.S. liners and foreign-flag tramps, shippers see little difference between them. For the shippers, cost remains the major factor in shipping decisions.

The basic problem for the shipper is to secure transportation of his goods to his customers. The water carrier is generally not the only mode of transportation involved. Packaged goods moving between inland points of the United States and foreign countries must be transported by several modes of transportation. Traditionally, the task of the traffic manager or freight forwarder has consisted of selecting one of several entry ports, one of several railroads or trucking firms, one of several shipping lines, and then comparing total rates, schedules, and so on. Each carrier mode operates independently, providing service and rates to the shipper primarily in terms of its own operations. Thus, a vessel operator offers a service that is pier-to-pier in scope and is only a part of the total service required by the shipper.

In building the total transport package, shippers and forwarders increasingly found during the 1960's that the vessel service offered by liners or tramps on a pier-to-pier basis was hard to differentiate. Pier operations on either end of the trip were often the same for any service. Congestion was the normal condition; loss and damage rates were comparable; and loading and unloading rates and costs were similar for liners and tramps. Thus, the delays of getting through the piers often negated any time savings the liner service might generate by faster ships or regularized schedules. And contrary to the popular view, U.S. liner companies have their share of old, World War II vessels as well as modern, efficient ships; and many first-rate tramp operators have some ships that can be classed as sister ships to the modern, efficient liners.

Moreover, breakbulk operations—be they liner or tramp—are not subject to dependable scheduling. Since there are usually many ports on a given voyage (14 is not a high number for a U.S. liner operator), a delay in one port—because of congestion, slow loading, or waiting for cargo—affects the remaining schedule, as well as the start of the next voyage. Further, liners attempt to adhere to port

---

ᵍTheir costs were also lower than U.S.-flag tramps because wages and benefits for foreign labor are lower than for U.S. seamen.

schedules even if the tonnage does not justify the call economically. A review of Maritime Administration data, for example, is replete with examples of liners making port calls for less than 1,000 measurement tons of cargo.[3]

Conversely, tramps do not have schedules, and usually enter a port only if there is sufficient cargo to justify the call. This mode of operation gives the tramps an advantage in servicing large parcels since tramps can give the large shipper direct service while the liner counterpart can not because of the need to maintain a fixed series of port calls. The liner's "speed" advantage is thus overcome.[h]

Tramp operators have an economic advantage over liner operators which allows tramps to undercut the liner conferences' published tariffs. To illustrate, we can compare and contrast a modern C-4 operated as a liner and as a tramp. Although both ships have similar economic characteristics[i]–crew size, capital and operating costs, stevedoring costs, capacity and speed, to name a few–the tramp serves fewer ports and thus makes more round trips per year. The increased annual capacity is translated into higher total annual revenues for the tramp operator, even when charging lower rates than the liner.

Thus, the liner service is clearly a premium service in terms of its cost characteristics. From the individual shipper's viewpoint, it does not always make sense to use this service especially when comparable service at a lower price is available from the tramp.

Because the U.S. shipper and forwarder could not differentiate between liner and tramp service, tramp operations flourished in the late 1950's and early 1960's. And since there were no economies of scale in breakbulk operations, a one-ship fleet was almost as efficient as a 50-ship fleet. In fact, some would argue that, with a high load factor in one vessel, a one-ship fleet was more efficient than the large fleets committed to fixed schedules. Thus, shippers and forwarders were solicited not only by U.S. liner operators and foreign-flag liners but by a multitude of small shipping companies serving the high seas on an inducement basis very successfully. Thus, during the late 1950's and early 1960's, the U.S.-flag operator had a tough job in getting the shipper and forwarder to choose him, and there was no way of limiting competition.

To summarize, the pressure from foreign operators was a result of two factors:

i) Liners fleets–both U.S.-flag and others–lost cargo to tramp operators who were able to offer service which more nearly met the needs of individual, large-volume shippers.

---

[h]Lest too much emphasis be placed on breakbulk ship speed, it should be noted that stevedoring operation delays may overcome any advantage either tramp or liner may have in a given situation.

[i]There can be substantial differences in these characteristics, particularly if the liner is U.S.-flag and the tramp is a foreign-flag ship with lower construction and labor costs. For illustrative purposes, however, we have taken the same ship operated in two different manners. See Appendix D for cost assumptions.

ii) U.S.-flag tramp operators did not share in the increasing market penetration by tramps because, without operating subsidy, they were unable to match the costs of foreign tramps.

Consequently, both sectors of the U.S.-flag fleet lost out—primarily to foreign tramps.

Because both U.S. and foreign liners served many ports on a semi-fixed schedule, their cost structure (reflected in conference rates) was higher than tramp rates. Thus, while liner services met the *national* goals of providing reliable service to many ports, the liner companies put themselves at a cost and service disadvantage in competing with the tramps, especially for the cargo of large-volume, discriminating shippers.

In the early and middle 1960's, U.S.-flag lines continued to lose ground, and efforts of U.S. operators to build a more efficient fleet—from the point of view of cost and service—were unsuccessful. Many lines tried to lower costs by increasing the effective annual capacity of the vessel through faster unloading gear on the ships. But in some cases these efforts to put a larger, more modern breakbulk ship on berth actually raised costs; and in no case did an American operator make a major breakthrough in improving the breakbulk vessel. The congestion in port terminals was in no way eliminated or reduced, and as volume grew, delays in handling cargo increased proportionately. During the 1960's, the shipper was offered equally poor service by all carriers of all flags and not surprisingly, therefore, looked for the lowest rates. Generally speaking, these were offered by foreign-flag tramps.

These, then, were the major reasons that U.S. participation in commercial general cargo ocean trade slid from 25% in 1958 to 8% in 1967.

Inherent Inefficiencies in the Breakbulk System. A full picture of the breakbulk industry is not gained simply by looking at its competitive structure. If there are factors which have fallen heaviest on the U.S.-flag fleet, there are also inherent inefficiencies which penalize all ocean carriers and all international shippers equally.

The Shipper Problem. When cargo moves in breakbulk or cartons, with no surrounding envelope or container, each package is a shipment. Shippers often label and move groups of packages as a single shipment, and efforts are made by rail and truck lines to keep a group shipment together. However, the carriers do not connect or interface smoothly: typical shipments move by truck to a forwarder, who consolidates the shipments for rail transport to a port; then the contents of the rail car are sorted before going to the pier for a final sorting and stowage aboard the ship. The possibilities for packages to be misrouted and separated are numerous. In short, breakbulk operations are not a system. Each carrier—trunk, rail and steamship—concentrates solely on moving cargo over its own segment, and the shipper or forwarder must construct his own system for every piece of cargo to be shipped. Such efforts frequently lead to frustration for the shipper as well as for the carrier attempting to regulate and plan its own business.

Because delays are frequent and the dependability of the service varies so widely, shippers have to plan on the longest door-to-door shipping time. Thus, if the normal shipping time of one month from Chicago to Japan sometimes stretches to two months, shippers have to assume that all shipments may take two months. This has a considerable effect on the inventory of the firm whose goods move over this route; a larger stock is necessary when goods are tied up in transit. Moreover, when delays occur, any one of several carriers may be involved, causing a considerable tracing problem. In addition, tracing a shipment or documenting a loss requires that the shipment be documented to cover every transportation mode in each country involved. As a result, there has developed a billion-dollar paperwork industry that both supports and strangles the international transportation industry.

All of these inefficiencies increase the direct costs incurred by shippers while many of the costs—for example, wasted time of shipper executives—are not measurable.

The Carrier Problem. Meanwhile, shipping operators have searched for ways to reverse the rising costs of cargo handling and pilferage and damage on the piers, and to lessen the time spent in port.

In the 1960's, cargo-handling costs rose rapidly, amounting to almost 30% of vessel-operating revenue in 1967 (see Appendix D). Since the handling of packaged general cargo is basically a labor-intensive process, offering little or no opportunity to utilize labor-saving capital equipment, there has been no way to offset the impact of wage increases. Cargo-handling costs per measurement ton rose approximately 6% a year between 1960 and 1966, with little or no increase in productivity.[j]

At the same time, pilferage and damage costs soared. Racketeering moved onto the piers, and theft became a major issue. Theft became so chronic in the South American trade, for example, that an order for shoes would be sent in two shipments: left shoes were sent first and right shoes followed. While this has reduced the incidence of theft, the consignee has had to assume the cost of sorting and reassembling the shipment. The increase in damage to shipments has resulted in further cost increases. Thus, the stevedoring problem is of major significance to vessel operators, U.S. and foreign alike.

The slow stevedoring process in turn creates other problems, resulting in inefficient utilization of the ship and fleet. Because of slow stevedoring, a ship must spend as much time in port as at sea, so that the ship is a warehouse as well as a transportation vehicle and the capital investment is productive for only half of the time. The slow, labor-intensive stevedoring problem also affects fleet economics, since unit costs are the same for a one-ship fleet as for a 100-ship fleet.

---

[j]Employment costs rose at a faster rate; this is only an estimate of the non-productive wage cost increases.[4]

The combination of the slow cargo-handling process and multiport scheduling limits the size of breakbulk ships. With package cargo stowed one atop the other, additional port calls require cargo on top to be moved out of the way for unloading lower packages and then handled again as more cargo is brought aboard. Above 15,000 measurement tons, vessel efficiency drops drastically; the unloading and loading problem becomes so difficult on a multiport basis that economics of scale, such as a 100,000-ton breakbulk ship (which would lower unit costs appreciably), are infeasible.

In summary, the handling of package cargo—with the shippers' package as the lowest common denominator—limited efficient vessel utilization by inhibiting fast turnaround, prevented economies of scale from obtaining in large-volume stevedoring operations, and limited operators in building large breakbulk vessels whose unit costs would decrease as volume increased. Until Grace, Matson, and Sea-Land experimented with the use of standard containers to hold non-standard shippers' packages, in the late 1950's, this situation had dominated ocean shipping for hundreds of years.

The Impact of New Technology. The new maritime shipping industry resulted from carriers' attempts to reduce the economic pressures on the U.S.-flag fleet. The basic problems were in the transfer of cargo at port, so U.S. companies focused on making this process more efficient. Using the concept of a standard unit of cargo to replace the individual packages customary in breakbulk shipments, the industry produced the container/containership and the barge/barge-carrying ship.

Barges or lighters are small, waterborne vessels which can be carried aboard large, oceangoing ships. These lighters can be unloaded and loaded from their mother ship outside congested ports, freeing the mother ship from the problems encountered by breakbulk vessels in size limitation and unproductive port time. In 1965 the first proponent of barge-carrying ships, Prudential Lines, announced its intention of building LASH vessels for its Mediterranean service; and Lykes announced its intention to build its version of barge-carrying ships, the SEABEE, shortly thereafter. However, the full economic characteristics of this system are not yet fully known.

Containers vary somewhat in size but are basically like truck trailers without wheels. They can be loaded with shippers' goods at any point in the trip from door-to-door but are most efficient when stuffed at the origin and unstuffed at the destination. Because they are standard units, they move readily between different modes of transportation, thereby promoting new potentials for service. In 1966 containerization was tested by Sea-Land in a major foreign market—the North Atlantic-United States route. In addition, several other operators tested container movements.

The change in the technology of the merchant shipping industry, then, is containerization, and the change in service is intermodalism. The full development of containerization and intermodalism is strategic to U.S. shipping companies, for it offers a means of enhancing America's competitive position in world markets and increasing the U.S.-flag share of the shipping market. Specifically, the development of the concept of the high-productivity ships attacks three problems:

i) It brings economies of scale to an industry that was heretofore devoid of such possibilities;
ii) it introduces capital-intensive processes to the labor-oriented stevedoring task, while reducing theft and damage;
iii) it offers an opportunity to differentiate shipper service by resolving the complex inland transportation issues in the development of an intermodal system.

The simple concept of consolidating packages into a standard unit of interchange between ships, docks, trucks and rail cars brings economies of scale to cargo-handling operations, dramatically increases the productivity of vessels, for the first time makes a large fleet more effective than a small one, and makes regularly scheduled service more efficient than a tramp operation. The change in the economic structure is so great as to raise serious questions about the effective competitiveness of tramp vessels for containerable cargo on major, high-volume trade routes.

By using containers as the standard unit of interchange—with a cellular containership, container cranes (on the ship or pier) and other supporting equipment—it is possible to achieve loading/unloading rates per berth hour of 1,000 tons[k] compared to 60 tons on breakbulk vessels. To understand fully the impact of this productivity, it is necessary to examine vessel utilization, with its impact on vessel costs and vessel revenue, and stevedoring costs.

The most significant effect of the dramatic speed of container loading/unloading is the increase achieved in annual lift capacity. Instead of the 1:1 sea-to-port-time ratio for breakbulk ships, a container vessel can achieve a 4:1 sea-to-port-time ratio. Thus, a modern C-4 breakbulk vessel might have an annual lift capacity of about 156,000 measurement tons, whereas a containership could average 560,000 measurement tons of lift capacity.[1]

The impact on vessel economics is equally dramatic. If freight rates remain unchanged, potential vessel revenue for containerships is four times that of the breakbulk ship, while in terms of vessel operating expense (excluding voyage expense) per ton of annual lift capacity, container vessel costs are almost one-half those of breakbulk ships. (See Table 2-2.) Clearly, a major breakthrough in vessel efficiency has been made with containerships.

The new ship types also radically change the economics of loading and discharging cargo. Instead of being labor intensive, container stevedoring operations are now capital intensive. The investment is in cranes, straddle

---

[k]Assumes that 480 40-foot containers are loaded and 480 containers are unloaded per 24-hour period (one off, one on, every three minutes).

[l]Technical notes on the computation of annual lift capacity are found in Appendix B.

Table 2-2

Comparison of Vessel Operating Costs:
1967

	C-4 Break-Bulk Ship	Containership
Annual Capacity	156,000	560,000
Vessel Costs:		
Vessel Operating Expense*	$1,367,000	$1,693,000
Vessel Depreciation	150,000	392,000
Container Cost	–	960,000
Total Vessel Cost	$1,517,000	$2,962,000
Cost per Ton of Capacity	$9.72	$5.29

*Excludes voyage expense and interest charges.

Source: See Appendix D for detailed explanation of cost assumptions.

carriers, and chassis for the containers. Container cranes can cost over a million dollars, and the auxiliary equipment, such as straddle carriers, costs as much as $100,000 per unit. In addition, a large parcel of land is required to store containers. Although the capital costs are higher than for breakbulk operations, they are fixed and do not increase as volume increases.

There are four distinct steps in the containership cargo-handling operation:

i) loading and unloading containers;
ii) moving containers between the pier and the container yard;
iii) stuffing and devanning the containers;
iv) terminal handling of the cargo.

It is estimated that the labor input to perform these functions amounted to $6.25 per measurement ton in 1967, or about one-half the breakbulk cost (see Appendix D). There are other port costs which are a function of volume: for example, if a pier lease (including cranes and supporting equipment) can be negotiated for $1,000,000 annually, when volume is at the 100,000-ton level, fixed costs are $10 per ton; however, if volume is at the 1,000,000-ton level, port charges are only $1 per ton. Thus, the potential to reduce cargo handling costs through the use of containerization is dependent on the volume put through the facility; and when sufficient volumes can be generated, containership operators can make significant breakthroughs in reducing stevedoring costs.

Because of the need to guarantee large volumes of containers for a pier facility, it is unlikely that a container vessel will be tramped from port to port. Thus, containerization—by dramatically changing the loading/unloading characteristics of the shipping industry—not only is changing vessel economics but is also changing the structure of cargo-handling costs.

The faster loading/unloading characteristics of the new system also allow much larger vessels to be built. While the size of breakbulk vessels has been limited to approximately 15,000 measurement tons for a vessel, vessels capable of carrying 2,000 20-foot container equivalents (or 32,000 to 40,000 measurement tons) are now possible and are on the drawing boards.

Container operations also enable large fleets to achieve economies not available to small companies. As the number of ships in the firm's fleet increases, fewer suits of containers are required per vessel. In other words, the productivity of containers is increased with larger-volume operations.

The implications of these changes are significant to liner organizations: the containership operator may have lower costs than the tramp line, and does have the potential to give significantly higher levels of service to shippers.[m] Thus, the poor commercial performance of liner operations in the 1950's and 1960's may be dramatically reversed in the 1970's.

Since the liner industry comprises the bulk of the U.S.-flag fleet, the U.S. Merchant Marine has a viable commercial future for the first time in many decades as well as a potential for increased contribution to national objectives. However, despite its pioneering in containerization, the U.S. fleet is still primarily breakbulk. The industry will need to make the costly transition from breakbulk operations to full container operations. Once the transition is made, the economics of containerization assure the liner operator a new competitive position.

Without a commercial future, the past contributions of the U.S. Merchant Marine to national objectives would be classified as an interesting academic exercise, since new building programs could not be assured. With containerization, the U.S. Merchant Marine has an incentive to continue and expand operations. Therefore, the past and potential contributions to the economic well-being of the nation become dynamic elements in the total view of the U.S. Merchant Marine. In Chapter 3 the past contributions of the fleet are documented. In Chapter 4 the future fleet size is projected and the impact of various fleet sizes on a combination of economic environments is measured. Finally, in Chapter 5, the key variables to the success of the U.S.-flag fleet are examined and a preliminary statement is made of how a joint industry-government partnership could realize the potentials of this industry.

---

[m]Chapter 5 is devoted to a more extensive treatment of this point.

3 The U.S. Merchant Marine During the Past Decade: 1958-1967

Introduction

Just as businesses and individuals need to keep account of their investments, so governments must periodically analyze and reassess their expenditures, primarily by calculating the return on their investments—or, in current terms, by determining the benefit/cost ratios for specific segments of the economy. This chapter assesses the benefits accruing to the United States from its investment in a Merchant Marine and quantifies both their magnitude and the related costs.

The contributions of the Merchant Marine can be classified in two broad areas:

i) benefits to the nation
ii) benefits to the industry

The benefits to the industry are measured by commercial performance, or profits. For the decade between 1958 and 1967, the performance of the U.S.-flag fleet has been characterized by a continuously diminishing carriage of U.S. foreign trade, both in terms of tons of commercial general cargo and in share of the market. While total U.S. foreign trade increased almost 75%—from 203.5 million measurement tons in 1958 to 353.1 million measurement tons in 1967—and the commercial general cargo category of U.S. foreign trade more than doubled (from 75.2 million tons to 180.2 million), the U.S.-flag carriage of commercial general cargo dropped by 25% during the period—from 18.8 million tons in 1958 to 14.0 million tons in 1967. Thus, the U.S.-flag fleet share of the overall U.S. foreign-trade market fell from 21.6% to 13.1% during the 10-year period, while its share of the commercial general cargo trade dropped from 25.0% to 7.8%. It should be noted that these declines were accompanied by a progressive aging of the fleet and by low profits.

Despite this adverse industry situation, the U.S. Merchant Marine has made substantial contributions to the nation. U.S.-flag carriage of trade accounted for a contribution of $7.3 billion to the balance of payments for the decade, thus lowering the substantial deficits which existed during this period. In defense, the fleet responded to national emergencies with sufficient rapidity to meet capacity requirements and to minimize the rate increases that usually accompany abrupt increases in demand. Quantification of some of these benefits indicates a substantial return on the nation's investment in the Merchant Marine, since for every dollar spent—in the form of direct and indirect subsidies—the nation received $4.17 in benefits.[1] Although not quantifiable, further benefits accrued to the nation because a foreign-flag fleet would not have employed higher-cost American labor, built in expensive American shipyards, or responded reliably to the defense needs of the United States.

Government Intervention and the
U.S.-Flag Fleet

As indicated above, the existence of a U.S.-flag fleet has benefited the nation in a number of ways. While these benefits are of importance to the nation, some of them create additional costs to the maritime industry, expenditures which are not necessary to carry cargo and which have seriously damaged the competitive position of U.S.-flag lines (see Chapter 2). Without some incentive to the industry to assume these additional costs, the benefits to the nation would be forfeited.

Therefore, the government has intervened—by means of subsidy to the industry—to promote the fullest benefits to the nation from the Merchant Marine. These subsidies, both direct and indirect, are paid for meeting certain requirements concerning employment, construction, sailings and defense features. Thus, subsidies are actually compensation to the shipping industry for the higher costs incurred because of these requirements and ensure industry survival under the conditions of competitive disadvantage imposed for the achievement of national, rather than industry, goals. While, superficially, government intervention in the maritime industry appears to be a program for the direct benefit of the industry, the subsidy program is actually promulgated for the greater national interest.

The Program

The current relationship of the government to the U.S. Merchant Marine was formulated during the Roosevelt administration. At the time of its passage, a primary purpose of the Merchant Marine Act of 1936 was to create employment opportunities for seamen, shipbuilders and marine suppliers, an issue of primary importance in the Depression years, but less vital today. Due to U.S. involvement in three wars, justification for a strong U.S. Merchant Marine has come to emphasize defense requirements. In addition, the positive contribution of the fleet to the balance of payments account has made the commercial capability of the fleet increasingly important over the past decade. Despite these changes in emphasis, the Merchant Marine Act of 1936 (as amended), through the use of its regulatory and promotional powers, has remained the mechanism for maritime policy.

Regulatory Provisions. The regulatory features of the Act set up mandatory procedures to promote employment, construction, defense, trade, and financial responsibility.

All recipients of government subsidy must employ a substantial percentage of American citizens in the crew: 90% for directly subsidized operators and 75% for indirectly-subsidized companies.

American-built ships are mandatory for directly subsidized lines as well as for carriers wishing to enjoy cargo and rate preferences or to carry Department of Defense (DOD) cargo. Chartered vessels may not be operated under subsidy except in times of emergency. The Act also specifies that recipients of direct subsidy must be willing and able to obtain a sufficient number of vessels of the size, type, speed, and equipment to meet competitive conditions. Under this provision, the Mariner-class vessel represented an attempt to design a standardized vessel which would cut production costs and provide vessels of advanced design for the fleet. Under present government policies, another standard merchant vessel is being planned for the future.

The Navy must approve the design of all directly subsidized vessels, and all special features required for national defense are paid for by the government. In addition, the government may requisition any U.S.-flag vessel in time of national emergency.

The deployment of directly subsidized vessels is regulated in order to provide essential and regular service. This has given rise to the trade route concept, whereby companies are required to serve specified ports with scheduled calls of some definite frequency. Furthermore, limitations are set on services so that lines receiving direct subsidy may not engage in: coastwise trade; the operation of nonsubsidized vessels in competition with subsidized vessels; the operation of foreign-flag vessels competing with U.S.-flag ships on an essential line of trade; enterprises unrelated to shipping; or the sale of ancillary services to the subsidized portions of their own operations.

For directly subsidized firms, the government specifies the recapture of one-half of profits in excess of 10%, up to the amount of subsidy. Other provisions (such as dividend restrictions) are designed to ensure financial responsibility. To provide adequate capital for new construction, firms are required to contribute to a reserve fund.

The effect of such regulations has been accurately observed by investigators of Northwestern University's Transportation Center: "These restrictions suggest that subsidized companies forego many potential advantages in exchange for the subsidy, but waivers may be granted and often are. To a considerable degree, the operators become instruments of governmental policy, entering into contracts with the Maritime Administration."[2] The policies promoted by the regulatory provisions of the Act are not always mutually compatible, and the present condition of the Merchant Marine is to some extent a result of the varied and sometimes conflicting roles it is required to play.

Promotional Provisions. Subsidies are of two types—direct and indirect. Direct payments are made to operators who meet the numerous restrictions detailed above; in addition, certain types of indirect subsidies are available to these operators. However, indirect subsidies are also extended to other lines meeting less stringent manning requirements than the directly subsidized operators. It should be stressed that the basic programs of the Merchant Marine Act concentrate on government support for equipping and manning of the fleet and for financing its construction. Minimal commitment is made for trade promotion or the improvement of cargo-handling systems.

In 1970, 14 U.S. liner operators are under contract to receive an operating differential subsidy (ODS) designed to bring their costs in line with those of foreign operators. Since payroll costs represent the major operating expense, ODS is primarily aimed at ensuring employment for American workers. Trained officers are provided through government support of the Merchant Marine Academy. For operators not receiving direct subsidy, manning requirements are somewhat less stringent.

The construction differential subsidy (CDS), provided to offset the added expense of building vessels in American shipyards, is of major benefit to American shipyards rather than to the Merchant Marine. To encourage investment in ship construction, subsidized companies are granted tax deferments on earnings voluntarily committed to the construction reserve fund. (This is not strictly a subsidy since payment is simply deferred.) Construction loans, mortgage insurance and moratoria on mortgage-interest payments are also available; and research and development grants are made for studies to improve vessel design. Operators ineligible for CDS may participate in vessel-exchange, trade-out and conversion programs by means of a reserve fleet maintained by the government.

Since the U.S. government is the largest single shipper in the world, its policies concerning carriage of its trade have major implications for the maritime industry. These are specified in the Cargo Preference Act, which requires all government cargo to be shipped in U.S.-flag vessels,[a] with rate-preference privileges extended, enabling U.S.-flag vessels to bid above world rates on certain shipments. All operators with American-built ships are eligible to participate in this program. Thus, this program constitutes a basic subsidy to operators ineligible for direct subsidy.

While promotional activities for commercial cargo are supported by the maritime industry, the government does participate by: statistical monitoring of the fleet's performance; participation in trade conferences; production of brochures; and promoting development of port and cargo-handling systems by a research-grant program.

Costs of the Government Program

Table 3-1 presents data on direct-subsidy expenditures from 1958 through 1967. Operating differential subsidy totaled $1,805 million for the 10-year period, with a generally upward trend, from $141 million in 1958 to $216 million in 1967. Meanwhile, construction differential subsidy amounted to $827 million for the decade, fluctuating from a low of $28 million in 1958 to a peak of $122 million in 1961.

Since indirect-subsidy funds are not appropriated—and some indirect subsidies do not involve the actual outlay of funds—the calculation of indirect-

---

[a]In practice, only Department of Defense cargo travels principally in American ships.

33

Table 3-1

**Operating and Construction
Differential Subsidies: 1958-1967
(Dollars in Thousands)**

Year	Operating Differential Subsidy (ODS Net Payable)	Construction Differential Subsidy (CDS Paid)*
1967	$216,217	$ 90,116
1966	199,050	77,954
1965	184,472	80,535
1964	204,227	83,293
1963	192,199	86,798
1962	177,490	117,857
1961	168,618	122,176
1960	163,026	88,659
1959	159,380	51,365
1958	140,741	28,046

*Since construction differential subsidy data are reported on a fiscal-year basis, it was necessary to convert to a calendar-year basis by averaging two fiscal years.

Sources: U.S. Department of Commerce, Maritime Administration, *1968 Annual Report of the Maritime Administration* (Washington, D.C.: Government Printing Office, 1969), and from data furnished by the Maritime Administration's Office of Government Aid. Hereafter, the Maritime Administration will be abbreviated as Marad.

subsidy costs is more difficult. Two programs—rate preference and ship exchange—involve calculable indirect-subsidy cost to the government. The total bill for the rate-preference programs amounted to about $600 million for the decade (see Table 3-2), and it is estimated that only 4.1% of this amount was received by directly subsidized operators.[3]

The costs of the ship-exchange program are approximately half that of rate preference, or $301 million, for the period from 1960 (when this program was instituted) through 1967. This subsidy was received entirely by the indirectly subsidized operators.[b]

The total amount of subsidy to the U.S. Merchant Marine is summarized in Table 3-3. Construction differential subsidy is shown separately because this program benefits the shipyard owners rather than the fleet operators. All subsidies amounted to $3,532 million for the decade, or $2,706 million excluding CDS.

Effects of Government Programs

The results of government regulation and subsidy can be assessed in a number of ways, both quantitative and qualitative. The most immediate effect of the programs is upon the size of the fleet; so much subsidy supports so many ships. These ships are simply a means to promote the carriage of trade, which in turn affects both the commercial performance of the fleet and the benefits which accrue to the nation. The ultimate measure of subsidy is its success in fulfilling its goal of amplifying net national benefits.[c] Each of these quantifiable elements:

  i) fleet size
 ii) commercial performance
iii) net national benefits

will be examined in more detail in later sections of this chapter.

There are other effects, which are expressed in terms other than ships constructed or tons of cargo carried. Ideally, government programs should produce benefits without creating side effects. However, the government is never a pure catalytic agent. The entire structure of the U.S. Merchant Marine has been affected by the government programs designed only to enhance national benefits. One major result has been the introduction of artificial differentiations among ocean carriers, with the industry split into three segments—directly subsidized liner, indirectly subsidized liner, and tramp-irregular. Each segment is characterized primarily by its relationship to the government.

---

[b]Because of the magnitude of these indirect subsidies, the less familiar but more accurate term "indirectly-subsidized" operators has been substituted for "nonsubsidized" operators.

[c]See note 1 for this chapter, p. 290.

Table 3-2

**Estimated Indirect Subsidy from Rate
Preference Program: 1958-1967
(Dollars in Thousands)**

Year	Title I PL 480	Title IV PL 480*	Total
1967	$ 59,085	$ 9,282	$ 68,367
1966	63,910	11,837	75,747
1965	61,201	6,851	68,052
1964	73,255	3,477	76,732
1963	78,176	1,125	79,301
1962	58,282	1,173	59,455
1961	49,765	–	49,765
1960	54,205	–	54,205
1959	36,827	–	36,827
1958	30,779	–	30,779
Total	$565,485	$33,745	$599,230

Note: Represents the difference between the U.S.-flag rates and the foreign-flag rates on the quantities required to be carried on U.S. vessels to comply with the 50% requirement contained in the Cargo Preference laws.

*Title IV did not become effective until 1962.

Source: From data furnished by U.S. Department of Agriculture, Commodity Credit Corporation, Financial Analysis Branch.

Table 3-3

**Summary of Subsidy Costs: 1958-1967
(Dollars in Thousands)**

		Indirect Subsidy				
Year	ODS	*Rate Preference*	*Ship Exchange Program*	Subtotal	CDS	Total
1967	$ 216,217	$ 68,367	$ 64,000	$ 348,584	$ 90,116	$ 438,700
1966	199,050	75,747	44,000	318,797	77,954	396,751
1965	184,472	68,052	38,000	290,524	80,535	371,059
1964	204,227	76,732	52,000	332,959	83,293	416,252
1963	192,199	79,301	47,000	318,500	86,798	405,298
1962	177,490	59,455	32,000	268,945	117,857	386,802
1961	168,618	49,765	12,000	230,383	122,176	352,559
1960	163,026	54,205	12,000	229,231	88,659	317,890
1959	159,380	36,827	–	196,207	51,365	247,572
1958	140,741	30,779	–	171,520	28,046	199,566
Total	$1,805,420	$599,230	$301,000	$2,705,650	$826,799	$3,532,449

Sources: Tables 3-1, 3-2, and computations
based on *Ship Exchange Report Status*
(Washington, D.C.: Marad, Office of Government Aid, May 1969, mimeo).

The subsidized segment can be characterized by its close and continuing contact with the Maritime Administration and the Maritime Subsidy Board. Direct subsidy has enabled this segment to replace its fleet and maintain a greater degree of commercial vigor than the average indirectly subsidized liner or tramp counterparts. However, maintaining eligibility for subsidy is a complex responsibility, and industry effort is divided between attention to commercial market requirements and the politics of subsidy.

The indirectly subsidized firms—both liner and tramp—have become equally involved with the government. Close and continuing contact between these operators and government agencies responsible for shipping government-impelled cargoes has evolved because these cargoes constitute a large part of the business of this segment (see Table 3-13). Moreover, dependence on the government has been assured by the prohibition against foreign-built ships in this reserved trade. Without construction subsidy and without permission to use foreign-built ships in their primary market, the indirectly-subsidized firms have been unable to replace their fleets without the use of trade-outs from the National Defense Reserve Fleet, a fleet which is rapidly becoming depleted of useful ships.

The existence of these artificially created divisions has been an obstacle to the development of a comprehensive maritime program. The underlying community of interest of the Merchant Marine is obscured as segments compete with each other, sometimes using the regulations governing other segments as weapons in their competitive strategies.

Government programs have also affected industry strategy through their concentration on a vessel-replacement policy which has ignored the importance to foreign trade of port and cargo-handling systems and has thereby stifled innovation in transportation service. The provision of subsidy for vessels alone, combined with the complexities of meeting regulatory requirements to maintain eligibility for subsidy, has inadvertently distracted the industry from viewing the transport system as a whole and has created an obsessive concern with vessel and ocean operations.

Government regulations requiring American construction of merchant vessels has made the Merchant Marine dependent on government aid to finance new vessels. Although other factors contribute to investment decisions to build ships, the industry could not have afforded U.S. construction costs without subsidy. Thus, the most direct effect of government intervention can be seen in the size, composition, and condition of the fleet.

The Size and Composition of the U.S.-Flag Fleet: 1958-1968

Although the economics of maritime shipping and the nature of government policy are bound to change over the next decade, some portion of the capacity of the U.S. Merchant Marine in 1976 will consist of vessels being used today.

Therefore, the starting point for an investigation of both the past and future of the Merchant Marine must be a determination of the size, composition and condition of the present fleet.

As indicated previously, the present fleet is divided into three segments: subsidized, indirectly-subsidized and tramp/irregular. The data for each segment were derived from *Vessel Inventory Report*[4] for the years 1958-1966, and from *Status of United States Flag Merchant Fleet*[5] for 1966, 1967 and 1968.

Since the composition of the fleet varies from year to year in number and size of ships, all vessels were converted to a standard measurement unit called the General Purpose Ship (GPS). The standard vessel was defined as a conventional general cargo freighter with an annual capacity of 149,408 tons, based on the following assumptions regarding the characteristics of the GPS.

Gross capacity in measurement tons = 20,000
Number of days in service per year = 350
Length in nautical miles of an average round trip = 13,500
Ship service speed in knots = 18
Sea-to-port-time ratio = 1:1 (175 days at sea, 175 days in port)
Ratio of usable measurement tons to total measurement
    tons of capacity = .667[6]

See Appendix B for the technical notes used to develop the factors for each ship type as well as for the tabulation of GPS values by year and ship type.

Growth, Composition and Age of the
U.S.-Flag Fleet

By 1958, the ships produced in the massive ship construction programs of World War II were reaching middle age. In a few years the fleet would have faced block obsolescence unless attention were given to vessel replacement.

Table 3-4 presents figures on the actual number of ships at the end of each year from 1958 to 1968. During this period, a slight increase—from 591 ships in 1958 to 617 in 1968—was registered. From this table, it appears that, after reaching a low of 563 in 1961, the industry was in the process of rebuilding the fleet. However, examination of Table 3-5 indicates an almost steady growth in GPS equivalent ships—from 339 in 1958 to over 500 in 1968. As older ships dropped out of the fleet, they were replaced by larger and faster breakbulk and container vessels. Table 3-6 expresses this trend in another fashion, showing the increase in individual ship size as a percentage of GPS.

As shown in Table 3-7, all segments of the industry—subsidized liner, indirectly subsidized liner and tramp/irregular—experienced increases in capacity. The subsidized-liner segment accounted for almost 50% of the fleet capacity in 1968 compared to nearly 57% in 1958; the indirectly subsidized

Table 3-4

Size of U.S.-Flag Fleet in Foreign Trade
Classified by Segment: 1958-1968
(Number of Ships at End of Year)

Year	Subsidized Liner	Indirectly-Subsidized Liner	Tramp/ Irregular	Total
1968	303	150	164	617
1967	315	145	156	616
1966	322	132	150	604
1966	322	143	135	600
1965	318	119	136	573
1964	317	131	137	585
1963	317	135	138	590
1962	298	133	144	575
1961	277	148	138	563
1960	278	144	144	566
1959	293	142	159	594
1958	305	139	147	591

Note: The data for 1967 and 1968 differ from those for the earlier years in that only those *ships in domestic service* at the end of the year were excluded, whereas for 1966 (and earlier) *all ships* belonging to companies thought to be primarily in domestic trade were excluded. To indicate the differences in the two methods of establishing ship count, the 1966 data are presented on both bases. This method is used in Tables 3-4 through 3-7.

Sources: *Status of United States Flag Merchant Fleet, as of December 31, 1966, 1967, and 1968* (Washington, D. C.: Marad, Office of Government Aid) and *Vessel Inventory Report, 1958-1966* (Washington, D. C.: Marad, Office of Trade Promotion).

Table 3-5

**Size of U.S.-Flag Fleet in Foreign Trade
in GPS Equivalents, Classified by
Segment: 1958-1968 (GPS Ships at End
of Year)**

Year	Subsidized Liner	Indirectly-Subsidized Liner	Tramp/ Irregular	Total
1968*	249.682	117.844	141.599	509.125
1967*	233.131	106.978	135.015	475.124
1966*	231.669	89.673	120.170	441.512
1966	230.961	93.397	111.835	436.193
1965	221.336	72.800	114.609	408.745
1964	216.550	82.793	113.608	412.951
1963	214.625	78.374	107.480	400.479
1962	197.061	75.184	102.771	375.016
1961	178.273	82.344	91.440	352.057
1960	174.510	80.621	80.148	335.279
1959	183.353	79.869	76.037	339.259
1958	191.166	79.083	69.001	339.250

*See Table 3-4.   Sources: Appendix Tables B-3 through B-8.

liner segment accounted for 23% in both years; and the tramp/irregular segment increased from 20% to 28%.

Most additions to the fleet since 1966 have been in the form of container capacity. The total number of such vessels grew from 22 to 63 between 1966 and 1968, while the breakbulk fleet dropped from 546 to 518 vessels (see Table 3-8). The number of fully containerized vessels in the subsidized fleet jumped from one in 1966 to 19 in 1968. The increase in capacity is even more

41

Table 3-6

**Average GPS Factors For U.S.-Flag
Fleet in Foreign Trade: 1958-1968**

Year	GPS Factor	Year	GPS Factor
1968*	.825	1963	.679
1967*	.771	1962	.652
1966*	.731	1961	.625
1966	.727	1960	.592
1965	.713	1959	.571
1964	.706	1958	.574

*See Table 3-4.   Source: Derived from Tables 3-4 and 3-5.

striking. Table 3-9 shows the rapid expansion of the container fleet, from 3.8 million measurement tons of annual lift capacity in 1966 to 13.6 million measurement tons in 1968; container capacity in the subsidized segment grew from 261,000 measurement tons in 1966 to nearly 5.2 million measurement tons in 1968.

It should be noted that the average subsidized containership had greater capacity than the container vessels in the indirectly subsidized fleet, since this latter group relied on conversion of older vessels for their container capacity, while the subsidized segment grew by building new containerships, as well as by converting larger breakbulk vessels.

Despite these changes, the U.S.-flag fleet was expanding less rapidly than the world fleet and in 1968 was still operating substantial numbers of older ships. The U.S. fleet accounted for 7.0% of world capacity in 1958 and 6.7% in 1968. Moreover, the average age of the ships in the U.S.-flag fleet in 1968 was 19 years.[d]

[d]This is an arithmatic average of all ships in the fleet at the end of 1968. However, of 617 ships in the 1968 fleet, 169 were built in 1945; 124, in 1944; and 55, in 1943. Thus, over one-half of the fleet was at least 22.5 years old at the end of 1968 and nearing the statutory age of retirement.[7]

Table 3-7

U.S.-Flag Annual Lift Capacity In
Foreign Trade, Classified by Segment:
1958-1968 (Measurement Tons in
Thousands)

Year	Subsidized Liner	Indirectly-Subsidized Liner	Tramp/ Irregular	Total
1968*	37,304	17,607	21,156	76,067
1967*	34,832	15,983	20,172	70,987
1966*	34,613	13,398	17,954	65,965
1966	34,507	13,954	16,709	65,170
1965	33,069	10,877	17,124	61,070
1964	32,354	12,370	16,974	61,698
1963	32,067	11,710	16,058	59,835
1962	29,442	11,233	15,355	56,030
1961	26,635	12,303	13,662	52,600
1960	26,073	12,045	11,975	50,093
1959	27,394	11,933	11,361	50,688
1958	28,562	11,816	10,309	50,687

*See Table 3-4.   Source: Derived from Table 3-5.

U.S.-Flag Performance in International Trade

The economic health of the U.S. shipping industry—and thus its benefits to the nation—depend indirectly upon the magnitude of the total market and directly upon the extent to which the U.S. fleet participates in this market. The U.S. foreign-trade market (in measurement tons) has risen nearly 75% in the decade, compared to a 40% growth in the U.S.-flag fleet lift capacity. Market growth has outstripped the U.S.-flag fleet's capacity to carry it, so that foreign operators are carrying a greater share of U.S. trade today than a decade ago (87% in 1967 vs. 78% in 1958).

Published historical data on U.S. exports and imports are recorded by type of carriage—liner or nonliner—rather than by type of cargo carried.[8] With the introduction of containerization, traditional patterns of carriage are changing since container vessels, unlike the general cargo ships of the past, do not have facilities to top off with bulk. In order to obtain a workable data base for future predictions and to observe past performance in cargo markets, therefore, it was necessary to estimate and classify foreign trade tonnage for commercial, government-impelled and DOD shipments as general cargo or bulk. Tanker tonnages of liquid cargo are excluded, since the focus of this study is exclusively on the dry cargo market.

It should be noted that throughout this report, tonnages in foreign trade are expressed in totals rather than in separate export and import figures. Although imbalances of trade on individual routes—as revealed by export/import data— do affect the performance of the fleet, this type of detailed inquiry is secondary to the larger matter of fleet performance which is revealed by totaled figures.

Total Market Size and Characteristics

The amount of U.S. foreign trade carried by all flags increased from 203.5 million measurement tons in 1958 to 353.1 million measurement tons in 1967 according to the figures in Table 3-10. It is significant that total trade is a composite of three types of market which respond to different factors:

  i) Commercial;
 ii) Government-Impelled;
iii) Department of Defense.

The commercial market has been the most important category of U.S. international trade, ranging between 84% and 89% of the total. Within the commercial market, general cargo assumed greater importance than bulk shipments over the decade: in 1958, general cargo constituted 44% of the total commercial market; by 1968, it had grown to almost 58% of total commercial cargo.

The government-impelled market, which is governed by PL 480 and the

Table 3-8

Size of U. S.-Flag Fleet in Foreign Trade: 1966-1968 (Number of Ships at End of Year)

Year and Use	Subsidized Liner				Indirectly-Subsidized Liner			
	Break-bulk	Con-tainer	Bulk	Subtotal	Break-bulk	Con-tainer	Bulk	Subtotal
1968								
In Foreign Trade	169	13	–	182	56	19	3	78
TCMST*	49	–	–	49	28	13	–	41
Temporarily Inactive	61	6	–	67	19	11	–	30
Laid Up	5	–	–	5	–	–	1	1
Total	284	19	–	303	103	43	4	150
1967								
In Foreign Trade	258	2	–	260	65	19	4	88
TCMST*	39	–	–	39	35	13	–	48
Temporarily Inactive	12	–	–	12	4	5	–	9
Laid Up	4	–	–	4	–	–	–	–
Total	313	2	–	313	104	37	4	145
1966								
In Foreign Trade	287	1	–	288	63	6	4	73
TCMST*	33	–	–	33	39	3	–	42
Temporarily Inactive	–	–	1	1	4	10	–	14
Laid Up	–	–	–	–	3	–	–	3
Total	320	1	1	322	109	19	4	132

Table 3-8 (*continued*)

Year and Use	Tramp/Irregular Break-bulk	Con-tainer	Bulk	Subtotal	All Segments Break-bulk	Con-tainer	Bulk	Total
1968								
In Foreign Trade	56	–	20	76	281	32	23	336
TCMST*	58	1	7	66	135	14	7	156
Temporarily Inactive	13	–	4	17	93	17	4	114
Laid Up	4	–	1	5	9	–	2	11
Total	131	1	32	164	518	63	36	617
1967								
In Foreign Trade	39	–	22	61	362	21	26	409
TCMST*	71	–	7	78	145	13	7	165
Temporarily Inactive	8	–	2	10	24	5	2	31
Laid Up	4	–	2	6	8	–	2	10
Total	122	–	33	155	539	39	37	615
1966								
In Foreign Trade	37	2	20	59	387	9	24	420
TCMST*	73	–	7	80	145	3	7	155
Temporarily Inactive	4	–	2	6	8	10	3	21
Laid Up	3	–	2	5	6	–	2	8
Total	117	2	31	150	546	22	36	604

*Time charter to Military Sea Transportation Service (MSTS).

Source: *Status of the United States Flag Merchant Fleet, as of December 31, 1966, 1967, 1968* (Washington, D. C.: Marad, Office of Government Aid).

Table 3-9

**U. S.-Flag Annual Lift Capacity in Foreign
Trade: 1966-1968 (Measurement Tons
in Thousands)**

Year and Use	Subsidized Liner				Indirectly-Subsidized Liner			
	Breakbulk	*Container*	*Bulk*	*Subtotal*	*Breakbulk*	*Container*	*Bulk*	*Subtotal*
1968								
In Foreign Trade	19,045	3,536	–	22,581	5,474	3,508	461	9,443
TCMST*	5,605	–	–	5,605	2,177	2,215	–	4,392
Temporarily Inactive	7,149	1,641	–	8,790	1,692	1,933	–	3,625
Laid Up	328	–	–	328	–	–	147	147
Total	32,127	5,177	–	37,304	9,343	7,656	608	17,607
1967								
In Foreign Trade	28,777	522	–	29,299	6,006	3,029	608	9,643
TCMST*	4,171	–	–	4,171	2,757	2,215	–	4,972
Temporarily Inactive	1,088	–	–	1,088	465	903	–	1,368
Laid Up	274	–	–	274	–	–	–	–
Total	34,309	522	–	34,832	9,228	6,147	608	15,983
1966								
In Foreign Trade	30,872	261	–	31,133	5,990	1,206	608	7,804
TCMST*	3,113	–	–	3,113	2,833	401	–	3,234
Temporarily Inactive	–	–	367	367	469	1,756	–	2,225
Laid Up	–	–	–	–	135	–	–	135
Total	33,985	261	367	34,613	9,427	3,363	608	13,398

47

Table 3-9 (*continued*)

Year and Use	Tramp/Irregular				All Segments			
	Break-bulk	*Con-tainer*	*Bulk*	*Subtotal*	*Break-bulk*	*Con-tainer*	*Bulk*	*Total*
1968								
In Foreign								
Trade	4,493	–	5,820	10,313	29,012	7,044	6,281	42,337
TCMST*	5,272	766	2,460	8,498	13,054	2,981	2,460	18,495
Temporarily								
Inactive	1,059	–	704	1,763	9,900	3,574	704	14,178
Laid Up	311	–	271	582	639	–	418	1,057
Total	11,135	766	9,255	21,156	52,605	13,599	9,863	76,067
1967								
In Foreign								
Trade	2,991	–	6,562	9,553	37,774	3,551	7,170	48,495
TCMST*	6,120	–	2,615	8,735	13,048	2,215	2,615	17,878
Temporarily								
Inactive	801	–	666	1,467	2,354	903	666	3,923
Laid Up	283	–	134	417	557	–	134	691
Total	10,195	–	9,977	20,172	53,733	6,669	10,585	70,987
1966								
In Foreign								
Trade	2,869	196	5,771	8,836	39,731	1,663	6,379	47,773
TCMST*	6,067	–	1,941	8,008	12,013	401	1,941	14,355
Temporarily								
Inactive	335	–	457	792	804	1,756	824	3,384
Laid Up	184	–	134	318	319	–	134	453
Total	9,455	196	8,303	17,954	52,694	3,820	9,278	65,965

*Time Charter to MSTS.

Source: Derived from Appendix Tables B-3, B-4, and B-5.

Table 3-10

Total U.S. Foreign Trade: 1958-1967
(Measurement Tons in Thousands)

	Commercial			Government-Impelled			DOD	
Year	General Cargo	Bulk*	Subtotal	General Cargo	Bulk†	Subtotal	General Cargo‡	Total
1967	180,242	132,815	313,057	10,542	10,946	21,488	18,542	353,087
1966	158,150	137,970	296,120	11,202	14,847	26,049	16,684	338,853
1965	149,790	131,797	281,587	11,296	13,926	25,222	12,472	319,281
1964	144,744	122,578	267,322	9,892	17,041	26,933	9,825	304,080
1963	121,302	105,866	227,168	13,354	17,657	31,011	9,487	267,666
1962	111,768	99,156	210,924	10,798	17,593	28,391	8,883	248,198
1961	105,768	86,201	191,969	12,466	14,295	26,761	7,613	226,343
1960	102,628	91,893	194,521	11,960	15,399	27,359	6,786	228,666
1959	96,118	93,701	189,819	10,794	10,756	21,550	7,535	218,904
1958	75,226	94,801	170,027	14,642	11,002	25,644	7,832	203,503

*Does not include any bulk shipments sent in tankers.

†Tanker shipments are included here since these are primarily grain. All Department of Agriculture and all tanker shipments were treated as bulk. AID, GSA and other tonnage shipped in liners and tramps were treated as general cargo and were converted to measurement tons.

‡Data were converted from a fiscal-year basis to a calendar-year basis by averaging two years. All DOD tonnage was considered to be general cargo.

Sources: Port of New York Authority; Marad, Office of Maritime Promotion, *Annual Reports*, 1958-1968. Military Sea Transportations Service (MSTS), *Fiscal Reports*, 1958-1968.

annual level of foreign aid appropriations, fluctuated randomly in tonnage, dropping from 13% of total trade in 1958 to 6% in 1967. In 1967, the market amounted to 21.5 million measurement tons, almost evenly divided between bulk and general cargo.

The Department of Defense carryings exhibited the greatest percentage growth over the decade, from 7.8 million measurement tons to 18.5 million, or 137%. This increase was due to the Vietnam conflict, but such trends are subject to rapid reversal with changes in military policy.

U.S. Share in U.S. Foreign Trade

Although the overall U.S. foreign trade market grew in volume by 75% during the decade, 1958-1967, U.S.-flag tonnage increased only 5%, from 43.9 million measurement tons in 1958 to 46.1 million measurement tons in 1967 (see Table 3-11). Consequently, the U.S.-flag share of the nation's foreign trade market declined from 21.6% in 1958 to 13.1% in 1967, as indicated in Table 3-12. The decline in the U.S.-flag share of commercial general cargo was even more severe, and the fleet actually carried fewer tons of commercial cargo in 1967 than in 1958, dropping from 24.3 million measurement tons in 1958 to 18.6 million measurement tons in 1967.

In order to establish a base for projecting fleet performance in 1976, it was necessary to estimate the distribution of tonnage carried by type of cargo for each segment in 1967; these estimates are presented in Table 3-13. The proportion of total trade carried by each segment corresponds closely to the distribution of capacity shown in a previous section: subsidized liners carried almost half the trade, or 48%; indirectly-subsidized liners, about 24%; and tramps carried slightly more, or 28%.

The types of cargo and market categories from which each segment drew its revenue differentiated the segments quite markedly. While all segments of the fleet relied heavily on government-impelled and DOD cargo, the subsidized liner segment continued to carry substantial proportions of commercial cargo. Thus, almost 55% of the tonnage carried by the directly-subsidized segment was commercial cargo, while the recipients of indirect subsidy—both liner and nonliner—substituted government and military cargoes for commercial carryings, with commercial tonnage amounting to only 22% of indirectly-subsidized liner carriage, and 30% of total tramp tonnage.

The Health of the U.S. Maritime Industry

The participation of the U.S.-flag fleet in carriage of government cargoes did not offset the effects of the commercial slide. The moderate growth of the fleet during the period, therefore, resulted not in greater prosperity for the industry but in declining load factors and lower return on investment (ROI).

Table 3-11

U.S.-Flag Carriage of U.S. Foreign Trade: 1958-1967 (Measurement Tons in Thousands)

Year	Commercial			Government-Impelled			DOD	Total
	General Cargo	Bulk	Subtotal	General Cargo	Bulk	Subtotal	General Cargo	
1967	14,006	4,621	18,627	4,924	4,018	8,942	18,542	46,111
1966	14,586	5,271	19,857	5,438	5,932	11,370	16,684	47,911
1965	13,168	5,436	18,604	7,250	6,853	14,103	12,473	45,180
1964	18,226	5,533	23,759	7,374	8,336	15,710	9,826	49,295
1963	14,690	4,156	18,846	9,540	9,349	18,889	9,488	47,223
1962	15,354	2,607	17,961	8,210	8,887	17,097	8,884	43,942
1961	15,408	3,796	19,204	7,426	7,207	14,633	7,613	41,450
1960	18,214	5,848	24,062	5,510	7,500	13,010	6,786	43,858
1959	18,046	6,261	24,307	4,694	4,998	9,692	7,535	41,534
1958	18,782	5,491	24,273	6,710	5,132	11,842	7,832	43,947

Notes: Source data for commercial and government-impelled cargoes were reported in long tons and converted to measurement tons. Because DOD data were reported by fiscal year, conversion to calendar years was made by averaging two fiscal years.

Sources: Marad, Division of Cargo Promotion, *Annual Reports,* 1958-1968; MSTS, *Fiscal Reports,* 1958-1968; commercial tonnage breakdown estimated on the basis of 1960-1963 data contained in Ernst & Ernst, *Review of Merchant Fleet Replacement* (Washington, D.C.: August 1965).

Table 3-12

**U.S.-Flag Market Share of U.S.
Foreign Trade: 1958-1967**

Year	Commercial			Government-Impelled			DOD	Total
	General Cargo	*Bulk*	*Subtotal*	*General Cargo*	*Bulk*	*Subtotal*	*General Cargo*	
1967	7.8%	3.5%	6.0%	46.7%	36.7%	41.6%	100.0%	13.1%
1966	9.2	3.8	6.7	48.5	40.0	43.6	100.0	14.1
1965	8.8	4.1	6.6	64.2	49.2	55.9	100.0	14.2
1964	12.6	4.5	8.9	74.5	48.9	58.3	100.0	16.2
1963	12.1	3.9	8.3	71.4	52.9	60.9	100.0	17.6
1962	13.7	2.6	8.5	76.0	50.5	60.2	100.0	17.7
1961	14.6	4.4	10.0	59.6	50.4	54.7	100.0	18.3
1960	17.7	6.4	12.4	46.1	48.7	47.6	100.0	19.2
1959	18.8	6.7	12.8	43.5	46.5	45.0	100.0	19.0
1958	25.0	5.8	14.3	45.8	46.6	46.2	100.0	21.6

Sources: Derived from Tables 3-10 and 3-11.

Table 3-13

U.S.-Flag Carriage of Foreign Trade:
1967 (Measurement Tons in Thousands)

Segment	Commercial			Government-Impelled			DOD	Total
	General Cargo	*Bulk*	*Subtotal*	*General Cargo*	*Bulk*	*Subtotal*	*General Cargo*	
Subsidized Liner	11,178	1,016	12,194	3,511	496	4,007	6,158	22,359
Indirectly-Subsidized Liner	1,972	436	2,408	619	212	831	7,679	10,918
Total Liner	13,150	1,452	14,602	4,130	708	4,838	13,837	32,277
Tramp	856	3,169	4,025	794	3,310	4,104	4,705	12,834
Total	14,006	4,621	18,627	4,924	4,018	8,942	18,542	46,111

Notes: Source data for commercial and government-impelled cargoes were reported in long tons and converted to measurement tons. Because DOD data were reported by fiscal year, conversion to a calendar year was made by averaging two fiscal years.

Sources: Derived from: MSTS, *Fiscal Reports,* 1966, 1967; Marad, Division of Trade Studies and Division of Cargo Promotion *Annual Reports,* 1966, 1967; and Ernst & Ernst, *Review of Merchant Fleet Replacement* (Washington, D.C., August 1965).

The average vessel utilization rate for the U.S.-flag fleet, which in 1958 was over 85%, declined to about 65% in 1967.

Data for return on investment corroborate the fact that declining market share and vessel utilization had an adverse financial impact on the U.S. maritime industry. The return on investment figures for the directly-subsidized segment are shown in Table 3-14. During the period 1958-1967, the subsidized liner segment—although operating with government subsidy—was receiving returns on investment ranging between 3.5% and 7.3%. Clearly, the Merchant Marine was neither profiting greatly from the government nor responding well to opportunities in the commercial market.

Benefits of the U.S.-Flag Fleet to the Nation

Although the commercial performance of the U.S.-flag fleet was deteriorating over the decade 1958-1967, the fleet made substantial contributions to the

53

Table 3-14

Return on Investment for Subsidized Liners: 1958-1967 (Dollars in Thousands)

Year	Stockholders' Investment	Earnings After Taxes	Return on Investment
1967	$966,904	$33,979	3.51%
1966	955,820	61,847	6.47
1965	907,677	39,157	4.31
1964	880,296	53,527	6.08
1963	835,650	44,750	5.36
1962	804,466	37,905	4.71
1961	774,472	28,481	3.68
1960	747,492	27,235	3.64
1959	728,784	29,835	4.09
1958	709,094	52,000	7.33

Note: The 1967 data are not strictly comparable with those for earlier years since they were taken from the Maritime Administration's *Annual Report*.

Sources: *Combined Financial Statement of Lines Holding Operating Differential Subsidy Contracts Under the Provisions of the Merchant Marine Act* (Washington, D. C.: Committee of American Steamship Lines, 1958-1966), and Marad, *Annual Report* (Washington, D. C.: Government Printing Office, 1968).

nation during those years, particularly in defense and in balance of payments. These contributions will continue to be vital to the nation as long as the United States maintains its current priorities. Despite the potential benefits, however, no industry can remain healthy indefinitely unless it is able to respond to profit and growth opportunities. The value of the fleet's benefits to the nation, in the long run, will depend on improvements in the commercial posture of the U.S. Merchant Marine. Unless the commercial side of the industry is improved, the industry as a whole will be unable to continue performing the services that have made it valuable to the nation in the past.

Balance of Payments Benefits [9]

The U.S. balance of payments is an accounting summary of transactions between U.S. entities and foreign entities. During the ten-year period, 1958-1967, the nation recorded annual deficits in its balance of payments in all but one year, with the ten-year deficits totaling approximately $27.4 billion.

A deficit in balance of payments affects the nation directly in three vital areas: interest rates, employment and prices. A deficit means the U.S. government is likely to maintain high interest rates in order to retain U.S. and foreign capital invested in the United States and to prevent further gold outflows. For the consumer, this is reflected in higher interest charges for mortgages and consumer loans, and credit is also more difficult to obtain when money is scarce. High interest rates for business can mean lower levels of domestic business investment, which translates into less employment for workers and lower profits for business. The cost of money is one component of price, and as the cost of money increases significantly, prices rise on many commodities. The balance of payments is related to other elements of the economy as well, but interest rates, employment and prices suffice to demonstrate the importance of keeping adverse balances low.

Two major factors in the chronic balance of payments deficits of the last ten years have been American foreign aid programs and overseas military expenditures. Since neither has declined radically in magnitude, the balance of payments role played by other contributors is crucial. The U.S. Merchant Marine is one such contributor and has furnished $7.3 billion in ten years to offset the large deficits.

The international ocean shipping operations of the U.S. Merchant Marine are reflected in the transportation sector of the balance of payments. Therefore, the balance of payments impact of U.S. merchant shipping is counted as the loss that would be sustained in the transportation sector of the U.S. balance of payments if the shipping services provided by the U.S. fleet were performed by the fleet of another country.

In many types of economic analysis, balance of payments impact is characterized only as receipts of foreign currency reflected in the balance of payments accounts. However, in assessing the balance of payments importance of the U.S. Merchant Marine in the context of alternative sources of transportation, it is equally important to consider the services it provides to U.S. customers which avoid additional payments of dollars to foreign shipping operators. Therefore, the balance of payments impact of the U.S. Merchant Marine is the sum of *two* elements:

i) Net improvement in U.S. foreign exchange position, consisting of revenue from foreign nationals.
ii) Dollar retention, consisting of revenue from U.S. nationals that would otherwise be paid out to foreign vessel operators.

The U.S. Merchant Marine, as an industry, is a major source of foreign exchange. For example, in 1967, gross shipping revenues received from foreign sources totaled $692 million. These revenues for services provided to foreigners are reflected in the balance of payments as *receipts.* Expenditures made in foreign countries by U.S. vessels and their operators in the extension of these services give rise to payments. These *expenditures,* called port charges, include such items as fuel, stores, repairs, stevedoring, labor fees, agents' commissions. Payments made by U.S. entities to foreign shipping operators exert a *negative* effect on our balance of payments, while the port charges paid by these foreign operators in the United States have a *positive* effect.

The total balance of payments impact of U.S. shipping services from 1958-1967, as derived from two sources—net improvement in foreign exchange position and net dollar retention—amounted to $7.3 billion. The detailed data are presented in Table 3-15.

National Security Benefits

The benefits to national security afforded by the U.S. Merchant Marine generally fall into two categories:

i) Availability of shipping capacity;
ii) Cost savings.

The U.S. Merchant Marine has been the mainstay of our defense sealift capability, carrying, on the average, two-thirds of the Military Sea Transportation Service cargo for the fiscal years 1958-1968 (see Figure 3-1). A survey of available figures from 1958 to 1966 on ton-mile carriage reveals a commercial share closer to 75%. This percentage remained high despite the marked increase in demand due to the Vietnam war, indicating that the fleet committed substantially more tonnage to the defense sector during the period.

The increased capacity was made available by several means—time charter and shipping contract (see Table 3-16). From FY 1963 to FY 1968, charter

56

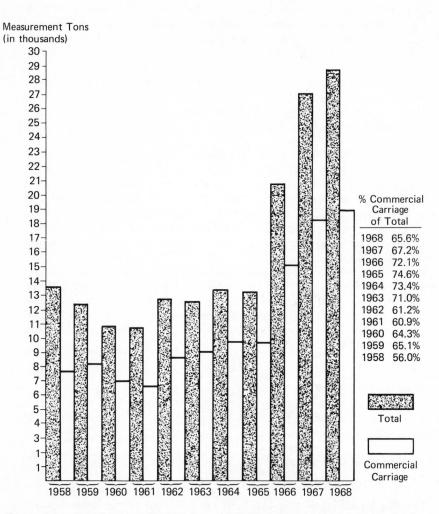

Figure 3-1   Distribution of MSTS Cargo: FY 1958-1968. (Source: Table 3-16)

Table 3-15

Balance of Payments Impact of U.S. Merchant Shipping Operations: FY 1958-1967 (Dollars in Millions)

	1967	1966	1965	1964	1963	1962	1961	1960	1959	1958
Gross Revenue										
Freight Receipts:										
Export	$ 523	$ 541	$ 519	$ 599	$ 538	$ 479	$ 424	$ 428	$ 359	$ 429
Import	378	500	375	380	340	339	290	346	358	336
Between Foreign Countries	161	139	152	158	154	177	155	136	140	130
Passenger Fares:										
Foreign Citizens	8	10	8	11	10	10	9	19	20	24
U. S. Citizens	68	68	72	92	102	83	80	84	85	88
Department of Defense	815	647	330	325	314	303	246	249	289	294
Charter Fees Received	8	10	9	9	9	10	8	8	7	8
Total Revenue	$1,961	$1,915	$1,465	$1,574	$1,467	$1,401	$1,212	$1,270	$1,258	$1,309
Deductions										
Port Charges:										
Abroad (Non-DOD)	$282	$ 294	$281	$317	$288	$260	$231	$167	$155	$170
Domestic (Non-DOD)	378	436	372	402	376	371	325	421	402	414
Foreign and Domestic DOD	204	163	91	92	89	85	67	68	76	68
Total Port Charges	$864	$ 893	$744	$811	$753	$716	$623	$656	$633	$652
Adjustment for Lower Port Charges	–	–	–	–	–	–	–	137	131	136
Net Port Charges	$864	$ 893	$744	$811	$753	$716	$623	$519	$502	$516
Charter Fees Paid	98	110	89	83	83	26	38	36	8	35
Total Deductions	$962	$1,003	$833	$894	$836	$742	$661	$555	$510	$551
Balance of Payments Impact	$999	$ 912	$632	$680	$631	$659	$551	$715	$748	$758

Note: Because original data was reported by fiscal year and averaging two years would obscure the marked shifts, a fiscal-year basis has been used for this table.

Source: Harbridge House, Inc., *The Balance of Payments and the U. S. Merchant Marine* (Boston: 1968), reprinted in Appendix C.

Table 3-16

MSTS Dry Cargo Traffic: FY 1958-1968 (Measurement Tons in Thousands)

Fiscal Year	Government		Commercial					Total MSTS Cargo Lift
	MSTS	GAA (or NSA)	Time Charter	Voyage Charter	Berth Term	Shipping Contract	Subtotal	
1968	4,326.4	5,544.4	8,761.9	90.2	987.7	9,024.4	18,864.2	28,735.0
1967	3,750.4	5,155.4	7,512.5	432.5	1,933.1	8,341.1	18,219.2	27,125.0
1966	3,326.2	2,401.3	6,033.9	105.0	1,583.7	7,425.9	15,148.5	20,876.0
1965	3,321.2	98.1	2,096.6	323.2	697.1	6,678.1	9,795.0	13,214.3
1964	3,466.1	105.1	1,714.2	541.0	721.4	6,878.5	9,855.1	13,426.3
1963	3,332.9	102.1	667.4	744.9	663.6	7,043.8	9,119.7	12,554.7
1962	3,905.7	114.7	607.8	436.1	636.8	6,966.3	8,647.0	12,667.4
1961	4,071.9	149.8	254.0	19.6	500.8	5,803.6	6,578.0	10,799.7
1960	3,756.2	131.7	165.6	122.1	513.8	6,191.8	6,993.3	10,881.2
1959	4,047.8	269.3	613.8	14.6	610.5	6,838.5	8,077.4	12,394.5
1958	5,492.5	466.9	383.1	59.2	708.5	6,436.3	7,587.1	13,546.5

Source: MSTS, *Fiscal Reports*, 1958-1968.

carriage of MSTS dry cargo increased from 1.4 million to 8.9 million measurement tons, or more than 500%. During the same period, berth term and shipping contract cargo increased only 2.3 million measurement tons, or 30%.

Because military needs cannot be predicted in advance, rapidity of response is essential. The rapidity of buildup is especially striking when the quarterly data on number of cargo ships under time charter to MSTS are examined. For example, the number of ships under time charter more than tripled in the three-month period between July and October 1965, as shown in Table 3-17.

The benefits derived by the nation from the availability of sealift capability are not readily quantifiable. Meeting national security needs is a goal ultimately measured in terms of survival not in dollars. As Admiral Moorer, current chairman of the Joint Chiefs of Staff and former Chief of Naval Operations, testified in congressional hearings, foreign-flag vessels involve political risks and "are not certainly as dependable and you cannot count on them as well as we can those that are part of the U.S. Merchant Marine."[10]

The availability of the U.S.-flag fleet does have a calculable effect on the costs of ocean transportation to the Department of Defense. The relative effect on costs, reflected by rate savings, varies depending on the DOD cargo demand level. At war or military emergency levels, the savings are greater than in peacetime situations. Since the short-run supply of shipping is relatively fixed, an increase in demand pushes the shipping price upward. However, the availability of the U.S.-flag ships, which can be diverted from their usual commercial trade, provides a "safety valve," helping to keep rates lower.[e] The difference between what was actually paid to ship military cargoes and an estimate of what might have been paid in the absence of the U.S.-flag fleet is the measure of the benefits derived from the U.S. Merchant Marine in national security.

The fiscal years 1959-1965 inclusive were taken as a period of "normal" and increasing military demand. For this seven-year time span, the average annual commercial carriage (non MSTS nucleus fleet or non GAA ships) of DOD cargo was approximately 8.4 million measurement tons, ranging from a low of 6.6 million measurement tons in fiscal year 1961 to a high of 9.9 million measurement tons in fiscal year 1964. MSTS peacetime savings were derived in two components—savings in time charter rates and savings in liner-type carriage. For each component a relevant index of world rates was compared to a similar index of MSTS rates, and the difference was then applied to the MSTS cargo bill. Tables 3-18 and 3-19 present the data and calculations. If the rates paid by MSTS for movement of DOD cargo had fluctuated on the same basis as comparable world rates during the period, 1959-1965, the increased costs to MSTS would have totaled $145 million.

---

[e]Such diversion does not contribute to higher rates in the commercial sector necessarily because foreign-flag operators are available to carry commercial cargo abandoned by U.S. operators in response to the nation's defense needs. There is, of course, a negative impact on the balance of payments from the increased use of foreign-flag vessels, which has been accounted for in the balance of payments calculations.

Table 3-17

**Privately Owned Cargo Ships Under
Time Charter to MSTS: January 1965 -
July 1966**

As of Beginning of Month	No. of Ships
January 1965	14
April 1965	17
July 1965	·33
October 1965	111
January 1966	108
April 1966	129
July 1966	139

Source: MSTS, *Fiscal Reports*, 1965-1967.

During military emergencies these savings in rates are even greater. Because of the availability of reliable past data, the Korean period (1951-1952) was selected as a "typical" post-World-War-II military emergency. The analysis is based in part on data developed by Leonard Rappings in the Northwestern study of the U.S. Merchant Marine.[11] Table 3-20 illustrates the war-emergency savings accruing to the nation as a result of the availability of the U.S.-flag fleet. The savings are estimated to total $3.9 billion for the two-year period.

The facts available on MSTS rates for the Vietnam emergency period confirm rate stability for the U.S.-flag fleet similar to that of the Korean period. The unweighted average of low bids for breakbulk military cargo on MSTS Route 01 (U.S. West Coast to the Far East) rose from $25.92 per measurement ton in fiscal year 1968 to $28.07 per measurement ton in fiscal year 1970, an increase of 8%.[12] Data developed for fiscal years 1966-1968 on rates per measurement ton for total commercial carriage of MSTS cargo show great stability. In 1966, the average rate was $27.60 per measurement ton with relatively little cargo going by container vessel. In 1967 and 1968, with from 25% to 50% of the cargo containerized, the average rates were $29.10 per measurement ton and $32.10 per measurement ton, respectively. Since breakbulk rates average

Table 3-18

Estimated MSTS Time-Charter Savings: FY 1959-1965

Fiscal Year	World Dry-Cargo, Time-Charter Index*	MSTS Dry-Cargo, Time-Charter Index*	Ratio of World Index to MSTS Index	Time Charter Bill†		Estimated Savings†
				Actual	*Based on World Rates*	
1965	155	46	3.37	$21,992	$ 74,113	$ 52,121
1964	137	43	3.19	16,635	53,066	36,431
1963	124	77	1.61	11,524	18,554	7,030
1962	102	81	1.26	11,127	14,020	2,893
1961	127	76	1.67	4,364	7,288	2,924
1960	116	92	1.26	3,628	4,571	943
1959	102	82	1.24	11,413	14,152	2,739
Total				$80,683	$185,764	$102,081

Note: In previous tables, information on the decade 1958-1967 has been provided. A number of unsuccessful attempts were made to find indices for MSTS time charter saving which would be compatible with given data or would include all 10 years. For this reason 1957 and 1966-67 are not included.

*1958 = 100.

†Expressed in thousands of dollars.

Sources: "Time-Charter Index"; *Norwegian Shipping News*, 2A, 1970: 159-160; MSTS, *Fiscal Reports*, 1959-1966.

Table 3-19

Estimated MSTS Liner-Type Savings: FY 1959-1965

Fiscal Year	World Liner Index*	MSTS Liner Index*	Ratio of World Index to MSTS Index	MSTS Liner Bill†		Estimated Savings†
				Actual	Based on World Rates	
1965	115	111	1.04	$ 198,706	$ 206,654	$ 7,948
1964	112	106	1.06	201,253	213,328	12,075
1963	108	102	1.06	199,167	211,117	11,950
1962	107	101	1.06	188,033	199,315	11,282
1961	102	104	0.98	152,543	149,492	−3,051
1960	99	98	1.01	155,159	156,711	1,552
1959	98	99	0.99	171,486	169,771	−1,715
Total				$1,266,347	$1,306,388	$40,041

Note: Data for 1958, 1966-1967 are unavailable.

*1958 = 100.

† Expressed in thousands of dollars.

Sources: "Time Charter Index," Norwegian Shipping News, 2A, 1970, p. 159-160; MSTS, *Fiscal Reports*, 1959-1965.

Table 3-20

MSTS War Emergency Savings: 1950-1953

Year	Savings as %'s of Prevailing Prices*	Military Freight Costs	Estimated Savings
1950	5.75%	$500	$ 29
1951	369.00	800	2,952
1952	119.00	800	952
1953	13.00	300	39

Note: 1950 and 1953 represent peacetime years and are shown for contrast only. Costs are expressed in millions of dollars.

Sources: MSTS, *Fiscal Reports,* 1950-1954, and Ferguson, et al., *Economic Value,* p. 241.

*Derivation of savings percentages developed in Ferguson, et al., *Economic Value.*

60% of the container rate,[f] the adjusted average rates for 1967 and 1968 would be at the same level or lower than the 1966 MSTS commercial rates. This was accomplished despite a 20% increase in carriage.

Thus, the cost of maintaining a reserve surge capacity is reduced because of the commercial capability of the present system. Vessels in the U.S. Merchant Marine are providing balance of payments benefits, employment of U.S. merchant seamen, tax revenues to the government, trade development and international diplomatic "functions" as they remain available for defense requirements.

Summary of Past Benefits and Costs of the U.S. Merchant Marine

The benefits and costs of the U.S. Merchant Marine for the years 1958-1967 are presented in Table 3-21. For this ten-year period, the U.S. Merchant Marine has contributed $11.3 billion in benefits to the U.S. economy as opposed to costs of $2.7 billion. In other words, the U.S. Merchant Marine has—for each

---

[f]A definitional difference since MSTS breakbulk does not include stevedoring, while container rates include loading and unloading costs.

Table 3-21

**Benefit/Cost Analysis of the U.S.
Merchant Marine: 1958-1967
(Dollars in Millions)**

Year	Benefits			Costs*				Net Benefits
	Balance of Payments	National Security†	Total	ODS	Rate Preference‡	Ship Exchange Program‡	Total	
1967	$ 999	$ 400	$ 1,399	$ 216	$ 68	$ 64	$ 348	$1,051
1966	912	400	1,312	199	76	44	319	993
1965	632	400	1,032	185	68	38	291	741
1964	680	400	1,080	204	77	52	333	747
1963	631	400	1,031	192	79	47	318	713
1962	659	400	1,059	178	59	32	269	790
1961	551	400	951	167	50	12	231	720
1960	715	400	1,115	163	54	12	229	886
1959	748	400	1,148	159	37	–	196	952
1958	758	400	1,158	141	31	–	172	986
Total	$7,285	$4,000	$11,285	$1,806	$599	$301	$2,706	$8,579

*CDS has been omitted from costs because it is a subsidy solely to shipyards.

†Average per year; does not reflect nonquantifiable "availability" factor.

‡Indirect subsidies.

Sources: Tables 2-3, 2-15, and 2-18 through 2-20.

dollar of cost—returned approximately $4.17 in benefits. In contrast, construction and river-control projects undertaken by the U.S. Army Corps of Engineers are frequently justified by benefit/cost ratios of 1.5 to 2.0.

Although it is difficult to distribute the precise sources of costs and benefits among the various segments of the industry, an approximation was made of the benefit/cost ratio for the subsidized liner segment: the subsidized liner segment supplied approximately $3.66 in benefits for every $1 of costs for the period, 1958-1967. Again, we can only conclude that the U.S. Merchant Marine in general—and the subsidized liner segment specifically—has not only performed a vital economic function but has also returned benefits to the country far greater than the investment the nation has made in them.

4

The Potential of the
U.S. Merchant Marine

Introduction

The government contracts of all but one of the currently subsidized lines will expire in 1976. Since present programs—or modifications of them—can be expected to receive careful evaluation at that time, this chapter treats the period 1970 to 1976 to determine how the industry will perform during this period.

These years are crucial ones for the U.S. Merchant Marine. The physical and commercial decline of the fleet makes change imperative; the growth of containerization makes change inevitable. Government response to the need for change can be instrumental in determining the level of benefits which will accrue from the introduction of new technology into the operations of the U.S.-flag fleet.

The most immediate effect of government programs is upon the size of the fleet. This chapter seeks first to quantify the impact of alternative construction programs and related subsidies upon the size of the fleet and then to measure the economic consequences of these alternatives upon industry health and national benefits. This analysis involves five steps:

 i) Estimating the level of U.S. foreign trade in 1976, including an evaluation of the impact of technological change;
 ii) Identifying alternative construction programs;
iii) Aging the existing (1968) fleet;
 iv) Deriving the range of possible U.S.-flag fleet sizes in 1976;
  v) Quantifying the commercial performance and national benefits of this range of 1976 U.S.-flag fleets.

Trade Projections

Three published studies were examined as possible sources for trade projections.

Litton Systems, Inc., *Ocean Shipping: Demand and Technology Forecast*[1]
U.S. Interagency Maritime Task Force, *The Merchant Marine in National Defense and Trade: A Policy and a Program*[2]
U.S. Navy Department, *Sealift Requirements Study*[3]

Each of these studies was inadequate for our analysis for a number of reasons. A minor difficulty was the use of 1975 as a projection date in all of these studies rather than 1976. A more compelling reason was the incompatibility of data bases. For instance, the 1975 estimates range from approximately 350 million[4] to 475 million measurement tons[5], because of different definitions of cargo categories, inclusion or exclusion of DOD/government cargoes in the base year data, and incomplete information at the time of the study. Not surprisingly, the annual growth rates do not present a consistent pattern either, varying from a low of 1.7% in the Litton study to a high of 3.8% for the Interagency Task Force Study.[6]

Because no existing study provided a reliable basis for projection, the authors chose to develop their own projections for the significant components of the market: commercial general cargo and dry bulk; government-impelled general cargo and dry bulk; and defense carryings. Commercial general cargo and dry bulk tonnage forecasts were derived from time-series analyses based on the period, 1958-1967. Department of Defense and government-impelled cargo carriage was estimated by the authors. From Table 4-1, it is seen that commercial general cargo is predicted to grow at a 4.5% annual rate, while the commercial dry bulk projection indicates a rate of 4.0%. Since government-impelled tonnage in 1976 is estimated to remain at about the same level as in 1967 (at about 21 million measurement tons), and DOD carriage may decrease to 7.5 million tons, the overall rate of increase, according to our estimates, appears to be about 3.6% (also, see Figure 4-1).

The fleet that will respond to the markets just outlined has been shaped since 1965 by a major technological change—containerization—which has in turn promoted other economic and institutional realignments, such as intermodalism. Another technological revolution of this magnitude would make predictions extremely difficult. Therefore, the authors have surveyed briefly the potential of other technological changes for affecting the industry as markedly as has containerization.

Technological experiments are now being conducted in three primary fields:

power plants,
ship design, and
computer applications.

Continued experimentation with technological systems such as nuclear power, hydrofoil, and computerized management systems can be expected; but none of the developments in these areas promises to have revolutionary commercial application by 1976.

Another development which could interfere with predictions would be increased competition from air freight. The international trade of the U.S. has been carried almost exclusively by water up to the present because the cost structure of air freight has not been competitive with ocean shipping. The air cargo industry is now developing larger planes which encourage greater emphasis on air freight by the airlines. Current studies indicate that a Boeing 747, with a 60% load factor and a rate of $0.20 per ton-mile, has a profit potential almost four times that of a B-707 all-cargo freighter.[7] Thus, airlines

Table 4-1

**Summary of U.S. Foreign Trade
Projections: 1976 (Measurement
Tons in Thousands)**

	1967	1976	Annual Growth Rate
Commercial:			
General Cargo	180,242	267,100	4.47%
Dry Bulk	132,815	188,800	3.99
Government-Impelled:			
General Cargo	10,542	10,000	−0.59
Dry Bulk	10,946	11,000	0.05
Department of Defense*	18,542	7,500	−9.57
Total	353,087	484,400	3.58%

*Assumed to be all general cargo.

Sources: Table 3-10 gives 1967 volume of trade. The rate of growth is based on a time-series analysis of commercial cargo and estimates of the stability of the government-impelled market with the decline in DOD cargo levels to pre-Vietnam volumes.

will be in a better position to compete with ocean carriers for goods whose value or perishability makes time savings a significant factor.

This competition will result in ocean cargo vessels losing some high value, international cargo to the air freight industry. However, the rise in air freight will have a minimal impact on the overall rising volume of waterborne general cargo. In 1966, total U.S. air exports and imports amounted to approximately 347,000 short tons.[8] This number is expected to increase fivefold by 1976. However, air cargo will still be less than one percent of the estimated 277 million measurement tons of U.S. foreign trade in commercial and government-impelled general cargo.

Alternative Government Policies

Because of the dependence of the maritime industry upon the government for fleet replacement, the role of government in the future is a crucial determinant

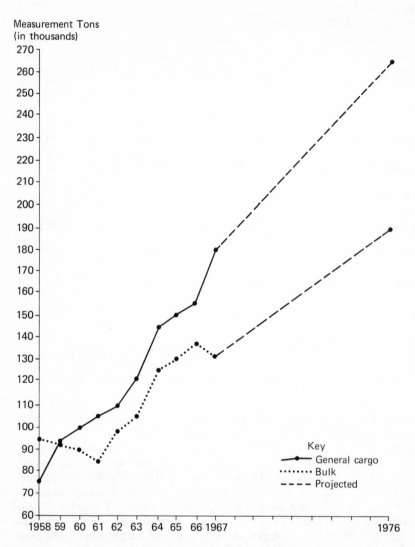

Figure 4-1   U.S. Foreign Commercial Trade 1958-1967 and Estimated 1976. (Source: Tables 3-10 and 4-1)

of the U.S.-flag fleet size. Proposed federal maritime policies and supporting programs were reviewed, therefore, in order to establish possible funding levels and resultant ship construction programs. Other subsidy features of the programs, such as operating differential subsidy which depend upon fleet size and composition, were varied accordingly.[a]

Our survey indicated that there is no dearth of policies and programs now in existence or advocated by industry members, by the Federal government or by federally-sponsored groups. Among the programs reviewed were:

The Merchant Marine Act of 1936;[9]
HR 13940 and S2650, a bill before Congress designed to "provide a new maritime program";[10]
the Interagency Maritime Task Force report, setting forth views of various government agencies;[11]
The Maritime Evaluation Committee report, a study carried out by a special group formed under the auspices of the Department of Commerce;[12]
the views of maritime labor, as represented by the comments of Joseph Curran (President, National Maritime Union) and Paul Hall (President, Seamen's International Union of North America) before the Congress in 1968;[13]
President Nixon's statements on proposed maritime programs.[14]

These policies were placed in four general categories according to their potential impact on fleet size. The primary element of each is the level (and mechanism) for funding ship construction, but other government-controlled factors which could affect the choice to build more ships are also included in the assumptions. The four alternatives are:

As Is. Under this program the current maritime policy and supporting programs would be continued. The appropriations for CDS would remain at $80 million annually with CDS and ODS reserved for present directly-subsidized operators.

Increased Funding. Under this program CDS would be increased to $200 million annually with a corresponding increase in ODS; CDS and ODS would be available only to the present group of directly-subsidized operators.

Extended Benefits. Under this program all segments of the general cargo freighter fleet would be eligible for both CDS and ODS, with increased

[a]Changes in government-controllable factors which do not affect fleet size and are not derived from it will be covered indirectly by approximating their impact upon fleet performance. For example, while we cannot conjecture what the exact effect would be of a more vigorous endorsement of bilateralism by the U.S. Government, it is clear that bilateralism is one method of increasing the U.S. flag fleet share of foreign trade. Therefore, the effect of bilateralism can be approximated by increasing the share significantly and observing the changes in return on investment and the benefit/cost ratios.

amounts of both available.^b CDS would be limited to $300 million annually with commensurate increases in ODS. The trade route concept and other responsibilities of the Merchant Marine Act of 1936, as amended, would remain in force for ODS recipients, and no vessel built under this program would be permitted in cabotage.

Build Foreign. Under this program construction subsidy would be abolished in favor of liberalizing use of foreign-built ships by all segments of the fleet. Vessels built in foreign yards would be allowed to register under the U.S. flag, to carry government-impelled and DOD cargoes, and to receive ODS. ODS allocations would be limited to $300 million annually, which is approximately the sum of 1967 ODS and CDS costs. The trade route concept and other responsibilities of the Merchant Marine Act of 1936, as amended, would remain in force for ODS recipients, and no vessel built under this program would be permitted in cabotage.

Although each policy has as its goal the establishment of a U.S. Merchant Marine best able to meet national objectives, the proposed policies and programs are contradictory in many respects, reflecting the conflicting views and desires of the various groups advocating them. The four government policies basically propose different construction programs, resulting in different U.S.-flag fleet sizes in 1976.^c

Alternative U.S.-Flag Fleet Sizes in 1976

The government policy alternatives provide the basis for projecting various sizes for the U.S.-flag fleet in 1976. The fleet will consist of "old" ships remaining from the 1968 fleet, and "new" ships constructed in the intervening period. The number of "old" ships will remain the same for all alternatives, while the number of "new" ships will vary according to the alternative.

Aging Analysis

In order to determine which of the 1968 ships will remain in the 1976 fleet, the 1968 fleet was examined using the following assumptions:[15]

---

^bDistinguished from the current administration's proposal by the exclusion of bulk carriers and tankers from support.

^cWhile the last two alternatives are distinguished by their mechanisms for funding ship construction, the size of the fleets produced is assumed to be identical. It has been assumed that the increased amounts of ODS under the *Build Foreign* alternative will support approximately the same number of ships as will be built under the *Extended Benefits* program, and that with the assurance of operating subsidy, the Merchant Marine operators will invest the same amount of their own funds in ship construction as under the *Extended Benefits* program. Since the cost of ships is lower in foreign yards, the *Build Foreign* program will result in a fleet size identical to that of the *Extended Benefits* program.

i) The directly-subsidized liner segment will retain its ships for 20 years, after which time the ships will become part of the indirectly-subsidized and/or tramp fleet for the remaining five years of their economic life.
ii) Container conversions were assumed to have an economic life of 10 years after conversion.[d]
iii) No passenger ships will remain in service by 1976.
iv) The Ship Exchange Program will have been completed as a source of additional ships.

The aging analysis indicates that 206 ships (with an annual lift capacity of 33.2 million measurement tons) in the (1968) fleet will also be part of the 1976 U.S.-flag fleet (see Tables 4-2 and 4-3). It should be noted that the capacity remaining in 1976 will consist principally of C-4 vessels, some 15% of which are containerships—some converted and some new.

New Construction (1969-1976)

If it is assumed that the industry will utilize the total amount of CDS funding available under each alternative construction program, the number of ships to be built during the eight-year period ranges from 55 to 208 (see Table 4-4). All post-1968 ships were assumed to be high technology vessels with the following characteristics:

Type	Container Vessel[e]
Total Cost	$21,000,000[f]
Cost to Owner	$9,450,000
Speed	22 knots
Gross Capacity	1,200 20′ equivalent containers or 38,400 measurement tons
GPS	3.754

In addition to the vessels built under these construction programs, about 10 privately-financed vessels will be built for the present indirectly-subsidized operators, Sea-Land and Matson. These are ships which are under construction or have been contracted for delivery before 1976.

---

[d]This information was developed in conversations with Maritime Administration officials.

[e]Although a container vessel is used as the "typical" high technology vessel for purposes of measuring capacity, it should be recognized that there are other types, such as LASH and SEABEE.

[f]At U.S. construction prices. Under *Build Foreign* the total cost equals the cost to owner.

Table 4-2

Size of the U. S.-Flag Fleet in 1968
and Those Ships Remaining in 1976
(Number of Ships at End of Year)

Ship Type	1968			1976		
	Subsidized Liners	Indirectly-Subsidized and Tramp	Total	Subsidized Liners	Indirectly-Subsidized and Tramp	Total
C-1	3	3	6	–	–	–
C-2	60	87	147	–	–	–
C-3	111	52	163	54	2	56
C-4	103	38	141	79	48	127
C-5	5	–	5	5	–	5
C-7	4	–	4	4	–	4
Passenger	13	–	13	–	–	–
Victory	4	56	60	–	1	1
T 2 and T 3	–	31	31	–	10	10
EC 2	–	12	12	–	–	–
Reefers	–	16	16	–	–	–
All Others	–	19	19	–	3	3
Total	303	314	617	142	64	206

Note: Although some of the ships have been converted to containerships or have been reconstructed, they are classified according to the designated ship type.

Source: Derived from Status of the United States Flag Merchant Fleet, as of December 31, 1968 (Washington, D. C.: Marad, Office of Government Aid).

Table 4-3

Annual Lift Capacity of the U.S. Flag-Fleet in 1968 and Those Remaining in 1976 (Measurement Tons in Thousands)

Ship Type	1968			Remaining in 1976 Fleet		
	Subsidized Liners	Indirectly-Subsidized and Tramp	Total	Subsidized Liners	Indirectly-Subsidized and Tramp	Total
C-1	192	193	385	–	–	–
C-2	5,040	7,380	12,420	–	–	–
C-3	12,208	6,053	18,261	6,335	311	6,646
C-4	15,725	6,022	21,747	12,429	7,510	19,939
C-5	1,555	–	1,555	1,555	–	1,555
C-7	1,549	–	1,549	1,549	–	1,549
Passenger	725	–	725	–	–	–
Victory	310	4,368	4,678	–	71	71
T2 and T3	–	8,376	8,376	–	2,194	2,194
EC 2	–	848	848	–	–	–
Reefers	–	730	730	–	–	–
All Others	–	4,793	4,793	–	1,230	1,230
Total	37,304	38,763	76,067	21,868	11,316	33,184

Note: Although some of the ships have been converted to containership or have been reconstructed, they are classified according to the designated ship type.

Source: *Status of United States Flag Merchant Fleet as of December 31, 1968* (Washington, D.C.: Marad, Office of Government Aid).

Table 4-4

**Number of Ships and Capacity Added
to Fleet Under Each Alternative
Construction Policy: January 1, 1969,
to December 31, 1976**

Alternative Policies	Annual Level of CDS	Number of Ships	Annual Lift Capacity*
A. As Is	$ 80,000,000	55	31,285
B. Increased Funding	200,000,000	139	77,962
C. Extended Benefits	300,000,000	208	116,663
D. Build Foreign	none	208	116,663

Note: Figures reflect only ships produced directly by government funding and therefore do not include 10 ships built by Sea-Land and Matson to be delivered in this period. Under the Build Foreign alternative, it has been assumed that the industry will invest the same amount in ship construction as it would under the policy of Extended Benefits.

*Expressed in thousands of measurement tons.

Source: See text and Appendix D for assumptions about costs and capacity.

U.S.-Flag Fleet in 1976

Table 4-5 presents a summary of the number of ships and annual lift capacity of the U.S.-flag fleet in 1976 under the alternative construction programs. Under Alternative A (*As Is*), the 1976 capacity of 78.2 million measurement tons closely approximates the capacity of the 1968 U.S.-flag fleet, which was 76.1 million measurement tons. However, instead of a 1968 fleet with capacity divided almost equally between subsidized operators and indirectly-subsidized liner/tramp operators, the 1976 proportions become two-thirds for subsidized liners and one-third for the remaining segments. Thus, it appears that the vigor of indirectly-subsidized operators like Sea-Land and Matson are the exception, and that the indirectly-subsidized U.S.-flag fleet will gradually deteriorate with age. The other construction alternatives provide for capacity increases over 1968 levels of 65% and 116%, respectively, or 125.3 million and 164.0 million measurement tons.

Even with these large increases in capacity, the number of ships in the 1976 fleet will decline from 617 in 1968 to a maximum of 424 by 1976. Although under Alternative A (*As Is*), the U.S. would have less than half as many ships

Table 4-5

**Size and Capacity of U.S.-Flag Fleet
According to Alternative Construction
Policies: 1976**

Alternative Policies	No. of Ships	Annual Lift Capacity*
As Is		
Subsidized Liner	197	52,716
Indirectly-Subsidized Liner		
and Tramp	74	25,511
Total	271	78,227
Increased Funding		
Subsidized Liner	281	99,830
Indirectly-Subsidized Liner		
and Tramp	74	25,511
Total	355	125,341
Extended Benefits		
Subsidized Liner	350	138,531
Indirectly-Subsidized Liner		
and Tramp	74	25,511
Total	424	164,042
Build Foreign		
Subsidized Liner	350	138,531
Indirectly-Subsidized Liner		
and Tramp	74	25,511
Total	424	164,042

Note: The figures for indirectly-subsidized liner and tramp include 10 ships built by Sea-Land and Matson without subsidy.

*Expressed in thousands of measurement tons.

Source: Derived from Tables 4-2 through 4-4.

in 1976 as it had in 1968, the impact on frequency of service would not be as severe as these figures imply, because the improved turnaround times for high technology vessels permit more trips per vessel.

Economics of the Alternative Fleets

Because of the magnitude of the investment required to bring into being a substantially new fleet, it seems reasonable to assume that future private investment in the U.S. Merchant Marine will be forthcoming only if there is some assurance that a reasonable return will be earned. Furthermore, it should be noted that the Merchant Marine Act of 1936 (as amended) calls for a reasonable return on investment.

Profitability, or return on investment, is a function of the relationship between volume of trade, rates, costs, and investment. In the case of the Merchant Marine there exist certain factors which significantly limit the ability of individual carriers to increase profitability through either unique cost reductions or rate variations. Theoretically, since essentially the same technology is available to all operators, efficiencies are equally available to all.[g] As regards rate charges, the conference system effectively rules out pricing action as a competitive weapon for members of the conference; that is, rates charged by individual operators on a particular trade route will be the same. Consequently, increasing volume carried (market share) through more frequent sailings and other forms of superior service are the principal ways in which a carrier, or group of carriers (such as the U.S.-flag fleet), can increase its profitability and thereby, its return on investment. Therefore, the following analysis has been structured to show return on investment for a range of possible market shares for each of Alternatives A, B and C/D.

Market Share Assumptions

Two major sets of assumptions were established regarding the U.S.-flag fleet share of the U.S. foreign trade market—one applied to the 1967 subsidized liner segment of the industry, and used for government policy programs which apply to the subsidized segment only: Alternative A (*As Is*) and Alternative B (*Increased Funding*); and the other applied to all segments and used for government policy programs which extend direct subsidy to all segments: Alternative C (*Extended Benefits*) and Alternative D (*Build Foreign*).

Alternatives A and B. Based on the subsidized liner tonnage, it was assumed that:

---

[g]This assumption recognizes the economies of scale available to larger firms under containerization but assumes that such economies are available to smaller firms through pooling arrangements or consortia.

i) the commercial bulk share of the market would remain essentially the same as in 1967 (at 1%);
ii) the government-impelled general cargo share would increase somewhat (from 33% to 40%) while the government-impelled bulk share remained about the same (5%);
iii) the subsidized liner share of defense tonnage would amount to 50% (up from 33% in 1967);
iv) the commercial general cargo tonnage would vary over a range from the smallest market share that would produce a profit to the highest market share corresponding to the maximum theoretical capacity of the respective fleets (see Tables 4-6 through 4-9).

Alternatives C and D. Based on total U.S.-flag fleet carriage, it was assumed that:

i) the commercial bulk share of the market would remain the same (at 3.5%);
ii) the government-impelled share of the market would rise to 50% for both general cargo and bulk shipments (from 47% and 37%, respectively);
iii) the U.S.-flag fleet would carry all defense tonnage;
iv) the commercial general cargo would vary so as to indicate the lowest share producing a profit and the highest share possible according to the fleet capacity (see Tables 4-10 and 4-11).

The utilization rates (or load factors) for the various market share assumptions used in Tables 4-6 through 4-11 are presented in Table 4-12 and indicate that:

i) under Alternative A, the subsidized segment can earn a "reasonable" return with an *overall* market share of 5.8% and a 53% utilization rate;
ii) Alternative B requires an 8.2% share of the market with a 40% utilization rate to realize a 10% return on investment;
iii) for Alternatives C and D, a 15.8% share of the market plus a 47% utilization rate are the requisites for a "reasonable" return.

Rate Assumptions

In order to estimate 1976 revenue for the U.S.-flag fleet, it was necessary to establish a rate schedule which might occur in the 1976 environment. First, however, the 1967 rates for the various types of cargo were derived, and these are presented in Table 4-13. One of the possibilities considered was to use the 1967 rate structure to derive 1976 revenues, and *pro forma* profit and loss data were computed on this basis. However, further reflection indicated that the higher expense levels posited for 1976 would require an increase in freight rates—but not necessarily at the same level as the expense rise.[h] To err on the

---

[h]About 50% rise in expense is projected. See Appendix D.

Table 4-6

**Subsidized-Liner Market Shares Under
As Is Program: 1976 (Percentage of
Total U.S. Foreign Trade)**

	1967	1976		
	Actual	*Lowest Profitable*	*Reasonable Return*	*Maximum Capacity*
Commercial				
General Cargo	6.2	2.84	6.7	15.92
Bulk	0.8	1.0	1.0	1.0
Subtotal	3.9	2.1	4.3	9.7
Government-Impelled				
General Cargo	33.3	40.0	40.0	40.0
Bulk	4.5	5.0	5.0	5.0
Subtotal	18.6	21.2	21.2	21.2
DOD				
General Cargo	33.2	50.0	50.0	50.0
Total Trade	6.3	3.7	5.8	10.9

Note: Market share for the subsidized segment alone has been calculated since this is the segment affected by this alternative. Cf. treatment of Extended Benefits and Build Foreign in Table 4-7. The meaning of lowest profitable share and maximum capacity share is self evident. Approximately 10% return on investment constitutes the reasonable return.

Sources: Tables 4-1 and 4-4 plus Appendix E.

Table 4-7

**Subsidized-Liner Market Shares Under
As Is Program: 1976 (Measurement
Tons in Thousands)**

	1967	1976		
	Actual	*Lowest Profitable*	*Reasonable Return*	*Maximum Capacity*
Commercial				
General Cargo	11,178	19,285	29,381	89,642
Bulk	1,016	1,888	1,888	1,888
Subtotal	12,194	21,173	31,269	91,530
Government-Impelled				
General Cargo	3,511	4,000	4,000	4,000
Bulk	496	550	550	550
Subtotal	4,007	4,550	4,550	4,550
DOD				
General Cargo	6,158	3,750	3,750	3,750
Total Trade	22,359	29,473	39,569	99,850

Note: See Table 4-6 for sources and notes.

Table 4-8

**Subsidized-Liner Market Share Under
Increased Funding Program: 1976
(Percentages of Total U.S. Foreign
Trade)**

	1967	1976		
	Actual	*Lowest Profitable*	*Reasonable Return*	*Maximum Capacity*
Commercial				
General Cargo	6.2	8.0	11.0	33.56
Bulk	0.8	1.0	1.0	1.00
Subtotal	3.9	5.1	6.9	20.10
Government-Impelled				
General Cargo	33.3	40.0	40.0	40.0
Bulk	4.5	5.0	5.0	5.0
Subtotal	18.6	21.2	21.2	21.2
DOD				
General Cargo	33.2	50.0	50.0	50.0
Total Trade	6.3	6.5	8.2	20.6

Note: See Table 4-6.   Sources: Tables 4-1 and 4-5 plus Appendix E.

Table 4-9

**Subsidized-Liner Market Shares
Under Increased Funding
Program: 1976 (Measurement
Tons in Thousands)**

	1967	1976		
	Actual	*Lowest Profitable*	*Reasonable Return*	*Maximum Capacity*
Commercial				
General Cargo	11,178	21,368	29,381	89,642
Bulk	1,016	1,888	1,888	1,888
Subtotal	12,194	23,256	31,269	91,530
Government-Impelled				
General Cargo	3,511	4,000	4,000	4,000
Bulk	496	550	550	550
Subtotal	4,007	4,550	4,550	4,500
DOD				
General Cargo	6,158	3,750	3,750	3,750
Total Trade	22,359	31,556	39,569	99,830

Note: See Table 4-6.   Source: Tables 4-1 and 4-5 plus Appendix E.

84

Table 4-10

**U.S.-Flag Market Shares of U.S.
Foreign Trade Under Extended Benefits
and Build Foreign Programs: 1976
(Percentage of Total U.S. Foreign Trade)**

	1967	1976		
	Actual	*Lowest Profitable*	*Reasonable Return*	*Maximum Capacity*
Commercial				
General Cargo	7.8	13.38	19.5	52.2
Bulk	3.5	3.50	3.5	3.5
Subtotal	6.0	9.30	12.9	32.0
Government-Impelled				
General Cargo	46.7	50.0	50.0	50.0
Bulk	36.7	50.0	50.0	50.0
Subtotal	41.6	50.0	50.0	50.0
DOD				
General Cargo	100.0	100.0	100.0	100.0
Total Trade	13.1	12.5	15.8	33.9

Note: See Table 4-6. The market shares in this table are calculated for the entire fleet because the entire fleet would receive the benefits from these alternative programs. Under the assumptions of the study, the size of the fleet would be the same under either program; therefore, they are considered together in this exhibit.

Source: Tables 4-1 and 4-5 plus Appendix E.

Table 4-11

**U.S.-Flag Market Shares of U.S.
Foreign Trade Implied by Extended
Benefits and Build Foreign Program:
1976 (Measurement Tons in
Thousands)**

	1967	1976		
	Actual	*Lowest Profitable*	*Reasonable Return*	*Maximum Capacity*
Commercial				
General Cargo	14,006	35,738	52,085	139,434
Bulk	4,621	6,608	6,608	6,608
Subtotal	18,627	42,346	58,693	146,042
Government-Impelled				
General Cargo	4,924	5,000	5,000	5,000
Bulk	4,018	5,500	5,500	5,500
Subtotal	8,942	10,500	10,500	10,500
DOD				
General Cargo	18,542	7,500	7,500	7,500
Total Trade	46,111	60,346	76,693	164,042

Note: See Table 4-10.   Sources: Tables 4-1 and 4-5 plus Appendix E.

Table 4-12

**U.S.-Flag Fleet Load Factors for
Specified Market Share Assumptions
and Alternative Construction
Programs: 1976**

Construction Program	Overall Market Share	Commercial Cargo Market Share	Load Factor	
			Subsidized Segment	*Total U.S. Flag Fleet*
A. As Is	3.7%	2.84%	33.7%	−
	5.8	6.70	53.3	−
	10.9	15.92	100.0	−
B. Increased Funding	6.1	7.22	29.5	−
	8.2	11.00	39.6	−
	20.6	33.56	100.0	−
C/D Extended Benefits and Build Foreign	12.5	13.38	−	36.8%
	15.8	19.50	−	46.8
	33.9	52.20	−	100.0

Note: Market shares for A and B are for the subsidized-liner segment, while U.S.-flag fleet market share has been used for C and D. The selected market shares are the lowest profitable, reasonable return, and maximum capacity developed in Tables 4-6 through 4-11.

Sources: Tables 4-1, and 4-5 through 4-11.

Table 4-13

**1967 Rate Schedule by Type of
Cargo (Dollars per Measurement
Ton)**

Commercial		Government-Impelled		DOD
General Cargo	*Bulk*	*General Cargo*	*Bulk*	*General Cargo*
$36.35*	$8.00†	$50.00‡	$18.00§	$24.00**

*Derived as follows:

Vessel Operating Revenue-Freight Only (assumes that this includes government-impelled tonnage as well as shipping agreement portion of DOD).	$696,236,000

Less

Estimated Revenue for Commercial Bulk, Government-Impelled, and DOD	289,998,000
Estimated Commercial General Cargo Revenue	$406,238,000

Divided by:

1967 Commercial General Cargo Tonnage	11,178,000

Equals:

Revenue per Measurement Ton	$36.34

†Weighted average cost of commercial dry bulk as reported in *Final Report Projection of Ocean Freight Rates,* George G. Sharp, Inc., New York, 9 January 1967.

‡Estimated from existing tariffs. It should be noted that voyage length affects rates for general cargo and that commercial general cargo in the U.S. trade is destined primarily for Europe while voyages for government-impelled cargoes are longer.

§Estimated from existing tariffs.

**Derived from MSTS, *Fiscal Report,* 1968.

conservative side, revenues were initially 25% above those derived from using the 1967 freight rates.

This was then modified to conform with our observation that revenue per ton bears a varying relationship to market share. The increase in market share is usually more rapid than the rise in revenue per ton.[i] Therefore, the 25% increase in revenues was applied only to the 1967 market-share levels of 6% for the subsidized segment and 8% for the entire U.S.-flag fleet. The rates of increase for the remaining increments were then interpolated from past data on the relationship between revenue and increased market shares.

Cost Assumptions

Before it was possible to set up *pro forma* profit and loss statements for the various construction alternatives and the range of market share assumptions, it was necessary to:

i) Establish expense data that would apply to the ship types presently in the Merchant Marine and remaining in the fleet in 1976;
ii) Estimate the 1976 costs of operating the new containerships entering the fleet in 1968 and subsequent years.

A detailed description of the cost assumptions and analysis is presented in Appendix D.

Return on Investment

The revenue and expense data for each of the fleet construction alternatives and a range of market share possibilities, with the resulting figures for return on investment, are shown in Figures 4-2 through 4-4 and in Tables 4-14 through 4-16. The implications of these key exhibits are important to the decisions on the levels of funding required by the U.S. Merchant Marine in the next six years.

In recent years, the industry return on investment has *averaged* about 5%. To maintain this level of earnings, the following market shares of commercial general cargo would be required for each of the fleet alternatives.[j]

---

[i]The variation stems in part from the relationship between freight rates and commodity values—higher value goods generally are charged higher rates. The present U.S.-flag trade is composed of a large portion of high value goods. As the U.S. increases its market share, it will have to resort to carrying lower-value, lower-rated goods, and thus market share will grow faster than revenue levels.

[j]Fleet A numbers 271 ships; Fleet B, 355 ships; Fleet C/D, 424 ships.

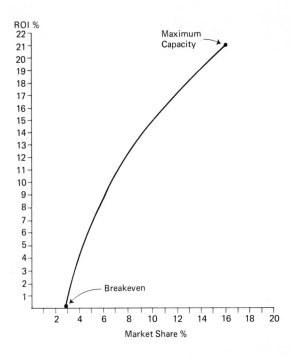

Figure 4-2   Estimated Return on Investment and Market Shares for Subsidized Segment Under As Is Construction Program: 1976. (Source: Appendix E-1)

90

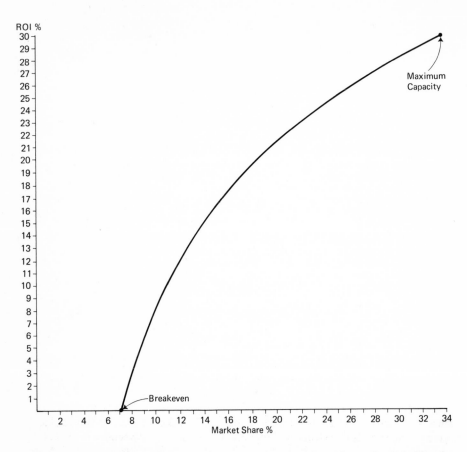

Figure 4-3   Estimated Return on Investment and Market Shares for Subsidized Segment Under Increased Funding Construction Program: 1976. (Source: Appendix E-2)

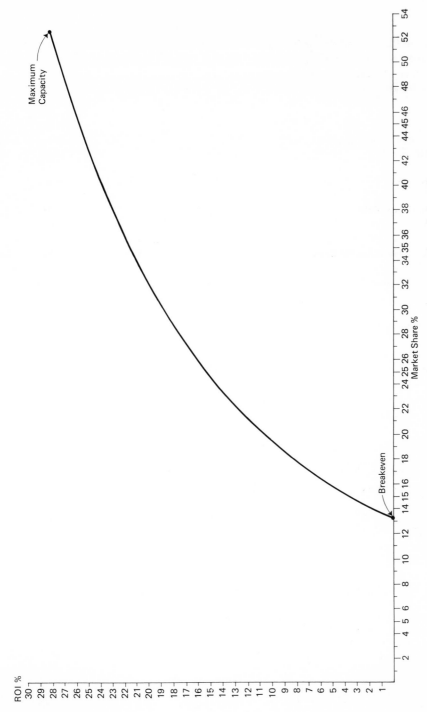

Figure 4-4 Estimated Return on Investment and Market Shares for U.S.-Flag Fleet Under Extended Benefits Construction Program: 1976. (Source: Appendix E-3)

Table 4-14

**Estimated Return on Investment for
Subsidized Segment Based on As Is
Program and Selected Market Shares:
1976 (Dollars in Thousands)**

Commercial General Cargo Market Share	*15.92%*	*6.7%*	*2.84%*
Total Revenue	2,273,565	1,254,373	799,992
Total Vessel Expense	409,033	409,033	409,033
Total Voyage Expense	994,702	521,656	323,666
Total Terminated Voyage Expense	1,403,735	930,689	732,699
Terminated Voyage Profit or Loss	869,830	323,684	67,293
Operating Differential Subsidy	141,100	141,100	141,100
Net Terminated Voyage Profit or Loss	1,010,930	464,784	208,393
Other Deductions:			
Depreciation	51,750	51,750	51,750
Container Leasing	59,520	59,520	59,520
Administrative and General	272,830	150,520	96,000
Other Deductions (including interest)	500	500	500
Subtotal	384,600	262,290	207,770
Earnings before Federal Income Taxes	626,330	202,494	623
Federal Income Taxes	125,266	40,499	125
Earnings after Federal Income Taxes	501,064	161,995	498
Additions to Stockholders' Investment	1,417,955	639,050	47,726
Stockholders' Investment at End of Year	2,384,859	1,605,954	1,014,630
Return on Investment	21.0%	10.1%	0.0%

Note: The selected market shares are maximum capacity, reasonable return, and lowest profitable ones.

Sources: Appendixes D and E.

Table 4-15

**Estimated Return on Investment
for Subsidized Liner Segment Based
on Increased Funding Program and
Selected Market Shares : 1976
(Dollars in Thousands)**

Commercial General Cargo *Market Share*	*35.56%*	*11%*	*7.22%*
Total Revenue	4,134,185	1,735,987	1,313,598
Total Vessel Expense	600,310	600,310	600,310
Total Voyage Expense	1,689,044	661,276	489,080
Total Terminated Voyage Expense	2,289,354	1,261,586	1,089,390
Terminated Voyage Profit or Loss	1,844,831	474,401	224,201
Operating Differential Subsidy	196,100	196,100	196,100
Net Terminated Voyage Profit or Loss	2,040,931	670,501	420,301
Other Deductions:			
Depreciation	87,740	87,740	87,740
Container Leasing	140,160	140,160	140,160
Administrative and General	496,100	208,320	157,630
Other Deductions (including interest)	34,600	34,600	34,600
Subtotal	758,600	470,820	420,130
Earnings before Federal Income Taxes	1,282,331	199,681	171
Federal Income Taxes	256,466	39,936	34
Earnings after Federal Income Taxes	1,025,865	159,745	137
Additions to Stockholders' Investment	2,451,390	633,144	34,432
Stockholders' Investment at End of Year	3,418,294	1,600,048	1,001,336
Return on Investment	30.0%	10.0%	0.0%

Note: See Table 4-14.   Sources: Appendixes D and E.

Table 4-16

**Estimated Return on Investment for
U.S.-Flag Fleet Based on Extended
Benefits Program and Selected Market
Shares: 1976 (Dollars in Thousands)**

Commercial General Cargo Market Share	*52.2%*	*19.5%*	*13.38%*
Total Revenue	$6,406,897	$3,016,270	$2,364,947
Total Vessel Expense	926,702	926,702	926,702
Total Voyage Expense	2,708,581	1,231,071	954,561
Total Terminated Voyage Expense	$3,635,283	$2,157,773	$1,881,263
Terminated Voyage Profit or Loss	$2,771,614	$ 858,497	$ 483,684
Operating Differential Subsidy	240,000	240,000	240,000
Net Terminated Voyage Profit or Loss	$3,011,614	$1,098,497	$ 723,684
Other Deductions:			
Depreciation	$ 145,100	$ 145,100	$ 145,100
Container Leasing	216,960	216,960	216,960
Administrative and General	768,830	361,950	283,790
Other Deductions (including interest)	77,500	77,500	77,500
Subtotal	$1,208,390	$ 801,510	$ 723,350
Earnings before Federal Income Taxes	$1,803,224	$ 296,987	$ 334
Federal Income Taxes	360,645	59,397	67
Earnings after Federal Income Taxes	$1,442,579	$ 237,590	$ 267
Additions to Stockholders' Investment	$3,824,014	$1,082,596	$ 74,021
Stockholders' Investment at End of Year	5,124,014	2,382,596	1,374,021
Return on Investment	28.2%	10.0%	0.0%

Note: See Table 4-14.   Sources: Appendixes D and E.

Fleet A:	Somewhat over 4% market share
Fleet B:	Slightly less than 9% market share
Fleet C/D:	About 16% market share

Thus, Fleets B, C and D need to raise their market share above the 1967 level just to attain a 5% return; only Fleet A appears to be in a favorable position for readily achieving past levels of returns. The preceding may be stated in a different way. If the market shares achieved in 1967 were to be maintained into 1976, again only the fleet postulated under Alternative A would show a positive return on investment (9%).

In view of the current rise in capital costs for starting and maintaining new technological systems, Harbridge House believes that a minimum return on investment of 10% is more nearly appropriate for the industry. To obtain such a return, the following market shares of commercial general cargo tonnage would be required for each of the fleet alternatives (see Tables 4-6 through 4-11).

Fleet A (Subsidized):	6.7% market share
Fleet B (Subsidized):	11.0% market share
Fleet C (U.S.-Flag):	19.5% market share

The 1967 market shares of commercial general cargo were 6.2% for the subsidized segment and 7.8% for the U.S.-flag fleet. Therefore, substantial increases in market share will be required to obtain a 10% return on investment for any of the fleet alternatives other than Alternative A.

The Nixon administration has suggested that an appropriate goal for the U.S. Merchant Marine would be a 30% share of the commercial general cargo market. Such a market share exceeds the capacity available under construction Alternative A. It is so very close to the theoretical capacity available under construction Alternative B, that the authors believe it is virtually unattainable. In the case of construction Alternatives C or D, a 30% market share, *if achieved*, would yield a return on investment of about 19%. However, in view of the declining trend of the past ten years, such an increase appears extremely unlikely.

In summary, it appears that the commercial value of the U.S. Merchant Marine, whatever the construction alternative selected, is completely dependent upon increasing the share of U.S. foreign trade carried by U.S.-flag vessels. Only in the case of the Alternative A does the possibility of maintaining a 5% return on investment, or increasing that return to 10%, seem readily attainable, since only a modest increase in market share would be required for the latter. Conversely, construction Alternatives C or D would require a nearly fourfold increase in current market share simply to ensure a 10% return on investment.

Future Benefits and Costs of the U.S.
Merchant Marine

The net quantifiable benefits derived from the presence of the U.S. Merchant Marine consist of the following components.

i) benefit areas
     balance of payments
     national security
ii) costs
     operating differential subsidy
     rate preference

Tables 4-17 and 4-18 compare the 1976 benefits and costs to the nation for the alternative fleet sizes under analysis:

i) based on the market shares yielding a "reasonable" rate of return on investment; and
ii) based on the smallest market share yielding a profit.

Benefits

The total balance of payments impact of the U.S. Merchant Marine can be approximated by subtracting total voyage expense from total revenue (see Appendix C). From Table 4-17 it can be seen that if market shares yielding a "reasonable" rate of return are achieved, the subsidized liner segment will produce balance of payments benefits of $733 million under Alternative A, and $1,075 million under Alternative B, while Alternative C will yield benefits in balance of payments of $1,785 million for the entire U.S.-flag fleet.

The previous discussion of national security benefits contributed by the U.S. Merchant Marine in the past focused on two areas:

i) availability of shipping capacity;
ii) cost savings.

For the period 1958-1967, DOD demand ranged between 13.5% and 26.1% of the U.S.-flag fleet capacity; the peacetime average (1958-1965) was 16%; and in 1966 and 1967, as DOD demand grew, the amount of capacity required to fulfill national security demand rose to 25.3% and 26.1% respectively.

Given the wide range of possible DOD levels in the future, will the U.S.-flag fleet under the three alternative construction programs have sufficient capacity to meet national security requirements? To overcome the difficulties of the short-of-all-out-war situation, the U.S. Merchant Marine has formulated a program called RESPOND, which provides a planned schedule of availability of sealift for various levels of DOD demand.

Table 4-17

**Estimated Benefits and Costs of the
U. S.-Flag Fleet: 1976 Reasonable
Return Market Shares**

	As Is*	Increased Funding*	Extended Benefits
No. of Ships at End of 1976	271	355	424
Share of Commercial General Cargo Market			
Necessary	6.70%	11.0%	19.50%
Benefits (in millions)			
Balance of Payments	$ 733	$1,075	$1,785
National Security	270†	319†	400
Subtotal	$1,003	$1,394	$2,185
Costs‡ (in millions)			
ODS	$ 141	$ 196	$ 240
Rate Preference	3§	3§	60
Subtotal	$ 144	$ 199	$ 300
Net Benefits (in millions)	$ 859	$1,195	$1,885
Benefit/Cost Ratio	7.0	7.0	7.3

*Subsidized segment only.

†It was assumed that national security benefits for these two alternative programs would be proportional to the capacity of the subsidized-liner segment.

‡CDS is not included since this program benefits shipyard owners rather than fleet operators.

§Estimated at 5% of the total program.

Table 4-18

**Estimated Benefits and Costs of the U.S.
Flag Fleet: 1976 Lowest Profitable
Market Shares**

	As Is*	Increased Funding*	Extended Benefits
No. of Ships at End of 1976	271	355	424
Share of Commercial General Cargo Market Necessary	2.84%	7.22%	13.38%
Benefits (in millions)			
Balance of Payments	$476	$825	$1,410
National Security	270†	319†	400
Subtotal	$746	$1,144	$1,810
Costs‡ (in millions)			
ODS	$141	$ 196	$ 240
Rate Preference	3§	3§	60
Subtotal	$144	$ 199	$ 300
Net Benefits (in millions)	$602	$ 945	$1,510
Benefit/Cost Ratio	5.2	5.7	6.0

*Subsidized segment only.

†It was assumed that national security benefits for these two alternatives programs would be proportional to the capacity of the subsidized-liner segment.

‡CDS is not included since this program benefits shipyard owners rather than fleet operators.

§Estimated at 5% of the total program.

Table 4-19 presents information on the annual measurement tonnage requirements for each stage; the expected sources of capacity; the relationship of the private U.S. Merchant Marine capacities under alternative construction programs A, B, and C to the DOD demand levels. From this analysis, the relative potential of each construction program for fulfilling national security requirements can be determined. For example, while the upper range of DOD needs would require 61% of the capacity available under the Alternative A, total DOD requirements would involve only 5% to 30% of the capacity under Alternative C. Thus, the capacity requirements under Stages IV and V for Alternative C approximate the relationship that existed in 1967 in supplying the DOD effort in Vietnam (assuming that the private U.S. Merchant Marine provides all the required sealift capability for each stage). If it is assumed that the MSTS nucleus fleet and the NDRF-GAA fleets are available and supply capacity in the amounts shown in Table 4-19 for each stage, the ability of the various U.S.-flag fleets to meet their share of DOD requirements is more favorable: there are only three instances (Stages IV and V under Alternative A and Stage V for Alternative B) where the U.S.-flag fleet would have fewer than three vessels available for other service for every ship engaged in DOD carriage (the relationship existing in 1967).

In the earlier discussion of national security benefits contributed by the U.S. Merchant Marine in the past, average cost savings per year (for a ten-year period consisting of two war-emergency years and eight peacetime years) amounted to $400 million (see Chapter 3, p. 64). Analysis of the future has turned up no new factors which might alter the supply and demand coefficients affecting these relationships and, accordingly, we have concluded that national security benefits of $400 million per year will accrue to the nation from the U.S.-flag fleet.

Costs of the U.S. Merchant Marine

The costs to the government fall into two principal areas: operating differential subsidy and rate preference costs. ODS will range from $141 million to $240 million depending upon the ship construction program, and we have assumed that rate preference costs will continue at current levels of approximately $60 million per year.[k] Because the enabling legislation for the Ship Exchange Program expires in 1970, costs have not been calculated for this program.

Net Benefits and Benefit/Cost Ratios

Tables 4-17 and 4-18 display the costs and benefits derived from alternatives at two different market shares. The net economic benefits accruing to the

[k]It should be noted that this is contrary to the proposed U.S. Merchant Marine Act of 1970.

Table 4-19

**Respond Program Requirements and
Sources by Stage and Ship Construction
Program (Thousands of Measurement Tons)**

	Peace I	Peace II	Stage I	Stage II	Stage III	Stage IV	Stage V
Annual Demand Level	7,500	12,800	17,100	21,000	28,000	39,000	48,000
Sources:							
MSTS-NUC	3,200	3,200	3,200	3,300	3,400	3,500	4,000
NDRF-GAA	——	——	500	1,700	5,000	7,000	9,000
Merchant Marine	4,300	9,600	13,400	16,000	19,600	28,500	35,000

Ship Construction Program:	DOD Merchant Marine Requirements as % of Estimated 1976 U. S.-Flag Fleet Capacity						
As Is	5.5%	12.3%	17.1%	20.5%	25.1%	36.4%	44.7%
Increased Funding	3.4	7.7	10.7	12.8	15.6	22.7	27.9
Extended Benefits/ Build Foreign	2.6	5.9	8.2	9.8	11.9	17.4	21.3

Ship Construction Program:	DOD Total Program Requirements as %'s of Estimated 1976 U. S.-Flag Fleet Capacity						
As Is	9.6%	16.4%	21.9%	26.8%	35.8%	49.9%	61.4%
Increased Funding	6.0	10.2	13.6	16.8	22.3	31.1	38.3
Extended Benefits/ Build Foreign	4.6	7.8	10.4	12.8	17.1	23.8	29.3

Sources: RESPOND Program submitted to Department of Defense by Committee of American Steamship Lines, 1968. Also, see Table 4-5 for projected capacity data.

nation in 1976 for the various fleet sizes under examination range from $602 million for a "breakeven" subsidized fleet to nearly $1.9 billion for a U.S.-flag fleet earning a "reasonable" rate of return. Predictably, large fleet sizes combined with larger market participation result in larger net benefits to the nation. For example, with a $300-million ship construction program and a 30% share of the commercial general cargo market, net national benefits would amount to $2.5 billion.

The ratios of benefits to costs based on a "reasonable" return on investment are 7.0 and over, which compares favorably with the actual 1967 ratio of 4.0 and the ten-year (1958-1967) average ratio of 4.2.

The Dilemma for Policy-Makers

The foregoing analysis presents a sobering picture to policy-makers who have been convinced of a need for change in the maritime industry. The safe path to adequate industry health with continued national benefits seems to be the maintenance of current construction programs. This is a low-risk policy, with little chance of either the industry or the nation not receiving a return on its investment. However, low risk is accompanied by low gains, particularly for the nation. The potential for increased benefits is severely circumscribed by the lack of capacity under the *As Is* construction program.

On the other hand, as the fleet size increases so does the potential for greatly increased benefits—but only at considerable commercial risk. For example, breakeven on a $300 million program requires almost a doubling of the 1967 commercial general cargo market share. Even at breakeven, however, this alternative would furnish the nation with nearly 50% more benefits than it received from its Merchant Marine in 1967. However, failure to achieve requisite market shares could have a disastrous effect on the nation's merchant fleet.

The problem for decision-makers, then, is whether to settle for traditional programs with traditional returns or to risk achieving the necessary increases in market shares in order to stimulate the commercial vigor of the fleet and to magnify the benefits to the nation. The risk can be justified only if there is some hope of improving the competitive position of the fleet and of winning a larger market share. The next chapter will discuss one means for accomplishing the higher goal.

5 The Role of Government and the U.S. Merchant Marine in our Evolving Transportation System

Introduction

Up to this point, this study has focused on the relationships of the U.S. Merchant Marine to the national economy by assessing:

i) the economic potential of U.S.-flag operations as an industry;
ii) the past contributions of the U.S.-flag fleet to national objectives;
iii) the potential profitability of the U.S.-flag fleet and the contributions of the industry to national objectives.

From this analysis it appears that the past investment in the U.S. Merchant Marine by the government/industry partnership has provided significant returns to the government. The faltering commercial performance is rapidly being changed by recent technological innovations. For those segments of the industry willing to adopt the new technology the outlook is bright, since the new cargo-handling techniques offer a means of differentiating service while increasing revenue potential. The new technology, moreover, has the potential to strengthen more than the maritime industry itself; the U.S. Merchant Marine—supported by appropriate government programs—can make a major contribution to the U.S. international transportation system.

The U.S. Merchant Marine is in a transitional period. The concept of transportation service is no longer simply pier-to-pier delivery; rather, the emerging concept is one of a door-to-door system with the steamship line providing through routing, liability and other supporting services, packaged in a through rate. Shipping lines are being transformed into transportation companies[a] and are playing a vital role in determining the shape of the U.S. international transportation system. In order for the nation to receive expanded benefits from a growing merchant marine, the government must play a policy role which allows companies to develop these systems.

Intermodalism: A New Transportation Service

As pointed up in Chapter 2, the impact of containerization on shipping economics can be substantial. Beyond the profit implications, containerization will also permit the development of intermodalism—the through move-

[a]Transportation companies refers to companies that are components of an intermodal transportation system on a **cooperative** basis; this **does not** necessarily imply mergers of different modes into one company.

ment of containers from inland origin across the ocean to another inland point without any intermediate handling of the cargo in the container. The economic potential of intermodalism is impressive—both in terms of direct cost reductions and of reduced transit time, leading to reduced inventory levels. However, unlike the cost-reducing effects for ocean shipping which come automatically from the introduction of containers, intermodal systems will have to be promoted and developed. In a technological sense, containerization eliminates many of the age-old barriers between the various transport modes. But these barriers are more than technological: they are built into the organization of the transportation industry and influence the thinking of most carrier managements. Moreover, land carriers have less stake in an international system because their trade is primarily domestic. Therefore, the managers of ocean carriers are the logical leaders in developing the full potential of the new technology for simplifying international freight transportation systems.

Potential Advantages of Intermodalism

Intermodal services, as such, do not necessarily lead to the degree of cost-saving possible from containerization, but they do offer profit potential through increased traffic, and may be more attractive to shippers than the available alternate services.

Faster and More Reliable Transit. The possibilities of rapid transfer from one carrier to another and of expedited service result in faster and more reliable transit. The payoff for the shipper comes from an ability to reduce inventories and thereby investment and other carrying costs. These are financial benefits which carriers providing intermodal service can produce for shippers, some portion of which should be reflected in increased carrier profits. In addition, more effective control of containers while on shore will increase productivity and carrier profits.

Simplified Supervision of Cargo. Breakbulk operations, characterized by stop-and-go movement of cargoes from origin to destination and transfer of cargo from one vehicle to another, vastly complicate the task of keeping track of cargo, thus increasing the costs of locating shipments. A through, intermodal service in readily identifiable containers presents the possibility of lessening these costly administrative burdens.

Lower Through-Cost Rates. On a door-to-door basis, the savings to shippers has and will continue to be very significant. For example, direct savings in packaging and pilferage can be realized if an intermodal system is operative. A survey by the National Academy of Sciences reported savings in this area amounting to as much as $18 per measurement ton for containerable cargo.[1]

Total general cargo movements in U.S. foreign trade equalled 191 million measurement tons, excluding DOD, in 1967. If only 10% of this tonnage were affected by these rate reductions, the annual savings would amount to $344 million for 1967; if only 50% of the total general cargo market is affected in the future, the annual savings could amount to $1.7 billion annually.

There have been no significant rate increases on the trade routes served by high technology ships supported by the intermodal transportation companies. In fact, there has been a decrease in the through-rate because companies are providing more service—such as local inland transportation—at no increase in rates. Shipping revenues for 191 million measurement tons of general cargo in the foreign trade of the United States in 1967 amounted to approximately $5 billion.[2] To this must be added the inland transportation charges in the countries of origin and destination which would add several billion dollars to total through cost. Therefore, the potential decrease in through transportation costs of an efficient intermodal transportation system is enormous. Even a one percent decrease in total through rates would mean a savings to shippers of well over $50 million annually.

Possibility of Rate Reductions. The lower handling costs of containerization should make possible rate reductions, as should the consolidation of small shipments. In addition, because of the concentrated nature of export-import traffic (especially import) the possibility of multi-car shipments of containers provides another basis for possible rate reductions. For example, if a 10% decrease in through costs can be achieved, the transportation savings in the shipping sector alone amount to more than $500 million. These cost and rate savings have a multiplier effect: as rates are lowered, U.S. products will become more competitive abroad.

The Competitive Effects of Intermodalism

Overall, the development of intermodal services will significantly change the competitive situation within the maritime industry. Because intermodalism will permit a shift from pier-to-pier operations to door-to-door operations, the market for tramp services would be curtailed sharply. Liner operators— both U.S.-flag and foreign-flag—will be the principal beneficiaries of inter-modalism. With high-speed, reliable and frequent service and the penetration of inland markets by containership operators, liners should quickly capture the bulk of the general cargo market on major trade routes. Intermodalism will permit liner companies to provide frequent, point-to-point service on high-volume trade routes which will—for the first time—be superior to those operated by tramps.

While the advantages of intermodalism in a technological sense are available to all ocean carriers, U.S.-flag operators should benefit most. Most U.S. trading partners have relatively small land masses, and distances between ports and principal export/import points are minimal. Consequently, the time and expense of inland transport at one end of U.S. foreign trade is relatively inconsequential. This is particularly fortunate since U.S. operators have fewer resources in making cooperative agreements with foreign land transportation companies than with domestic operators. In the United States, however, inland transport is of major importance due to the considerable distances between the seaboard and the major import/export centers, such as Chicago. Because of their greater familiarity with U.S. laws and business practices as well as with U.S. domestic carriers, U.S.-flag operators should have a major advantage over foreign-flag operators in developing intermodal services in the United States. For the first time, U.S.-flag operators should be able to make an important differentiation between their services and those of foreign-flag operators.

Inland Carriers

Intermodal container operations obviously require the direct involvement of inland carriers—railroads, truck lines and possibly barge lines—singly or in combination. While a single firm would be the most suitable unit for providing and coordinating multi-mode service, present laws and regulations appear to require that intermodal service be performed either in conjunction with certificated freight forwarders or through cooperative ventures between water and inland carriers. For the reasons discussed below, ocean carriers should take the lead in establishing arrangements for intermodal container services.

Inland Carrier Markets. Unlike ocean carriers in international service, inland carriers have only limited dependence on export/import traffic. Domestic carriage is by far the largest part of the traffic of most inland carriers. Since a given number of containers can be of crucial importance to an ocean carrier—while being of only marginal importance to the inland carrier—these inland carriers are not likely to expend great efforts on developing intermodal service. Therefore, the ocean carrier, whose stake is much greater, must take the lead.

Furthermore, the inland carrier must be concerned about the effect on domestic traffic of any special rates or services provided for export/import traffic. A rate advantageous in capturing export/import traffic might cause substantial losses on domestic traffic. This becomes of greater importance as cost of service begins to replace value of commodity as the basis for domestic rates. Also, if the use of containers in domestic traffic increases substantially, inland carriers may change present practices which are beneficial to container traffic such as carrying containers without wheels or returning empties free of charge. These arrangements will tend to be dictated by advantages to be gained in domestic traffic.

107

Inland Carrier Services. Inland movements of marine containers are currently being made under "piggy-back" or highway truck rates and services, which are largely structured around the capabilities of the highway truck. Essentially, this results in rates which reflect the relatively low weights permissible in over-the-road movements. These weights are well below those possible for fully-loaded marine containers. (Incidentally, they are also well below the capabilities of modern railroad equipment and roadbeds.) The rail rates for trailer on flatcar (TOFC), which are the models in most cases for container rates (COFC), were designed to permit recapture of traffic lost to trucks without at the same time eroding boxcar traffic.

Furthermore, most terminal facilities have been designed for transferring wheeled vehicles between highway and rail flatcar, and few terminals have facilities for handling containers without wheels. In this connection, it is not clear at present whether containers are more suitable for domestic intermodal services than are the highway trailers so widely used in these services.[b] If containers become more prevalent in domestic transportation, the way for widespread intermodal services in export/import traffic would be open; but if—as seems likely—domestic transportation continues to utilize wheeled vehicles, intermodal container services will be more difficult to develop because land carriers operations will not be structured for them.

This means that ocean carriers trying to develop intermodal container service must, at present, make do with rates and services which were not designed with marine containers in mind. Nevertheless, this should not preclude attempts to develop a rate structure and service pattern more nearly reflecting the capabilities of marine containers. There are indications that at least some railroads, if presented with sound analyses of traffic potentials, might be willing to design rates and services more nearly related to the capabilities and needs of intermodal container service.

Other Requirements for Intermodalism

In addition to making necessary arrangements with inland carriers, the development of intermodal service requires other new activities by ocean carrier management. Indeed, intermodal service is as much dependent upon effective management as it is on containers. Planning and control systems and the use of modern marketing techniques are particularly crucial, given the considerable cost of marine containers. As the containers in intermodal service move further away from dockside, the need—as well as the difficulty—for maintaining control increases. Effective reporting systems and computerized records will be necessary.

The development of intermodal service will require the use of modern marketing techniques which have not been widely understood or practiced

[b]The merger of the New York Central Railroad into the Penn Central has eliminated the principal major proponent of transport without wheels.

among transportation company managements. Origin and destination studies, and service packages tailored to the shipper's requirements, for example, will be indispensible. Basically, the need will be to develop a new concept of shipping in foreign trade as a through package rather than as a series of separate and distinct movements.

Conclusion

However difficult the task in fulfilling the promise of intermodalism to the development of the U.S. international transportation system, the goal of the U.S. Merchant Marine is clear: **to provide the basis of an integrated international intermodal transportation system with significant benefits in improved services and lower through costs.**

As employment was the objective of government support in the '30's, and defense the key requirement of the '50's and '60's, it is evident that the continued development of the U.S. transportation system will be the priority of the U.S. Merchant Marine in the '70's. And only a U.S. Merchant Marine can accomplish this. The U.S. cannot rely on foreign fleets supported by foreign governments to develop new technology and improve the U.S. international transportation system.

Foreign-flag carriers do not have the same interest, capability or opportunity to develop close working relationships with U.S. inland transportation companies, to resolve complicated tariff issues with the ICC, or to develop strategic logistic concepts with the Department of Defense. The foreign lines are interested in developing a transportation link with the United States rather than in contributing to the total transportation needs of this country.

In the area of rates, the record is clear. In the commercial market, foreign shipping lines work more closely with home country shippers and gear service to their needs. Further, since rebates are a legal practice in foreign countries (but not in the United States) foreign shippers may spend resources in attracting trade through rebates rather than improving the efficiencies of the transportation system to U.S. shippers. Finally, to the extent that foreign governments exercise control over their fleets (many are nationalized companies), the U.S. shipper could be at a disadvantage without the presence of a U.S.-flag fleet.

Action Requirements

The U.S. Government has played a major role in the development of the U.S. Merchant Marine since the passage of the 1936 Act. The major roles it has played have been in ship construction (and administration of the Reserve fleet), and in administration of the operating differential subsidy and cargo/rate preference programs.

In the future, the role of the government will necessarily be different because of two related factors: first, the U.S. fleet has great need for new high productivity ships (the Nixon Administration aims for 300 such ships over the next 10 years); and second, if the size of the U.S. Merchant Marine increases, an ambitious program of increasing U.S. market share will be required for the survival of the fleet.

The ships will almost surely represent a $6 billion investment by government and industry, without considering the sums that will be spent on auxiliary equipment and supporting systems. If the market-share goals are not achieved, the industry will face severe economic losses, and thus will not be able to fulfill its potential to government programs nor to the evolving U.S. international transportation system. The key role of the U.S. Government in the 1970's will be to assist the industry to increase market share from its present low of 6% to a share in the 20% to 30% range—a fivefold increase over present market-share levels.

This suggests that a government-industry coordinated effort must be developed to increase market share simultaneously with the decision to undertake a large ship construction program. Elements of this program are briefly discussed below. Certain of the elements involve direct action by government and the industry. Other elements require investigation of currently unresolved questions, after which action may or may not be called for.

For Action

Rationalization of the Industry. In a fundamental sense, the nation's shipping industry includes not only the companies engaged in the business, but also the several labor unions, port authorities and other local governmental agencies, a number of federal government regulatory agencies, and, on occasion, the Congress and executive. These various groups have created over the years, a structure of laws, regulations, contractual agreements, operating practices, and concepts which are based on the old, fragmented process of breakbulk shipping. For the technically possible door-to-door intermodal shipping of containers to become commonplace (and the U.S. Merchant Marine to benefit therefrom), this structure of institutions and their actions must be changed to conform to the new technology. As is generally true in such cases, change will not come easily. The forces for maintenance of the *status quo* are powerful, since in the short run, at any rate, everyone involved will appear to lose some hard-won advantage as a result of serious change. Consequently, there must be clear purpose and firm leadership if the necessary rationalization of the industry is to take place. This is without doubt the most important role for government in the coming years.

Development of Information. Because of the fragmented nature of traditional shipping operations, there is available relatively little information of the sort needed to plan and conduct intermodal operations in international trade. Data relating to the levels of U.S.-flag and foreign-flag service, projected volumes of cargo—both containerable and bulk, and emerging shipper preferences should be collected and available in data banks. Only with such information can the industry take full advantage of the market potential of the new technology, and active participation of government—our principal collector of statistics—is necessary.

National Marketing Program. In cooperation with the industry, government can do much to promote the use of U.S.-flag ships. Embassies, legations and consulates throughout the world are in touch with shippers and receivers, and there should be an organized program for acquainting these latter groups with the services provided locally by U.S.-flag ships. These same government agencies should be an important source of the market information for the data bank referred to above.

For Investigation

Bilateral Agreements. One area for study and possible action, is to investigate the possibility of bilateral agreements between the United States and its shipping partners. Such agreements would have the effect of confining the trade of any two countries to vessels carrying the flags of those two countries, and since the United States is a major trading partner of virtually all nations, the U.S.-flag fleet would obviously benefit. However, bilateral agreements would surely affect "third-flag" carriers, many of which are American. Consequently, the desirability of unilateralism for the United States calls for careful investigation.

Government-Impelled Cargo. At present, about 50 percent of government-impelled cargo—primarily military and AID cargoes—is carried in U.S.-flag ships, and the feasibility of increasing this percentage on all government cargo should be examined. Government cargo is currently carried by U.S.-flag fleets at rates somewhat above regular world rates. Carrying these cargoes at regular market rates or somewhat below market rates while increasing the portion carried represents a potential benefit for both government and the U.S.-flag fleet.

The future development and promise of the U.S. Merchant Marine is primarily dependent on the initiative of those steamship companies capable of making the transition from one-vessel operations to total transportation companies, but meaningful and directed government policies, which encourage this transition, are also essential.

For the first time in decades, the U.S. Merchant Marine has the potential to develop an economic and service advantage over its foreign-flag competition.

By continuing to lead the way in adopting the new capital-intensive technology and systems, an industry-government partnership working towards the common goal of developing strong transportation companies is capable of achieving a profitable industry with significant benefits to national objectives.

Appendixes

Appendix A
List of General
Cargo Commodities

Live Animals
Milk Dry Cond or Ev
Fish & Fish Products
Misc Grain Products
Bananas
Fruit & Veg Juices
Vegetables Canned
Sugar
Tea
Cocoa Beans
Hay & Fodder
Lard Greases &
  Margarine
Alcoholic Beverages
Hides & Skins, Raw
Oil Seed Flour
Nursery Stock
Synthetic Rubber
Umfd Cork
Lumber
Raw Cotton
Man-Made Fibers
Veg Fibers Nec
Natural Fertilizers
Limestone Flux
Salt
Clay & Refrac Min
Copper Ore & Conc
Bituminous Coal
Fixed Veg Oils Nec
Alcohols
Carbon Black
Boric Acid
Sulfuric Acid
Toluene
Chemicals Nec
Inks
Toilet Preparations
Plastic Materials
Meat Fresh or Frozen
Dairy Products
Rice
Fruits & Nuts, Fresh
Fruits, Dried
Nuts, Shelled

Veg Preps Nec
Edible Molasses
Spices
Coffee & Cocoa Preps
Grain Byproducts Nec
Misc Foods & Food
  Preps
Unmfd Tobacco
Fur Skins, Raw
Animal Mat Incl Shells
Crude Veg Mat Nec
Scrap & Recl Rubber
Post Poles Ties Fuel
  Wood
Waste Paper
Cotton Linters
Raw Wool
Other Textile Fibers
Marble & Stone Raw
Sulphur & Pyrites
Sand Gravel Crushed
  Stone
Nonmetallic Min Nec
Iron & Steel Scrap
Petroleum Waxes
Proc Anim & Veg Oils
Organic Chem Nec
Radioactive Material
Elem Oxides Halides
Mineral Tar
Wood-Based Chemicals
Dyes & Tanning Mat
Pharmaceuticals
Explosives
Insecticides
Meat Preparations
Eggs & Egg Products
Wheat Flour & Semol
Fruits, Frozen
Nuts Fruits & Preps
Vegs Fresh or Froz
Veg & Veg Preps
Inedible Molasses
Coffee Green or Roasted
Misc Animal Feeds

Animal Feeds Nec
Nonalcohol Beverages
Mfd Tobacco
Oil Seeds
Garden & Field Seeds
Crude Rubber
Fuel Wood
Posts Poles RR Ties
Pulp, All Types
Textile Waste Nec
Misc Veg & Textile
  Fibers
Phosphate Rock
Limestone Flux &
  Gypsum
Natural Abrasives
Nonmet Mineral & Slag
Ferrous Slag & Dross
Plat Uran Thor Ores
Soft Fixed Veg Oils
Hydrocarbons
Misc Inorganic Chem
Sodium Hydroxide
Inorganic Chem Nec
Benzene
Organic Products Nec
Figments & Paints
Essential Oils
Sporting Ammunition
Starches
Glues
Potassic Fertilizers
Leather
Footwear
Clothing
Other Woven Fabrics
Rubber Materials
Plastic Mfrs Nec
Tires Inc Aircraft
Worked Wood & Wood
  Mfrs
Wood Mfrs
Paper & Paperboard
Stationery Supplies
Building Mat Nec

Plate & Sheet Glass
Pig Iron
Steel Bars
Steel Rails
Steel Castings
Copper
Lead
Uranium & Thorium
Metal Transp Contain
Hand Tools
Heat & Cook Stoves
Lighting Fixtures
Office Mchy
Mchy for Special Ind
Valves & Fittings
Gas Engines & Diesels
Telecom Apparatus
Scientific Instruments
Sound Recorders
Road Motor Vehicles
Aircraft & Parts
Photo Supplies
Works of Art
Misc Manufactures
Ammonium Sulfate
Phosphatic Fertilize
Leather Mfrs
Furs & Mfrs
Yarn & Thread
Special Fabrics
Hyg & Conv Rubber Pr
Plastic & Rubber Mat
Plastic & Rub Mfrs Nec
Worked Wood Mfrs

Cork Mfrs
Newsprint
Bldg Cement & Lime
Clay Constr Mat
Glass Containers
Sponge Iron
Steel Plates & Sheet
Steel Wire
Ferroalloys
Nickel
Zinc
Misc Base Metals Nec
Nonelec Wire Prod
Cutlery
Cent Heating Equip
Cranes Draglines etc.
Metal Working Mchy
Mchy Nec
Steam Power Boilers
Elec Mot & Gen
Domestic Appliances
Scientific Apparatus
Electric Mchy Nec
Motorcycles
Ships & Boats
Musical Instruments
Jewelry
Gifts, US Art Retdetc
Nitrogen Fertilizers
Fertilizers Nec
Travel Goods
Fur Clothing
Woven Cotton Fabrics

Rugs & Tapestries
Tires & Tubes
Rubber Convey Belts
Veneers & Plywood
Worked Wood Nec
Paper Paperboard Mfrs
Printed Matter
Asphalt Building Prods
Mineral Mfrs Nec
Pottery
Steel Ingots
Steel Hoop & Strip
Steel Tubes
Silver & Platinum
Aluminum
Tin
Fin Met Struct Nec
Nails Screws etc.
Metal Household Mfrs
Sanitary Plumg Fixt
Agricultural Mchy
Textile & Leath Mchy
Heating Equipment
Int Comb Engines
Insul Wire & Cable
Electro-Medical App
Watches & Clocks
Rail Vehicles
Vehicles Nec
Furniture
Toys & Sporting Goods
Parachutes etc.
Precious Stones

Appendix B
Technical Notes on
Computation of GPS

A standardized unit—the General Purpose Ship (GPS)—was developed for computation of annual lift capacity. The standard vessel was defined as a conventional general cargo freighter with the following characteristics.

Gross capacity in measurement tons = 20,000
Number of days in service per year = 350
Length (in nautical miles) of an average round trip = 13,500
Ship service speed (in knots) = 18
Port/seatime ratio = 1:1 (175 days at sea, 175 days in port)
Ratio of usable measurement tons to total measurement tons of capacity = .667

The gross measurement ton capacity and speed figures were established arbitrarily (this procedure was valid since all ships in the fleet would be expressed as a fraction of the unit ship) to represent a modern breakbulk ship. The port/seatime ratio and length of round trip were developed from Maritime Administration Schedule 3002 data. Although the tabulation showed that approximately 53% of total voyage days were spent at sea, the lower figure of 50% has been used to adjust for the decreasing number of passenger ships. The ratio of usable measurement tons was derived from Ernst & Ernst, *Selected Commodity Costs for Oceanborne Shipments Via Common Carrier.*[1]

The general formula used to compute the GPS unit, using the above characteristics, was:

$$GPS \text{ Annual Lift Capacity} = .667 \times RTC \times GMT \times R$$

$$\text{where } RTC = \text{round-trip capacity factor}$$
$$GMT = \text{gross measurement-ton capacity}$$
$$R = \text{number of round trips per year}$$

The number of round trips per year was computed as follows:

$$R = \frac{D}{\dfrac{RTVL}{24S} + PT}$$

$$\text{where } D = \text{number of days in service per year}$$
$$RTVL = \text{round-trip voyage length (in nautical miles)}$$
$$S = \text{ship service speed (in knots)}$$
$$PT = \text{port time (equal to sea time)}$$

$$\text{Thus, } R = \frac{350}{\dfrac{13,500}{18 \times 24} + \dfrac{13,500}{18 \times 24}} = 5.600;$$

and GPS Annual Lift Capacity = .667(2 × 20,000) × 5.600 = 149,408.

All ship types in the U.S.-flag fleet can be described as a ratio of the unit GPS.

The fleet can be viewed in terms of three classes of ships: breakbulk, dry bulk, and containerships. It should be noted that the differences between the classes are twofold—port-to-sea time ratio and usable capacity.

Table B-1

**Summary of Ship Class Differences in
Port/Seatime Ratio**

	Breakbulk	Dry Bulk	Containership
1958-1965	1:1	1:3	1:2
1966-1968	1:1	1:3	1:3
1976	1:1	1:4	1:4
Ratio of Usable Capacity to Total Capacity	.667	1.000	.667

In order to simplify the computation of the GPS equivalent (factor) for each ship type, constants were developed to express the effect of the nonvariable items within each class. The basic equation used for all ship types is:

GPS Equivalent (I) $= GMT$ (I) $\times S$ (I) $\times$ Fac (I),

where GMT (I) $=$ gross measurement tonnage of the Ith ship;

$\quad S$ (I) $=$ speed of the I ship; the

$\quad FAC$ (I) $=$ constant for that class of ship, representing the impact of the class variables and those items which are constant for all classes (i.e. the percentage of usable capacity, round-trip voyage length, and annual operating days).

The computations of the GPS factors for the respective ship types are presented in Tables B-2; and detailed data for ship count, GPS equivalents and annual lift capacity for 1966-1968 are presented in Tables B-3, B-4, and B-5, while less detailed data for the earlier years (1958-1966) are given in B-6, B-7, and B-8.

Table B-2

GPS Factors for Specified Ship Types

Ship Type	Speed	Capacity (MT)	Constant	Annual Lift Capacity	GPS Factor
C1A	14	11,150	.415	64,782	.434
C1B	14	10,925	.415	63,474	.425
C1MAV1	10.5	5,950	.415	25,927	.174
C1MBTV	10.5	5,950	.415	25,927	.174
C2	15.5	12,975	.415	83,462	.559
C2F	15.5	12,975	.415	83,462	.559
C2S	15.5	15,150	.415	97,452	.652
C2SA1	15.5	15,150	.415	97,452	.652
C2SAJ1	15.5	12,975	.415	83,462	.559
C2SAJ2	15.5	12,600	.415	81,050	.542
C2SAJ3	15.5	13,525	.415	87,000	.582
C2SAJ4	15.5	12,350	.415	79,441	.532
C2SAJ5	15.5	12,000	.415	77,190	.517
C2SB1	15.5	13,119	.415	84,388	.565
C2SDG2	15.5	13,225	.415	85,070	.569
C2SE1	15.5	13,650	.415	87,804	.588
C2SV	15.75	13,275	.415	86,769	.581
C3	16.5	16,250	.415	111,272	.745
C3A	16	16,000	.415	106,240	.711
C3E	16	13,375	.415	88,810	.594
C3PC					.745
C3SA1	16	16,000	.415	106,240	.711
C3SA2	16.5	16,800	.415	115,038	.770
C3SA3	16.5	13,825	.415	94,667	.634
C3SA4	16.5	14,613	.415	100,063	.670
C3SA5	16.5	13,650	.415	93,468	.626
C3SBH1	16.7	16,075	.415	111,408	.746
C3SBH2	16.7	15,700	.415	108,809	.728
C3SBR1	16.5	11,425	.415	78,233	.524
C3S33A	18	12,392	.415	92,568	.620
C3S37A	17.7	14,075	.415	103,388	.692
C3S37B	18	13,800	.415	103,086	.690
C3S37C	17.7	14,125	.415	103,755	.694
C3S37D	18	14,050	.415	104,954	.702
C3S38A	18.5	14,975	.415	114,971	.770
C3S43A	18	16,350	.415	122,135	.817
C3S45A	18	16,300	.415	121,761	.815

(continued)

Table B-2 (*continued*)

Ship Type	Speed	Capacity (MT)	Constant	Annual Lift Capacity	GPS Factor
C3S46A	18.5	17,275	.415	132,629	.888
C3S46B	18.5	17,900	.415	137,427	.920
C3S76A	18.6	17,750	.415	137,012	.917
C4	17	17,800	.415	125,579	.841
C4SA1	17	16,925	.415	119,406	.799
C4SA3	17	16,925	.415	119,406	.799
C4SA4	17	16,525	.415	116,584	.780
C4SB2	17	17,800	.415	125,579	.841
C4SB5	17	17,800	.415	125,579	.841
C4S1A	20	19,150	.415	158,945	1.064
C4S1F	20	16,850	.415	139,855	.936
C4S1H	20	16,525	.415	137,158	.918
C4S1P	20	18,200	.415	151,060	1.011
C4S1Q	20	13,775	.415	114,333	.765
C4S1QA	20.4	18,125	.415	153,446	1.027
C4S1S	20	16,925	.415	140,478	.940
C4S1SA	20	16,925	.415	140,478	.940
C4S1T	20	16,075	.415	133,423	.893
C4S1U	20	17,800	.415	147,740	.989
C4S49A	20	12,450	.415	103,335	.692
C4S57A	21	15,400	.415	134,211	.898
C4S58A	20.5	16,775	.415	142,714	.955
C4S60A	21	16,700	.415	145,541	.974
C4S64A	21	16,425	.415	143,144	.958
C4S64B	20.8	18,725	.415	161,634	1.082
C4S65A	20	18,825	.415	156,248	1.046
C4S66A	20	18,738	.415	155,525	1.041
C4S69A	23	21,000	.415	200,445	1.342
C4S69B	23	20,250	.415	193,286	1.294
C5SAX1 C5S751	15	10,500	.934	147,105	.985
EC2	11	11,825	.415	53,981	.361
EC2AW1	11	12,625	.415	57,633	.386
EC2SC1	11	12,625	.415	57,633	.386
N3MA1	9	4,000	.415	14,940	.100

Table B-2 (*continued*)

Ship Type	Speed	Capacity (MT)	Constant	Annual Lift Capacity	GPS Factor
America					.436
P1S1DR					.396
P2N1MA	20	17,825	.415		
P2S11K	20	5,975	.415	49,593	.332
P2S11N					.229
P2S11V	21	3,925	.415	34,206	.229
P2S29A	23	8,125	.415	77,553	.519
P2S211A	20	10,650	.415	88,395	.592
P2S2R2					.230
P2S2R3	19	4,350	.415	34,300	.230
P2S2R10	19	3,625	.415	28,583	.191
P2S2R14					
P3S2DL2	23	5,125	.415	48,918	.327
P6S4DS1	32	4,900	.415	65,072	.436
R1SDH1	16	4,750	.415	31,540	.211
R2STAV1	18	8,000	.415	59,760	.400
SEC2	11	11,475	.415	52,383	.351
VC2SAP2	15.5	11,325	.415	72,848	.488
VC2SAP3	16.5	11,325	.415	77,548	.519
VC2SAP7					.488

Table B-3

**Detailed Data on Fleet Size, GPS
Equivalents and Annual Lift Capacity by
Ship Type and Use for Subsidized Liners:
1966-1968**

Ship Type and Item	1968				
	Foreign Trade	TCMST	Temporarily Inactive	Laid Up	Total
C1-A					
No. of Ships	0	0	1	0	1
GPS Equivalent	–	–	0.434	–	0.434
Annual Lift Capacity	–	–	64,843	–	64,843
C1-B					
No. of Ships	2	0	0	0	2
GPS Equivalent	0.850	–	–	–	0.850
Annual Lift Capacity	126,997	–	–	–	126,997
C2-S					
No. of Ships	2	2	1	0	5
GPS Equivalent	1.304	1.304	0.652	–	3.260
Annual Lift Capacity	194,828	194,828	97,414	–	487,070
C2-S-AJ1					
No. of Ships	19	3	3	0	25
GPS Equivalent	10.621	1.677	1.677	–	13.975
Annual Lift Capacity	1,586,862	250,557	250,557	–	2,087,976
C2-S-AJ4					
No. of Ships	2	0	0	0	2
GPS Equivalent	1.064	–	–	–	1.064
Annual Lift Capacity	158,970	–	–	–	158,970
C2-S-AJ5					
No. of Ships	1	3	4	0	8
GPS Equivalent	0.517	1.551	2.068	–	4.136
Annual Lift Capacity	77,244	231,732	308,976	0	617,952
C2-S-B1					
No. of Ships	13	5	1	1	20
GPS Equivalent	7.345	2.825	0.565	0.565	11.300
Annual Lift Capacity	1,097,402	422,077	84,416	84,416	1,688,311

Table B-3 (*continued*)

Ship Type and Item	1968				
	Foreign Trade	*TCMST*	*Temporarily Inactive*	*Laid Up*	*Total*
C-3					
No. of Ships	1	0	0	1	2
GPS Equivalent	0.745	–	–	0.745	1.490
Annual Lift Capacity	111,309	–	–	111,309	222,618
C3-S-A1					
No. of Ships	0	3	0	0	3
GPS Equivalent	–	2.133	–	–	2.133
Annual Lift Capacity	–	318,687	–	–	318,687
C3-S-A2					
No. of Ships	10	3	1	0	14
GPS Equivalent	7.700	2.310	0.770	–	10.780
Annual Lift Capacity	1,150,442	345,132	115,044	–	1,610,618
C3-S-A3					
No. of Ships	10	0	1	0	11
GPS Equivalent	6.340	–	0.634	–	6.974
Annual Lift Capacity	947,246	–	94,725	–	1,041,971
C3-S-A4					
No. of Ships	4	0	2	0	6
GPS Equivalent	2.680	–	1.340	–	4.020
Annual Lift Capacity	400,413	–	200,207	–	600,620
C3-S-A5					
No. of Ships	3	0	4	0	7
GPS Equivalent	1.878	–	2.504	–	4.382
Annual Lift Capacity	280,588	–	374,118	–	654,706
C3-S-BH1					
No. of Ships	4	0	1	0	5
GPS Equivalent	2.984	–	0.746	–	3.730
Annual Lift Capacity	445,834	–	111,458	–	557,292
C3-S-BH2					
No. of Ships	5	0	1	0	6
GPS Equivalent	3.640	–	0.728	–	4.368
Annual Lift Capacity	543,845	–	108,769	–	652,614

(*continued*)

Table B-3 (*continued*)

Ship Type and Item	1968				
	Foreign Trade	*TCMST*	*Temporarily Inactive*	*Laid Up*	*Total*
C3-S-BR1					
No. of Ships	3	0	0	0	3
GPS Equivalent	1.572	–	–	–	1.572
Annual Lift Capacity	234,869	–	–	–	234,869
C3-S-33A					
No. of Ships	2	1	5	0	8
GPS Equivalent	1.240	0.620	3.100	–	4.960
Annual Lift Capacity	185,266	92,633	463,165	–	741,064
C3-S-37A					
No. of Ships	6	3	0	0	9
GPS Equivalent	4.152	2.076	–	–	6.228
Annual Lift Capacity	620,342	310,171	–	–	930,513
C3-S-37B					
No. of Ships	1	2	1	0	4
GPS Equivalent	0.690	1.380	0.690	–	2.760
Annual Lift Capacity	103,091	206,184	103,091	–	412,366
C3-S-37C					
No. of Ships	2	5	1	0	8
GPS Equivalent	1.388	3.470	0.694	–	5.552
Annual Lift Capacity	207,378	518,446	103,689	–	829,513
C3-S-37D					
No. of Ships	4	0	1	0	5
GPS Equivalent	2.808	–	0.702	–	3.510
Annual Lift Capacity	419,538	–	104,884	–	524,422
C3-S-38A					
No. of Ships	2	0	2	0	4
GPS Equivalent	1.540	–	1.540	–	3.080
Annual Lift Capacity	230,088	–	230,088	–	460,176
C3-S-43A					
No. of Ships	1	2	0	0	3
GPS Equivalent	0.817	1.634	–	–	2.451
Annual Lift Capacity	122,066	244,133	–	–	366,199

Table B-3 (*continued*)

Ship Type and Item	Foreign Trade	TCMST	Temporarily Inactive	Laid Up	Total
			1968		
C3-S-46A					
No. of Ships	0	0	4	0	4
GPS Equivalent	–	–	3.552	–	3.552
Annual Lift Capacity	–	–	530,697	–	530,697
C3-S-46B					
No. of Ships	0	0	0	0	0
GPS Equivalent	–	–	–	–	–
Annual Lift Capacity	–	–	·–	–	–
C3-S-46B *(Containership)*					
No. of Ships	3	0	1	0	4
GPS Equivalent	4.208	–	1.374	–	5.582
Annual Lift Capacity	628,709	–	205,286	–	833,995
C3-S-76A					
No. of Ships	2	0	3	0	5
GPS Equivalent	1.834	–	2.751	–	4.585
Annual Lift Capacity	274,014	–	411,021	–	685,035
C4-S-A1 *(Containership)*					
No. of Ships	1	0	1	0	2
GPS Equivalent	1.171	–	1.171	–	2.342
Annual Lift Capacity	174,957	–	174,957	–	349,914
C4-S-1A					
No. of Ships	10	0	4	0	14
GPS Equivalent	10.640	–	4.256	–	14.896
Annual Lift Capacity	1,589,701	–	635,881	–	2,225,582
C4-S-1F					
No. of Ships	3	0	0	0	3
GPS Equivalent	2.808	–	–	–	2.808
Annual Lift Capacity	419,538	–	–	–	419,538

(*continued*)

Table B-3 (*continued*)

Ship Type and Item	1968				
	Foreign Trade	*TCMST*	*Temporarily Inactive*	*Laid Up*	*Total*
C4-S-1H					
No. of Ships	2	0	2	0	4
GPS Equivalent	1.836	–	1.836	–	3.672
Annual Lift Capacity	274,313	–	274,313	–	548,626
C4-S-1P					
No. of Ships	2	2	0	0	4
GPS Equivalent	2.022	2.022	–	–	4.044
Annual Lift Capacity	302,103	302,103	–	–	604,206
C4-S-1Q					
(Containership)					
No. of Ships	2	0	0	0	2
GPS Equivalent	2.944	–	–	–	2.944
Annual Lift Capacity	439,857	–	–	–	439,857
C4-S-1QA					
No. of Ships	3	0	0	0	3
GPS Equivalent	3.081	–	–	–	3.081
Annual Lift Capacity	460,326	–	–	–	460,326
C4-S-1S					
No. of Ships	3	0	0	0	3
GPS Equivalent	2.820	–	–	–	2.820
Annual Lift Capacity	421,331	–	–	–	421,331
C4-S-1SA					
No. of Ships	2	0	0	0	2
GPS Equivalent	1.880	–	–	–	1.880
Annual Lift Capacity	280,887	–	–	–	280,887
C4-S-1T					
No. of Ships	2	0	0	0	2
GPS Equivalent	1.786	–	–	–	1.786
Annual Lift Capacity	266,843	–	–	–	266,843

Table B-3 (*continued*)

Ship Type and Item	1968				
	Foreign Trade	*TCMST*	*Temporarily Inactive*	*Laid Up*	*Total*
C4-S-1U					
No. of Ships	6	0	0	0	6
GPS Equivalent	5.934	–	–	–	5.934
Annual Lift Capacity	886,587	–	–	–	886,587
C4-S-49A					
No. of Ships	4	0	0	0	4
GPS Equivalent	2.768	–	–	–	2.768
Annual Lift Capacity	413,561	–	–	–	413,561
C4-S-57A					
No. of Ships	2	5	4	0	11
GPS Equivalent	1.796	4.490	3.592	–	9.878
Annual Lift Capacity	268,336	670,842	536,674	–	1,475,852
C4-S-58A					
No. of Ships	3	0	3	0	6
GPS Equivalent	2.865	–	2.865	–	5.730
Annual Lift Capacity	428,054	–	428,054	–	856,108
C4-S-60A					
No. of Ships	0	2	4	0	6
GPS Equivalent	–	1.948	3.896	–	5.844
Annual Lift Capacity	–	291,047	582,093	–	873,140
C4-S-64A					
No. of Ships	0	3	0	0	3
GPS Equivalent	–	2.874	–	–	2.874
Annual Lift Capacity	–	429,399	–	–	429,399
C4-S-64A *(Containership)*					
No. of Ships	1	0	1	0	2
GPS Equivalent	1.504	–	1.506	–	3.010
Annual Lift Capacity	224,710	–	225,008	–	449,718

(*continued*)

Table B-3 (*continued*)

Ship Type and Item	1968				
	Foreign Trade	TCMST	Temporarily Inactive	Laid Up	Total
C4-S-64B					
No. of Ships	2	0	0	0	2
GPS Equivalent	2.164	–	–	–	2.164
Annual Lift Capacity	323,319	–	–	–	323,319
C4-S-65A					
No. of Ships	3	0	3	0	6
GPS Equivalent	3.138	–	3.138	–	6.276
Annual Lift Capacity	468,842	–	468,842	–	937,684
C4-S-66A					
No. of Ships	5	5	2	0	12
GPS Equivalent	5.205	5.205	2.082	–	12.492
Annual Lift Capacity	777,669	777,669	311,067	–	1,866,405
C4-S-69A					
No. of Ships	5	0	0	0	5
GPS Equivalent	6.710	–	–	–	6.710
Annual Lift Capacity	1,002,528	–	–	–	1,002,528
C4-S-69B					
No. of Ships	1	0	0	0	1
GPS Equivalent	1.294	–	–	–	1.294
Annual Lift Capacity	193,334	–	–	–	193,334
C5-S-73B *(Containership)*					
No. of Ships	1	0	0	0	1
GPS Equivalent	1.985	–	–	–	1.985
Annual Lift Capacity	296,575	–	–	–	296,575
C5-S-75A *(Containership)*					
No. of Ships	2	0	0	0	2
GPS Equivalent	4.930	–	–	–	4.930
Annual Lift Capacity	736,581	–	–	–	736,581

Table B-3 (*continued*)

Ship Type and Item	1968				
	Foreign Trade	TCMST	Temporarily Inactive	Laid Up	Total
C5-S-77A					
(Containership)					
No. of Ships	1	0	1	0	2
GPS Equivalent	1.746	–	1.746	–	3.492
Annual Lift Capacity	260,866	–	260,866	–	521,732
C7-S-68C					
(Containership)					
No. of Ships	1	0	1	0	2
GPS Equivalent	2.592	–	2.592	–	5.184
Annual Lift Capacity	387,266	–	387,266	–	774,532
C7-S-68D					
(Containership)					
No. of Ships	1	0	1	0	2
GPS Equivalent	2.592	–	2.592	–	5.184
Annual Lift Capacity	387,266	–	387,266	–	774,532
P2-S1-1K					
No. of Ships	2	0	0	0	2
GPS Equivalent	0.664	–	–	–	0.664
Annual Lift Capacity	99,207	–	–	–	99,207
P2-S1-1V					
No. of Ships	0	0	0	1	1
GPS Equivalent	–	–	–	0.229	0.229
Annual Lift Capacity	–	–	–	34,214	34,214
P2-S2-9A					
No. of Ships	2	0	0	0	2
GPS Equivalent	1.038	–	–	–	1.038
Annual Lift Capacity	155,086	–	–	–	155,086
P2-S2-11A					
No. of Ships	2	0	0	0	2
GPS Equivalent	1.184	–	–	–	1.184
Annual Lift Capacity	176,899	–	–	–	176,899

(*continued*)

Table B-3 (*continued*)

Ship Type and Item	1968				
	Foreign Trade	*TCMST*	*Temporarily Inactive*	*Laid Up*	*Total*
P2-S2-R14					
No. of Ships	1	0	0	0	1
GPS Equivalent	0.191	–	–	–	0.191
Annual Lift Capacity	28,537	–	–	–	28,537
P2-SC2-R3					
No. of Ships	2	0	0	0	2
GPS Equivalent	0.460	–	–	–	0.460
Annual Lift Capacity	68,728	–	–	–	68,728
P3-S2-DL2					
No. of Ships	0	0	0	0	0
GPS Equivalent	–	–	–	–	–
Annual Lift Capacity	–	–	–	–	–
P6-S4-DS1					
No. of Ships	–	0	0	0	1
GPS Equivalent	0.436	–	–	–	0.436
Annual Lift Capacity	65,142	–	–	–	65,142
VC2-S-AP3					
No. of Ships	2	0	2	0	4
GPS Equivalent	1.038	–	1.038	–	2.076
Annual Lift Capacity	155,086	–	155,085	–	310,171
Total	182	49	67	5	303
GPS Equivalent	151.139	37.519	58.831	2.193	249,682
Annual Lift Capacity	22,581,376	5,605,640	8,789,820	327,652	37,304,488

131

Table B-3 (*continued*)

Ship Type and Item	Foreign Trade	TCMST	Temporarily Inactive	Laid Up	Total
			1967		
C1-A					
No. of Ships	0	1	2	0	3
GPS Equivalent	–	0.434	0.868	–	1.302
Annual Lift Capacity	–	64,843	129,686	–	194,529
C1-B					
No. of Ships	2	1	0	0	3
GPS Equivalent	0.850	0.425	–	–	1.275
Annual Lift Capacity	126,997	63,498	–	–	190,495
C2-S					
No. of Ships	4	1	1	0	6
GPS Equivalent	2.608	0.652	0.652	–	3.912
Annual Lift Capacity	389,656	97,414	97,414	–	584,484
C2-S-A1					
No. of Ships	2	0	0	0	2
GPS Equivalent	1.304	–	–	–	1.304
Annual Lift Capacity	194,828	–	–	–	194,828
C2-S-AJ1					
No. of Ships	26	2	2	0	30
GPS Equivalent	14.534	1.118	1.118	–	16.770
Annual Lift Capacity	2,171,496	167,038	167,038	–	2,505,572
C2-S-AJ2					
No. of Ships	0	1	0	1	2
GPS Equivalent	–	0.542	–	0.542	1.084
Annual Lift Capacity	–	80,979	–	80,979	161,958
C2-S-AJ4					
No. of Ships	3	0	0	2	5
GPS Equivalent	1.596	–	–	1.064	2.660
Annual Lift Capacity	238,455	–	–	158,970	397,425
C2-S-AJ5					
No. of Ships	10	0	0	0	10
GPS Equivalent	5.170	–	–	–	5.170
Annual Lift Capacity	772,439	–	–	–	772,439

(*continued*)

Table B-3 (*continued*)

Ship Type and Item	1967				
	Foreign Trade	*TCMST*	*Temporarily Inactive*	*Laid Up*	*Total*
C2-S-B1					
No. of Ships	17	6	0	0	23
GPS Equivalent	9.605	3.390	–	–	12.995
Annual Lift Capacity	1,435,064	506,493	–	–	1,941,557
C-3					
No. of Ships	2	0	0	0	2
GPS Equivalent	1.490	–	–	–	1.490
Annual Lift Capacity	222,618	–	–	–	222,618
C3-E					
No. of Ships	1	0	0	0	1
GPS Equivalent	0.594	–	–	–	0.594
Annual Lift Capacity	88,748	–	–	–	88,748
C3-S-A1					
No. of Ships	0	2	1	0	3
GPS Equivalent	–	1.422	0.711	–	2.133
Annual Lift Capacity	–	212,458	106,229	–	318,687
C3-S-A2					
No. of Ships	15	3	2	0	20
GPS Equivalent	11.550	2.310	1.540	–	15.400
Annual Lift Capacity	1,725,663	345,132	230,088	–	2,300,883
C3-S-A3					
No. of Ships	11	0	0	0	11
GPS Equivalent	6.974	–	–	–	6.974
Annual Lift Capacity	1,041,971	–	–	–	1,041,971
C3-S-A4					
No. of Ships	6	0	0	0	6
GPS Equivalent	4.020	–	–	–	4.020
Annual Lift Capacity	600,620	–	–	–	600,620
C3-S-A5					
No. of Ships	7	0	0	0	7
GPS Equivalent	4.382	–	–	–	4.382
Annual Lift Capacity	654,706	–	–	–	654,706

Table B-3 (*continued*)

Ship Type and Item	1967				
	Foreign Trade	TCMST	Temporarily Inactive	Laid Up	Total
C3-S-BH1					
No. of Ships	5	0	0	0	5
GPS Equivalent	3.730	–	–	–	3.730
Annual Lift Capacity	557,292	–	–	–	557,292
C3-S-BH2					
No. of Ships	6	0	0	0	6
GPS Equivalent	4.368	–	–	–	4.368
Annual Lift Capacity	652,614	–	–	–	652,614
C3-S-BR1					
No. of Ships	0	0	3	0	3
GPS Equivalent	–	–	1.572	–	1.572
Annual Lift Capacity	–	–	234,869	–	234,869
C3-S-33A					
No. of Ships	8	0	0	0	8
GPS Equivalent	4.960	–	–	–	4.960
Annual Lift Capacity	741,064	–	–	–	741,064
C3-S-37A					
No. of Ships	6	3	0	0	9
GPS Equivalent	4.152	2.076	–	–	6.228
Annual Lift Capacity	620,342	310,171	–	–	930,513
C3-S-37B					
No. of Ships	4	0	0	0	4
GPS Equivalent	2.760	–	–	–	2.760
Annual Lift Capacity	412,366	–	–	–	412,366
C3-S-37C					
No. of Ships	2	6	0	0	8
GPS Equivalent	1.388	4.164	–	–	5.552
Annual Lift Capacity	207,378	622,135	–	–	829,513
C3-S-37D					
No. of Ships	5	0	0	0	5
GPS Equivalent	3.510	–	–	–	3.510
Annual Lift Capacity	524,422	–	–	–	524,422

(*continued*)

Table B-3 (*continued*)

Ship Type and Item	Foreign Trade	TCMST	Temporarily Inactive	Laid Up	Total
			1967		
C3-S-38A					
No. of Ships	4	0	0	0	4
GPS Equivalent	3.080	–	–	–	3.080
Annual Lift Capacity	460,176	–	–	–	460,176
C3-S-43A					
No. of Ships	2	0	1	0	3
GPS Equivalent	1.634	–	0.817	–	2.451
Annual Lift Capacity	244,133	–	122,066	–	366,199
C3-S-46A					
No. of Ships	4	0	0	0	4
GPS Equivalent	3.552	–	–	–	3.552
Annual Lift Capacity	530,697	–	–	–	530,697
C3-S-46B					
No. of Ships	4	0	0	0	4
GPS Equivalent	3.680	–	–	–	3.680
Annual Lift Capacity	549,821	–	–	–	549,821
C4-S-1A					
No. of Ships	14	0	0	0	14
GPS Equivalent	14.896	–	–	–	14.896
Annual Lift Capacity	2,225,582	–	–	–	2,225,582
C4-S-1F					
No. of Ships	3	0	0	0	3
GPS Equivalent	2.808	–	–	–	2.808
Annual Lift Capacity	419,538	–	–	–	419,538
C4-S-1H					
No. of Ships	4	0	0	0	4
GPS Equivalent	3.672	–	–	–	3.672
Annual Lift Capacity	548,626	–	–	–	548,626
C4-S-1P					
No. of Ships	2	2	0	0	4
GPS Equivalent	2.022	2.022	–	–	4.044
Annual Lift Capacity	302,103	302,103	–	–	604,206

Table B-3 (*continued*)

Ship Type and Item	1967				
	Foreign Trade	*TCMST*	*Temporarily Inactive*	*Laid Up*	*Total*
C4-S-1Q					
No. of Ships	2	0	0	0	2
GPS Equivalent	1.530	–	–	–	1.530
Annual Lift Capacity	228,594	–	–	–	228,594
C4-S-1QA					
No. of Ships	3	0	0	0	3
GPS Equivalent	3.081	–	–	–	3.081
Annual Lift Capacity	460,326	–	–	–	460,326
C4-S-1S					
No. of Ships	3	0	0	0	3
GPS Equivalent	2.820	–	–	–	2.820
Annual Lift Capacity	421,331	–	–	–	421,331
C4-S-1SA					
No. of Ships	2	0	0	0	2
GPS Equivalent	1.880	–	–	–	1.880
Annual Lift Capacity	280,887	–	–	–	280,887
C4-S-1T					
No. of Ships	2	0	0	0	2
GPS Equivalent	1.786	–	–	–	1.786
Annual Lift Capacity	266,843	–	–	–	266,843
C4-S-1U					
No. of Ships	6	0	0	0	6
GPS Equivalent	5.934	–	–	–	5.934
Annual Lift Capacity	886,587	–	–	–	886,587
C4-S-49A					
No. of Ships	4	0	0	0	4
GPS Equivalent	2.768	–	–	–	2.768
Annual Lift Capacity	413,561	–	–	–	413,561
C4-S-57A					
No. of Ships	8	3	0	0	11
GPS Equivalent	7.184	2.694	–	–	9.878
Annual Lift Capacity	1,073,347	402,505	–	–	1,475,852

(*continued*)

Table B-3 (*continued*)

Ship Type and Item	1967				
	Foreign Trade	TCMST	Temporarily Inactive	Laid Up	Total
C4-S-58A					
No. of Ships	6	0	0	0	6
GPS Equivalent	5.730	–	–	–	5.730
Annual Lift Capacity	856,108	–	–	–	856,108
C4-S-60A					
No. of Ships	6	0	0	0	6
GPS Equivalent	5.844	–	–	–	5.844
Annual Lift Capacity	873,140	–	–	–	873,140
C4-S-64A					
No. of Ships	5	0	0	0	5
GPS Equivalent	4.790	–	–	–	4.790
Annual Lift Capacity	715,664	–	–	–	715,664
C4-S-64B					
No. of Ships	2	0	0	0	2
GPS Equivalent	2.162	–	–	–	2.162
Annual Lift Capacity	323,319	–	–	–	323,319
C4-S-65A					
No. of Ships	6	0	0	0	6
GPS Equivalent	6.276	–	–	–	6.276
Annual Lift Capacity	937,684	–	–	–	937,684
C4-S-66A					
No. of Ships	5	5	0	0	10
GPS Equivalent	5.205	5.205	–	–	10.410
Annual Lift Capacity	777,669	777,669	–	–	1,555,338
C4-S-69A					
No. of Ships	3	0	0	0	3
GPS Equivalent	4.026	–	–	–	4.206
Annual Lift Capacity	601,517	–	–	–	601,517
C5-SAXI (Bulk)					
No. of Ships	0	0	0	0	0
GPS Equivalent	–	–	–	–	–
Annual Lift Capacity	–	–	–	–	–

Table B-3 (*continued*)

Ship Type and Item	Foreign Trade	TCMST	Temporarily Inactive	Laid Up	Total
			1967		
C5-S-77A					
(Containership)					
No. of Ships	2	0	0	0	2
GPS Equivalent	3.492	–	–	–	3.492
Annual Lift Capacity	521,732	–	–	–	521,732
P2-S1-1K					
No. of Ships	2	0	0	0	2
GPS Equivalent	0.664	–	–	–	0.664
Annual Lift Capacity	99,207	–	–	–	99,207
P2-S1-1V					
No. of Ships	0	0	0	1	1
GPS Equivalent	–	–	–	0.229	0.229
Annual Lift Capacity	–	–	–	34,214	34,214
P2-S2-9A					
No. of Ships	2	0	0	0	2
GPS Equivalent	1.038	–	–	–	1.038
Annual Lift Capacity	155,086	–	–	–	155,086
P2-S2-11A					
No. of Ships	2	–	–	–	2
GPS Equivalent	1.184	–	–	–	1.184
Annual Lift Capacity	176,899	–	–	–	176,899
P2-S2-R14					
No. of Ships	1	0	0	0	1
GPS Equivalent	0.191	–	–	–	0.191
Annual Lift Capacity	28,537	–	–	–	28,537
P2-SC2-R3					
No. of Ships	2	0	0	0	2
GPS Equivalent	0.460	–	–	–	0.460
Annual Lift Capacity	68,728	–	–	–	68,728

(*continued*)

Table B-3 (*continued*)

Ship Type and Item	1967				
	Foreign Trade	TCMST	Temporarily Inactive	Laid Up	Total
P3-S2-DL2					
No. of Ships	2	0	0	0	2
GPS Equivalent	0.654	–	–	–	0.654
Annual Lift Capacity	97,713	–	–	–	97,713
P6-S4-DS1					
No. of Ships	1	0	0	0	1
GPS Equivalent	0.436	–	–	–	0.436
Annual Lift Capacity	65,142	–	–	–	65,142
VC2-S-AP2					
No. of Ships	0	3	0	0	3
GPS Equivalent	–	1.464	–	–	1.464
Annual Lift Capacity	–	218,733	–	–	218,733
VC2-S-AP3					
No. of Ships	4	0	0	0	4
GPS Equivalent	2.076	–	–	–	2.076
Annual Lift Capacity	310,171	–	–	–	310,171
Total	260	39	12	4	315
GPS Equivalent	196.100	27.918	7.278	1.835	233.131
Annual Lift Capacity	29,299,207	4,171,171	1,087,390	274,163	34,831,921

Table B-3 (*continued*)

Ship Type and Item	1966 Foreign Trade	TCMST	Temporarily Inactive	Laid Up	Total
C1-A					
No. of Ships	2	1	0	0	3
GPS Equivalent	0.868	0.434	–	–	1.302
Annual Lift Capacity	129,686	64,843	–	–	194,529
C1-B					
No. of Ships	2	1	0	0	3
GPS Equivalent	0.850	0.425	–	–	1.275
Annual Lift Capacity	126,997	63,498	–	–	190,495
C2-F					
No. of Ships	1	0	0	0	1
GPS Equivalent	0.559	–	–	–	0.559
Annual Lift Capacity	487,070	97,414	–	–	83,519
C2-S					
No. of Ships	5	1	0	0	6
GPS Equivalent	3.260	0.652	–	–	3.912
Annual Lift Capacity	487,070	97,414	–	–	584,484
C2-S-A1					
No. of Ships	2	0	0	0	2
GPS Equivalent	1.304	–	–	–	1.304
Annual Lift Capacity	194,828	–	–	–	194,828
C2-S-AJ1					
No. of Ships	32	1	0	0	33
GPS Equivalent	17.888	0.559	–	–	18.447
Annual Lift Capacity	2,672,610	83,519	–	–	2,756,129
C2-S-AJ2					
No. of Ships	3	2	0	0	5
GPS Equivalent	1.626	1.084	–	–	2.710
Annual Lift Capacity	242,937	161,958	–	–	404,895
C2-S-AJ4					
No. of Ships	6	0	0	0	6
GPS Equivalent	3.192	–	–	–	3.192
Annual Lift Capacity	476,910	–	–	–	476,910

(*continued*)

Table B-3 (*continued*)

Ship Type and Item	Foreign Trade	TCMST	Temporarily Inactive	Laid Up	Total
			1966		
C2-S-AJ5					
No. of Ships	10	0	0	0	10
GPS Equivalent	5.170	–	–	–	5.170
Annual Lift Capacity	772,439	–	–	–	772,439
C2-S-B1					
No. of Ships	21	6	0	0	27
GPS Equivalent	11.865	3.390	–	–	15.255
Annual Lift Capacity	2,772,726	506,493	–	–	2,279,219
C-3					
No. of Ships	2	0	0	0	2
GPS Equivalent	1.490	–	–	–	1.490
Annual Lift Capacity	222,618	–	–	–	222,618
C3-E					
No. of Ships	1	0	0	0	1
GPS Equivalent	0.594	–	–	–	0.594
Annual Lift Capacity	88,748	–	–	–	88,748
C3-S-A1					
No. of Ships	0	3	0	0	3
GPS Equivalent	–	2.133	–	–	2.133
Annual Lift Capacity	–	318,687	–	–	318,687
C3-S-A2					
No. of Ships	18	2	0	0	20
GPS Equivalent	13.860	1.540	–	–	15.400
Annual Lift Capacity	2,070,795	230,088	–	–	2,300,883
C3-S-A3					
No. of Ships	11	0	0	0	11
GPS Equivalent	6.974	–	–	–	6.974
Annual Lift Capacity	1,041,971	–	–	–	1,041,971
C3-S-A4					
No. of Ships	6	0	0	0	6
GPS Equivalent	4.020	–	–	–	4.020
Annual Lift Capacity	600,620	–	–	–	600,620

Table B-3 (*continued*)

Ship Type and Item	1966				
	Foreign Trade	*TCMST*	*Temporarily Inactive*	*Laid Up*	*Total*
C3-S-A5					
No. of Ships	7	0	0	0	7
GPS Equivalent	4.382	–	–	–	4.382
Annual Lift Capacity	654,706	–	–	–	654,706
C3-S-BH1					
No. of Ships	5	0	0	0	5
GPS Equivalent	3.730	–	–	–	3.730
Annual Lift Capacity	557,292	–	–	–	557,292
C3-S-BH2					
No. of Ships	6	0	0	0	6
GPS Equivalent	4.368	–	–	–	4.368
Annual Lift Capacity	652,614	–	–	–	652,614
C3-S-BR1					
No. of Ships	3	0	0	0	3
GPS Equivalent	1.572	–	–	–	1.572
Annual Lift Capacity	234,869	–	–	–	234,869
C3-S-33A					
No. of Ships	8	0	0	0	8
GPS Equivalent	4.960	–	–	–	4.960
Annual Lift Capacity	741,064	–	–	–	741,064
C3-S-37A					
No. of Ships	8	1	0	0	9
GPS Equivalent	5.536	0.692	–	–	6.228
Annual Lift Capacity	827,123	103,390	–	–	930,513
C3-S-37B					
No. of Ships	1	3	0	0	4
GPS Equivalent	0.690	2.070	–	–	2.760
Annual Lift Capacity	103,091	309,275	–	–	412,366
C3-S-37C					
No. of Ships	2	6	0	0	8
GPS Equivalent	1.388	4.164	–	–	5.552
Annual Lift Capacity	207,378	622,135	–	–	829,513

(*continued*)

Table B-3 (*continued*)

Ship Type and Item	1966				
	Foreign Trade	*TCMST*	*Temporarily Inactive*	*Laid Up*	*Total*
C3-S-37D					
No. of Ships	4	1	0	0	5
GPS Equivalent	2.808	0.702	–	–	3.510
Annual Lift Capacity	419,538	104,884	–	–	524,422
C3-S-38A					
No. of Ships	4	0	0	0	4
GPS Equivalent	3.080	–	–	–	3.080
Annual Lift Capacity	460,176	–	–	–	460,176
C3-S-43A					
No. of Ships	3	0	0	0	3
GPS Equivalent	2.451	–	–	–	2.451
Annual Lift Capacity	366,199	–	–	–	366,199
C3-S-46A					
No. of Ships	4	0	0	0	4
GPS Equivalent	3.552	–	–	–	3.552
Annual Lift Capacity	530,697	–	–	–	530,697
C3-S-46B					
No. of Ships	4	0	0	0	4
GPS Equivalent	3.680	–	–	–	3.680
Annual Lift Capacity	549,821	–	–	–	549,821
C4-S-1A					
No. of Ships	14	0	0	0	14
GPS Equivalent	14.896	–	–	–	14.896
Annual Lift Capacity	2,225,582	–	–	–	2,225,582
C4-S-1F					
No. of Ships	3	0	0	0	3
GPS Equivalent	2.808	–	–	–	2.808
Annual Lift Capacity	419,538	–	–	–	419,538
C4-S-1H					
No. of Ships	4	0	0	0	4
GPS Equivalent	3.672	–	–	–	3.672
Annual Lift Capacity	548,626	–	–	–	548,626

Table B-3 (*continued*)

Ship Type and Item	1966				
	Foreign Trade	*TCMST*	*Temporarily Inactive*	*Laid Up*	*Total*
C4-S-1P					
No. of Ships	3	1	0	0	4
GPS Equivalent	3.033	1.011	–	–	4.044
Annual Lift Capacity	453,155	151,051	–	–	604,206
C4-S-1Q					
No. of Ships	2	0	0	0	2
GPS Equivalent	1.530	–	–	–	1.530
Annual Lift Capacity	228,594	–	–	–	228,594
C4-S-1QA					
No. of Ships	3	0	0	0	3
GPS Equivalent	3.081	–	–	–	3.081
Annual Lift Capacity	460,326	–	–	–	460,326
C4-S-1S					
No. of Ships	3	0	0	0	3
GPS Equivalent	2.820	–	–	–	2.820
Annual Lift Capacity	421,331	–	–	–	421,331
C4-S-1SA					
No. of Ships	2	0	0	0	2
GPS Equivalent	1.880	–	–	–	1.880
Annual Lift Capacity	280,887	–	–	–	280,887
C4-S-1T					
No. of Ships	2	0	0	0	2
GPS Equivalent	1.786	–	–	–	1.786
Annual Lift Capacity	266,843	–	–	–	266,843
C4-S-1U					
No. of Ships	6	0	0	0	6
GPS Equivalent	5.934	–	–	–	5.934
Annual Lift Capacity	886,587	–	–	–	886,587
C4-S-49A					
No. of Ships	4	0	0	0	4
GPS Equivalent	2.768	–	–	–	2.768
Annual Lift Capacity	413,561	–	–	–	413,561

(*continued*)

Table B-3 (*continued*)

Ship Type and Item	1966				
	Foreign Trade	*TCMST*	*Temporarily Inactive*	*Laid Up*	*Total*
C4-S-57A					
No. of Ships	11	0	0	0	11
GPS Equivalent	9.878	–	–	–	9.878
Annual Lift Capacity	1,475,852	–	–	–	1,475,852
C4-S-58A					
No. of Ships	6	0	0	0	6
GPS Equivalent	5.730	–	–	–	5.730
Annual Lift Capacity	856,108	–	–	–	856,108
C4-S-60A					
No. of Ships	6	0	0	0	6
GPS Equivalent	5.844	–	–	–	5.844
Annual Lift Capacity	873,140	–	–	–	873,140
C4-S-64A					
No. of Ships	5	0	0	0	5
GPS Equivalent	4.790	–	–	–	4.790
Annual Lift Capacity	715,664	–	–	–	715,664
C4-S-64B					
No. of Ships	2	0	0	0	2
GPS Equivalent	2.164	–	–	–	2.164
Annual Lift Capacity	323,319	–	–	–	323,319
C4-S-65A					
No. of Ships	3	0	0	0	3
GPS Equivalent	3.138	–	–	–	3.138
Annual Lift Capacity	468,842	–	–	–	468,842
C4-S-66A					
No. of Ships	6	0	0	0	6
GPS Equivalent	6.246	–	–	–	6.246
Annual Lift Capacity	933,202	–	–	–	933,202
C5-SAXI (Bulk)					
No. of Ships	0	0	1	0	1
GPS Equivalent	–	–	2.454	–	2.454
Annual Lift Capacity	–	–	366,647	–	366,647

Table B-3 (*continued*)

Ship Type and Item	1966				
	Foreign Trade	TCMST	Temporarily Inactive	Laid Up	Total
C5-S-77A					
(Containership)					
No. of Ships	1	0	0	0	1
GPS Equivalent	1.746	–	–	–	1.746
Annual Lift Capacity	260,866	–	–	–	260,866
P2-S1-1K					
No. of Ships	2	0	0	0	2
GPS Equivalent	0.664	–	–	–	0.664
Annual Lift Capacity	99,207	–	–	–	99,207
P2-S1-1V					
No. of Ships	1	0	0	0	1
GPS Equivalent	0.229	–	–	–	0.229
Annual Lift Capacity	34,214	–	–	–	34,214
P2-S2-9A					
No. of Ships	2	0	0	0	2
GPS Equivalent	1.038	–	–	–	1.038
Annual Lift Capacity	155,086	–	–	–	155,086
P2-S2-11A					
No. of Ships	2	0	0	0	2
GPS Equivalent	1.184	–	–	–	1.184
Annual Lift Capacity	176,899	–	–	–	176,899
P2-S2-R14					
No. of Ships	1	0	0	0	1
GPS Equivalent	0.191	–	–	–	0.191
Annual Lift Capacity	28,537	–	–	–	28,537
P2-SC2-R3					
No. of Ships	2	0	0	0	2
GPS Equivalent	0.460	–	–	–	0.460
Annual Lift Capacity	68,728	–	–	–	68,728

(*continued*)

146

Table B-3 (*continued*)

Ship Type and Item	1966				
	Foreign Trade	TCMST	Temporarily Inactive	Laid Up	Total
P3-S2-DL2					
No. of Ships	2	0	0	0	2
GPS Equivalent	0.654	–	–	–	0.654
Annual Lift Capacity	97,713	–	–	–	97,713
P6-S4-DS1					
No. of Ships	1	0	0	0	1
GPS Equivalent	0.436	–	–	–	0.436
Annual Lift Capacity	65,142	–	–	–	65,142
VC2-S-AP2					
No. of Ships	3	3	0	0	6
GPS Equivalent	1.464	1.464	–	–	2.928
Annual Lift Capacity	218,733	218,733	–	–	465,257
VC2-S-AP3					
No. of Ships	5	1	0	0	6
GPS Equivalent	2.595	0.519	–	–	3.114
Annual Lift Capacity	387,714	77,543	–	–	465,257
Total	288	33	1	0	322
GPS Equivalent	208.376	20.839	2.454	–	231.669
Annual Lift Capacity	31,133,038	3,113,511	366,647	–	34,613,196

Table B-4

**Detailed Data on Fleet Size, GPS
Equivalents and Annual Lift Capacity
by Ship Type and Use for Indirectly-
Subsidized Liner: 1966-1968**

Ship Type and Item	1968				
	Foreign Trade	TCMST	Temporarily Inactive	Laid Up	Total
C1-A					
No. of Ships	1	0	0	0	1
GPS Equivalent	.434	–	–	–	.434
Annual Lift Capacity	64,843	–	–	–	64,843
C2-S-AJ1					
No. of Ships	11	0	2	0	13
GPS Equivalent	6.149	–	1.118	–	7.267
Annual Lift Capacity	918,710	–	167,038	–	1,085,748
C2-S-B1					
No. of Ships	1	2	2	0	5
GPS Equivalent	.565	1.130	2.825	–	2.825
Annual Lift Capacity	84,416	168,831	168,831	–	422,078
C2-S-E1					
No. of Ships	4	8	0	0	12
GPS Equivalent	2.352	4.704	–	–	7.056
Annual Lift Capacity	351,408	702,815	–	–	1,054,223
C2-S-E1 *(Containership)*					
No. of Ships	3	0	0	0	3
GPS Equivalent	1.968	–	–	–	1.968
Annual Lift Capacity	294,035	–	–	–	294,035
C2-SE-A1 *(Containership)*					
No. of Ships	1	0	0	0	1
GPS Equivalent	.656	–	–	–	.656
Annual Lift Capacity	98,012	–	–	–	98,012

(*continued*)

Table B-4 (*continued*)

Ship Type and Item	1968				
	Foreign Trade	*TCMST*	*Temporarily Inactive*	*Laid Up*	*Total*
C2-SE-E1					
(Containership)					
No. of Ships	0	0	0	0	0
GPS Equivalent	–	–	–	–	–
Annual Lift Capacity	–	–	–	–	–
C3-S-A2					
No. of Ships	28	0	7	0	35
GPS Equivalent	21.560	–	5.390	–	26.950
Annual Lift Capacity	3,221,236	–	805,309	–	4,026,545
C3-S-A2					
(Containership)					
No. of Ships	2	0	0	0	2
GPS Equivalent	2.084	–	–	–	2.084
Annual Lift Capacity	311,366	–	–	–	311,366
C4-S-A1					
No. of Ships	0	3	0	0	3
GPS Equivalent	–	2.397	–	–	2.397
Annual Lift Capacity	–	358,131	–	–	358,131
C4-S-A1					
(Containership)					
No. of Ships	2	0	9	0	11
GPS Equivalent	2.342	–	10,539	–	12,881
Annual Lift Capacity	349,914	–	1,574,611	–	1,924,525
C4-S-A3					
No. of Ships	0	3	0	0	3
GPS Equivalent	–	2.397	–	–	2.397
Annual Lift Capacity	–	358,131	–	–	358,131
C4-S-A3					
(Containership)					
No. of Ships	6	0	1	0	7
GPS Equivalent	8.080	–	1.171	–	9.251
Annual Lift Capacity	1,207,217	–	174,957	–	1,382,174

Table B-4 (*continued*)

Ship Type and Item	1968				
	Foreign Trade	*TCMST*	*Temporarily Inactive*	*Laid Up*	*Total*
C4-S-B2 (*Containership*)					
No. of Ships	0	1	0	0	1
GPS Equivalent	–	.949	–	–	.949
Annual Lift Capacity	–	141,788	–	–	141,788
C4-S-B5					
No. of Ships	2	0	0	0	2
GPS Equivalent	1.682	–	–	–	1.682
Annual Lift Capacity	251,304	–	–	–	251,304
R1-S-DH1					
No. of Ships	2	5	1	0	8
GPS Equivalent	.422	1.055	.211	–	1.688
Annual Lift Capacity	63,050	157,625	31,525	–	252,200
R2-ST-AV1					
No. of Ships	2	6	0	0	8
GPS Equivalent	.800	2.400	–	–	3.200
Annual Lift Capacity	119,526	358,579	–	–	478,105
T2-SE-A2 (*Containership*)					
No. of Ships	1	7	1	0	9
GPS Equivalent	1.228	8.596	1.288	–	11.052
Annual Lift Capacity	183,473	1,284,311	183,473	–	1,651,257
VC2-S-AP2					
No. of Ships	4	1	5	0	10
GPS Equivalent	1.952	.488	2.440	–	4.880
Annual Lift Capacity	291,644	72,911	364,556	–	729,111
VC2-S-AP3					
No. of Ships	0	0	2	0	2
GPS Equivalent	–	–	1.038	–	1.038
Annual Lift Capacity	–	–	155,086	–	155,086

(*continued*)

Table B-4 (*continued*)

Ship Type and Item	Foreign Trade	TCMST	Temporarily Inactive	Laid Up	Total
Foreign Constr.					
No. of Ships	1	0	0	0	1
GPS Equivalent	.720	–	–	–	.720
Annual Lift Capacity	107,574	–	–	–	107,574
Ore Carrier (Bulk)					
No. of Ships	3	0	0	1	4
GPS Equivalent	3.085	–	–	.985	4.070
Annual Lift Capacity	460,924	–	–	147,167	608,091
Private (Containership)					
No. of Ships	4	5	0	0	9
GPS Equivalent	7.120	5.279	–	–	12.399
Annual Lift Capacity	1,063,785	788,725	–	–	1,852,510
Total	78	41	30	1	150
GPS	63.199	29.395	24.265	.985	117.844
Annual Lift Capacity	9,442,437	4,391,847	3,626,386	147,167	17,606,837

The column header "1968" spans all data columns.

Table B-4 (*continued*)

Ship Type and Item	1967				
	Foreign Trade	*TCMST*	*Temporarily Inactive*	*Laid Up*	*Total*
C1-A					
No. of Ships	1	0	0	0	1
GPS Equivalent	.434	–	–	–	.434
Annual Lift Capacity	64,843	–	–	–	64,843
C1-M-AV1					
No. of Ships	1	0	0	0	1
GPS Equivalent	0.174	–	–	–	0.174
Annual Lift Capacity	25,997	–	–	–	25,997
C2-S-AJ1					
No. of Ships	14	0	0	0	14
GPS Equivalent	7.812	–	–	–	7.812
Annual Lift Capacity	1,167,175	–	–	–	1,167,175
C2-S-B1					
No. of Ships	2	3	0	0	5
GPS Equivalent	1.130	1.695	–	–	2,825
Annual Lift Capacity	168,831	253,247	–	–	422,078
C2-S-E1					
No. of Ships	3	9	0	0	12
GPS Equivalent	1.764	5.292	–	–	7.056
Annual Lift Capacity	263,556	790,667	–	–	1,054,223
C2-S-E1 *(Containership)*					
No. of Ships	4	0	0	0	4
GPS Equivalent	2.990	–	–	–	2.990
Annual Lift Capacity	446,730	–	–	–	446,730
C2-SE-A1 *(Containership)*					
No. of Ships	1	0	0	0	1
GPS Equivalent	.656	–	–	–	.656
Annual Lift Capacity	98,012	–	–	–	98,012

(*continued*)

Table B-4 (*continued*)

Ship Type and Item	Foreign Trade	TCMST	Temporarily Inactive	Laid Up	Total
		1967			
C2-SE-E1					
(Containership)					
No. of Ships	2	0	0	0	2
GPS Equivalent	1.312	–	–	–	1.312
Annual Lift Capacity	196,023	–	–	–	196,023
C3-S-A2					
No. of Ships	28	0	3	0	31
GPS Equivalent	21.560	–	2.310	–	23.870
Annual Lift Capacity	3,221,236	–	345,132	–	3,566,368
C3-S-A2					
(Containership)					
No. of Ships	2	0	0	0	2
GPS Equivalent	2.084	–	–	–	2.084
Annual Lift Capacity	311,366	–	–	–	311,366
C3-S-45A					
(Containership)					
No. of Ships	2	0	0	0	2
GPS Equivalent	.968	–	–	–	.968
Annual Lift Capacity	144,627	–	–	–	144,627
C4-S-A1					
No. of Ships	0	3	0	0	3
GPS Equivalent	–	2.397	–	–	2.397
Annual Lift Capacity	–	358,131	–	–	358,131
C4-S-A1					
(Containership)					
No. of Ships	0	0	3	0	3
GPS Equivalent	–	–	3.513	–	3.513
Annual Lift Capacity	–	–	524,870	–	524,870
C4-S-A3					
No. of Ships	0	2	1	0	3
GPS Equivalent	–	1.598	.799	–	2.397
Annual Lift Capacity	–	238,754	119,377	–	358,131

Table B-4 (*continued*)

Ship Type and Item	Foreign Trade	TCMST	Temporarily Inactive	Laid Up	Total
			1967		
C4-S-A3					
(Containership)					
No. of Ships	3	0	1	0	4
GPS Equivalent	3,912	–	1.304	–	5.216
Annual Lift Capacity	584,484	–	194,828	–	779,312
C4-S-B2					
(Containership)					
No. of Ships	0	1	0	0	1
GPS Equivalent	–	.949	–	–	.949
Annual Lift Capacity	–	141,788	–	–	141,788
C4-S-B5					
No. of Ships	0	3	0	0	3
GPS Equivalent	–	2.523	–	–	2.523
Annual Lift Capacity	–	376,956	–	–	376,956
C5-S-AX1					
(Ore Carrier)					
No. of Ships	2	0	0	0	2
GPS Equivalent	1.970	–	–	–	1.970
Annual Lift Capacity	294,334	–	–	–	294,334
R1-S-DH1					
No. of Ships	3	6	0	0	9
GPS Equivalent	.633	1.266	–	–	1.899
Annual Lift Capacity	94,575	189,151	–	–	283,726
R2-ST-AV1					
No. of Ships	1	8	0	0	9
GPS Equivalent	.400	3.200	–	–	3.600
Annual Lift Capacity	59,763	478,106	–	–	537,869
T2-SE-A2					
(Containership)					
No. of Ships	1	7	1	0	9
GPS Equivalent	1.288	8.596	1.228	–	11.052
Annual Lift Capacity	183,473	1,284,311	183,473	–	1,651,257

(*continued*)

Table B-4 (*continued*)

Ship Type and Item	Foreign Trade	TCMST	Temporarily Inactive	Laid Up	Total
			1967		
VC2-S-AP2					
No. of Ships	9	1	0	0	10
GPS Equivalent	4.392	.488	–	–	4.880
Annual Lift Capacity	656,200	72,911	–	–	729,111
VC2-S-AP3					
No. of Ships	4	0	0	0	4
GPS Equivalent	2.076	–	–	–	2.076
Annual Lift Capacity	310,171	–	–	–	310,171
Private (Bulk)					
No. of Ships	2	0	0	0	2
GPS Equivalent	2.100	–	–	–	2.100
Annual Lift Capacity	313,757	–	–	–	313,757
Private (Containership)					
No. of Ships	4	5	0	0	9
GPS Equivalent	7.120	5.279	–	–	12.399
Annual Lift Capacity	1,063,785	788,725	–	–	1,852,510
Total	88	48	9	0	145
GPS	64.541	33.283	1.154	0	106,978
Annual Lift Capacity	9,642,941	4,972,747	1,367,680	0	15,983,368

Table B-4 (*continued*)

Ship Type and Item	Foreign Trade	TCMST	Temporarily Inactive	Laid Up	Total
			1966		
C1-M-AV1					
No. of Ships	1	0	0	0	1
GPS Equivalent	0.174	–	–	–	0.174
Annual Lift Capacity	25,997	–	–	–	25,997
C1-M-BV1					
No. of Ships	0	0	0	2	2
GPS Equivalent	–	–	–	0.348	0.348
Annual Lift Capacity	–	–	–	51,994	51,994
C2-S-AJ1					
No. of Ships	12	2	0	1	15
GPS Equivalent	6.708	1.118	–	.559	8.385
Annual Lift Capacity	1,002,229	167,038	–	83,519	1,252,786
C2-S-B1					
No. of Ships	1	8	0	0	9
GPS Equivalent	.565	4.520	–	–	5.085
Annual Lift Capacity	84,416	675,324	–	–	759,740
C2-S-E1					
No. of Ships	3	9	0	0	12
GPS Equivalent	1.764	5.292	–	–	7.056
Annual Lift Capacity	263,556	790,667	–	–	1,054,223
C3-S-A2					
No. of Ships	28	1	2	0	31
GPS Equivalent	21.560	.770	1.540	–	23.870
Annual Lift Capacity	3,221,236	115,044	230,088	–	3,566,368
C3-S-45A *(Containership)*					
No. of Ships	1	0	0	0	1
GPS Equivalent	.484	–	–	–	.484
Annual Lift Capacity	72,313	–	–	–	72,313

(*continued*)

Table B-4 (*continued*)

Ship Type and Item	Foreign Trade	TCMST	Temporarily Inactive	Laid Up	Total
			1966		
C4-S-A1					
No. of Ships	1	0	1	0	2
GPS Equivalent	.949	–	.882	–	1.831
Annual Lift Capacity	141,788	–	131,778	–	273,566
C4-S-A3					
No. of Ships	2	0	2	0	4
GPS Equivalent	1.598	–	1.598	–	3.196
Annual Lift Capacity	238,754	–	238,754	–	477,508
C4-S-B5					
No. of Ships	2	1	0	0	1
GPS Equivalent	1.682	.841	–	–	2.523
Annual Lift Capacity	251,304	125,652	–	–	376,956
C5-S-AX1 *(Ore Carrier)*					
No. of Ships	2	0	0	0	2
GPS Equivalent	1.970	–	–	–	1.970
Annual Lift Capacity	294,334	–	–	–	294,334
R1-S-DH1					
No. of Ships	3	6	0	0	9
GPS Equivalent	633	1.266	–	–	1.899
Annual Lift Capacity	94,575	189,151	–	–	283,726
R2-ST-AV1					
No. of Ships	1	8	0	0	9
GPS Equivalent	.400	3.200	–	–	3.600
Annual Lift Capacity	59,763	478,106	–	–	537,869
T2-SE-A1 *(Containership)*					
No. of Ships	0	0	1	0	1
GPS Equivalent	–	–	1.051	–	1.051
Annual Lift Capacity	–	–	157,028	–	157,028

Table B-4 (*continued*)

Ship Type and Item	1966				
	Foreign Trade	*TCMST*	*Temporarily Inactive*	*Laid Up*	*Total*
T2-SE-A2					
(Containership)					
No. of Ships	0	0	8	0	8
GPS Equivalent	–	–	9.824	–	9.824
Annual Lift Capacity	–	–	1,467,784	–	1,467,784
VC2-S-AP2					
No. of Ships	6	4	0	0	10
GPS Equivalent	2.928	1.952	–	–	4.880
Annual Lift Capacity	437,467	291,644	–	–	729,111
VC2-S-AP3					
No. of Ships	4	0	0	0	4
GPS Equivalent	2.076	–	–	–	2.076
Annual Lift Capacity	310,171	–	–	–	310,171
Built 1928					
(Containership)					
No. of Ships	0	1	0	0	1
GPS Equivalent	–	.741	–	–	.741
Annual Lift Capacity	–	110,711	–	–	110,711
Private (Bulk)					
No. of Ships	2	0	0	0	2
GPS Equivalent	2.100	–	–	–	2.100
Annual Lift Capacity	313,757	–	–	–	313,757
Private					
(Containership)					
No. of Ships	4	2	0	0	6
GPS Equivalent	6.638	1.942	–	–	8.580
Annual Lift Capacity	991,770	290,150	–	–	1,281,920
Total	73	42	14	3	132
GPS	52.229	21.642	14.895	.907	89.673
Annual Lift Capacity	7,803,430	3,233,487	2,225,432	135,513	13,397,862

Table B-5

**Detailed Data on Fleet Size, GPS
Equivalents and Annual Lift Capacity
by Ship Type and Use for Tramps:
1966-1968**

Ship Type and Item	1968				
	Foreign Trade	*TCMST*	*Temporarily Inactive*	*Laid Up*	*Total*
C1-A					
No. of Ships	0	0	1	0	1
GPS Equivalent	–	–	.434	–	.434
Annual Lift Capacity	–	–	64,843	–	64,843
C1-B					
No. of Ships	1	0	0	0	1
GPS Equivalent	.425	–	–	–	.425
Annual Lift Capacity	63,498	–	–	–	63,498
C2-S-AJ1					
No. of Ships	12	7	1	0	20
GPS Equivalent	6.708	3.913	.559	–	11.180
Annual Lift Capacity	1,002.229	584,634	83,519	–	1,670,383
C2-S-AJ2					
No. of Ships	1	1	0	0	2
GPS Equivalent	.542	.542	–	–	1.084
Annual Lift Capacity	80,979	80,979	–	–	161,958
C2-S-AJ4					
No. of Ships	2	0	0	0	2
GPS Equivalent	1.064	–	–	–	1.064
Annual Lift Capacity	158,970	–	–	–	158,970
C2-S-AJ5					
No. of Ships	2	0	0	0	2
GPS Equivalent	1.034	—	–	–	1.034
Annual Lift Capacity	154,488	–	–	–	154,488
C2-S-B1					
No. of Ships	11	9	2	3	25
GPS Equivalent	6.215	5.085	1.130	1.695	14,125
Annual Lift Capacity	928,571	759,740	168,831	253,247	2,110,388

Table B-5 (*continued*)

Ship Type and Item	Foreign Trade	TCMST	Temporarily Inactive	Laid Up	Total
			1968		
C2-S1-0G2					
No. of Ships	0	2	0	0	2
GPS Equivalent	–	1.138	–	–	1.138
Annual Lift Capacity	–	170,026	–	–	170,026
C3					
No. of Ships	2	1	0	0	3
GPS Equivalent	1.490	.745	–	–	2.235
Annual Lift Capacity	222,618	111,309	–	–	333,927
C3-S-A2					
No. of Ships	2	7	3	0	12
GPS Equivalent	1.540	5.390	2.310	–	9.240
Annual Lift Capacity	230,088	805,309	345,132	–	1,380,530
C4-S-A1					
No. of Ships	0	2	0	0	2
GPS Equivalent	–	1,598	–	–	1.598
Annual Lift Capacity	–	238,754	–	–	238,754
C4-S-A3					
No. of Ships	0	3	0	0	3
GPS Equivalent	–	2.397	–	–	2.397
Annual Lift Capacity	–	358,131	–	–	358,131
C4-S-A3 (Bulk)					
No. of Ships	2	0	0	0	2
GPS Equivalent	3.573	–	–	–	3.573
Annual Lift Capacity	533,835	–	–	–	533,835
C4-S-A4					
No. of Ships	0	3	0	0	3
GPS Equivalent	–	2.340	–	–	2.340
Annual Lift Capacity	–	349,615	–	–	349,615
C4-S-B2					
No. of Ships	0	1	0	0	1
GPS Equivalent	–	.841	–	–	.841
Annual Lift Capacity	–	125,652	–	–	125,652

(*continued*)

Table B-5 (*continued*)

Ship Type and Item	1968				
	Foreign Trade	TCMST	Temporarily Inactive	Laid Up	Total
EC2-S-C1					
No. of Ships	5	0	3	1	9
GPS Equivalent	1.930	–	1.158	.386	3.474
Annual Lift Capacity	288,357	–	173,014	57,671	519,043
EC2-S-C1					
(Bulk)					
No. of Ships	1	0	1	0	2
GPS Equivalent	.980	–	.413	–	1.393
Annual Lift Capacity	146,420	–	61,706	–	208,125
EC2-S-AW1					
(Bulk)					
No. of Ships	1	0	0	0	1
GPS Equivalent	.811	–	–	–	.811
Annual Lift Capacity	121,170	–	–	–	121,170
T2-SE-A1					
(Bulk)					
No. of Ships	11	6	2	1	20
GPS Equivalent	22.431	13.825	3.448	1.816	41.520
Annual Lift Capacity	3,351,371	2,065,566	515,159	271,325	6,203,420
T2-SE-A2					
(Bulk)					
No. of Ships	0	1	0	0	1
GPS Equivalent	–	2.641	–	–	2.641
Annual Lift Capacity	–	394,587	–	–	394,587
T3-S-A1					
(Bulk)					
No. of Ships	0	0	1	0	1
GPS Equivalent	–	–	.849	–	.849
Annual Lift Capacity	–	–	126,847	–	126,847
VC2-S-AP2					
No. of Ships	7	4	2	0	13
GPS Equivalent	3.416	1.952	.976	–	6.344
Annual Lift Capacity	510,378	291,644	145,822	–	947,844

Table B-5 (*continued*)

Ship Type and Item	Foreign Trade	TCMST	Temporarily Inactive	Laid Up	Total
			1968		
VC2-S-AP2					
(Bulk)					
No. of Ships	1	0	0	0	1
GPS Equivalent	1.402	–	–	–	1.402
Annual Lift Capacity	209,470	–	–	–	209,470
VC2-S-AP3					
No. of Ships	11	18	1	0	30
GPS Equivalent	5.709	9.342	.519	–	15.570
Annual Lift Capacity	852,970	1,395,770	77,543	–	2,326,283
Foreign Construction					
(Bulk)					
No. of Ships	1	0	0	0	1
GPS Equivalent	2.384	–	–	–	2.384
Annual Lift Capacity	356,189	–	–	–	356,189
Private					
(Bulk)					
No. of Ships	3	0	0	0	3
GPS Equivalent	7.374	–	–	–	7.374
Annual Lift Capacity	1,101,735	–	–	–	1,101,735
Private					
(Containership)					
No. of Ships	0	1	0	0	1
GPS Equivalent	–	5.129	–	–	5.129
Annual Lift Capacity	–	766,314	–	–	766,314
Total	76	66	17	5	164
GPS Equivalent	69.028	56.878	11.796	3.897	141,599
Annual Lift Capacity	10,313,336	8,498,030	1,762,416	582,243	21,156,025

(*continued*)

Table B-5 (*continued*)

Ship Type and Item	Foreign Trade	TCMST	Temporarily Inactive	Laid Up	Total
			1967		
C1-B					
No. of Ships	0	1	0	0	1
GPS Equivalent	–	.425	–	–	.425
Annual Lift Capaicty	–	63,498	–	–	63,498
C1-M-A V1					
No. of Ships	1	0	0	0	1
GPS Equivalent	.174	–	–	–	.174
Annual Lift Capacity	25,997	–	–	–	25,997
C2					
No. of Ships	0	0	0	1	1
GPS Equivalent	–	–	–	.559	.559
Annual Lift Capacity	–	–	–	83,519	83,519
C2-S-AJ1					
No. of Ships	3	10	1	0	14
GPS Equivalent	1.677	5.590	.559	–	7.826
Annual Lift Capacity	250,557	835,191	83,519	–	1,169,267
C2-S-B1					
No. of Ships	10	14	1	1	26
GPS Equivalent	5.650	7.910	.565	.565	14.690
Annual Lift Capacity	844,155	1,181,817	84,416	84,416	2,194,804
C2-S1-0G2					
No. of Ships	0	2	0	0	2
GPS Equivalent	–	1.138	–	–	1.138
Annual Lift Capacity	–	170,026	–	–	170,026
C3					
No. of Ships	1	2	0	0	3
GPS Equivalent	.745	1.490	–	–	2.235
Annual Lift Capacity	111,309	222,618	–	–	333,927
C3-S-A2					
No. of Ships	4	6	0	0	10
GPS Equivalent	3.080	4.620	–	–	7.700
Annual Lift Capacity	460,177	690,265	–	–	1,150,442

Table B-5 (*continued*)

Ship Type and Item	Foreign Trade	TCMST	Temporarily Inactive	Laid Up	Total
			1967		
C4-S-A1					
No. of Ships	0	0	2	0	2
GPS Equivalent	–	–	1.598	–	1.598
Annual Lift Capacity	–	–	238,754	–	238,754
C4-S-A3					
No. of Ships	0	1	2	0	3
GPS Equivalent	–	.799	1.598	–	2.397
Annual Lift Capacity	–	119,377	238,754	–	358,131
C4-S-A3 *(Bulk)*					
No. of Ships	2	0	0	0	2
GPS Equivalent	3.573	–	–	–	3.573
Annual Lift Capacity	533,835	–	–	–	533,835
C4-S-A4					
No. of Ships	0	3	0	0	5
GPS Equivalent	–	2.340	–	–	2.340
Annual Lift Capacity	–	349,615	–	–	349,615
C4-S-B2					
No. of Ships	0	1	0	0	1
GPS Equivalent	–	.841	–	–	.841
Annual Lift Capacity	–	125,652	–	–	125,652
EC2-S-C1					
No. of Ships	12	0	0	2	14
GPS Equivalent	4.632	–	–	.772	5.404
Annual Lift Capacity	692,058	–	–	115,343	807,401
EC2-S-C1 (Bulk)					
No. of Ships	1	0	0	2	3
GPS Equivalent	.980	–	–	.898	1.878
Annual Lift Capacity	146,420	–	–	134,168	280,588

(*continued*)

Table B-5 (*continued*)

Ship Type and Item	1967				
	Foreign Trade	TCMST	Temporarily Inactive	Laid Up	Total
ET1-S-C3					
(Bulk)					
No. of Ships	0	1	0	0	1
GPS Equivalent	–	.906	–	–	.906
Annual Lift Capacity	–	135,364	–	–	135,364
T2-SE-A1					
(Bulk)					
No. of Ships	14	5	1	0	20
GPS Equivalent	28.207	11.471	1.816	–	41.494
Annual Lift Capacity	4,214,351	1,713,859	271,325	–	6,199,535
T2-SE-A2					
(Bulk)					
No. of Ships	0	0	1	0	1
GPS Equivalent	–	–	2.641	–	2.641
Annual Lift Capacity	–	–	394,587	–	394,587
VC2-S-AP2					
No. of Ships	3	9	0	0	12
GPS Equivalent	1.464	4.392	–	–	5.856
Annual Lift Capacity	218.733	656,200	–	–	874,933
VC2-S-AP2					
(Bulk)					
No. of Ships	1	0	0	0	1
GPS Equivalent	1.402	–	–	–	1.402
Annual Lift Capacity	209,470	–	–	–	209,470
VC2-S-AP3					
No. of Ships	5	22	2	0	29
GPS Equivalent	2.595	11.418	1.038	–	15.051
Annual Lift Capacity	387,714	1,705,941	155,086	–	2,248,741
Foreign Construction					
(Bulk)					
No. of Ships	1	0	0	0	1
GPS Equivalent	2.384	–	–	–	2.384
Annual Lift Capacity	356,189	–	–	–	356,189

Table B-5 (*continued*)

Ship Type and Item	1967				
	Foreign Trade	*TCMST*	*Temporarily Inactive*	*Laid Up*	*Total*
Private (Bulk)					
No. of Ships	3	1	0	0	4
GPS Equivalent	7.374	5.129	–	–	12.503
Annual Lift Capacity	1,101,735	766,314	–	–	1,868,049
Total	61	78	10	6	155
GPS Equivalent	63.937	58.469	9.815	2.794	135,015
Annual Lift Capacity	9,552,700	8,735,737	1,466,441	417,446	20,172,324

(*continued*)

Table B-5 (*continued*)

Ship Type and Item	1966				
	Foreign Trade	*TCMST*	*Temporarily Inactive*	*Laid Up*	*Total*
C1-B					
No. of Ships	0	1	0	0	1
GPS Equivalent	–	.425	–	–	.425
Annual Lift Capacity	–	63,498	–	–	63,498
C2					
No. of Ships	0	1	0	0	1
GPS Equivalent	–	.599	–	–	.559
Annual Lift Capacity	–	83,519	–	–	83,519
C2 (Containership)					
No. of Ships	2	0	0	0	2
GPS Equivalent	1.312	–	–	–	1.312
Annual Lift Capacity	196,023	–	–	–	196,023
C2-S-AJ1					
No. of Ships	6	11	0	0	17
GPS Equivalent	3.354	6.149	–	–	9.503
Annual Lift Capacity	501,114	918,710	–	–	1,419,824
C2-S-B1					
No. of Ships	8	11	0	0	19
GPS Equivalent	4.520	6.215	–	–	10.735
Annual Lift Capacity	675,324	928,571	–	–	1,603,895
C2-S-E1					
No. of Ships	0	1	0	0	1
GPS Equivalent	–	.588	–	–	.588
Annual Lift Capacity	–	87,852	–	–	87,852
C2-S1-OG2					
No. of Ships	0	2	0	0	2
GPS Equivalent	–	1,138	–	–	1,138
Annual Lift Capacity	–	170,026	–	–	170,026

Table B-5 (*continued*)

Ship Type and Item	1966 Foreign Trade	TCMST	Temporarily Inactive	Laid Up	Total
C3					
No. of Ships	0	2	1	1	4
GPS Equivalent	–	1.490	.745	.745	2.980
Annual Lift Capacity	–	222,618	111,309	111,309	445,236
C3-S-A2					
No. of Ships	5	5	0	0	10
GPS Equivalent	3.850	3.850	–	–	7.700
Annual Lift Capacity	575,221	575,221	–	—	1,150,442
C4					
No. of Ships	0	1	0	0	1
GPS Equivalent	–	.841	–	–	.841
Annual Lift Capacity	–	125,652	–	–	125,652
C4-S-A3					
No. of Ships	2	0	0	0	2
GPS Equivalent	3.573	–	–	–	3.573
Annual Lift Capacity	533,835	–	–	–	533,835
C4-S-A3 *(Bulk)*					
No. of Ships	0	2	0	0	2
GPS Equivalent	–	1.560	–	–	1.560
Annual Lift Capacity	–	233,076	–	–	233,076
C4-S-A4					
No. of Ships	0	1	0	0	1
GPS Equivalent	–	.841	–	–	.841
Annual Lift Capacity	–	125,652	–	–	125,652
C4-S-B2					
No. of Ships	0	0	0	1	1
GPS Equivalent	–	–	–	.100	.100
Annual Lift Capacity	–	–	–	14,941	14,941

(*continued*)

Table B-5 (*continued*)

Ship Type and Item	1966				
	Foreign Trade	*TCMST*	*Temporarily Inactive*	*Laid Up*	*Total*
N3-MA1					
No. of Ships	4	4	0	0	8
GPS Equivalent	1.444	1.444	–	–	2.888
Annual Lift Capacity	215,745	215,745	–	–	431,490
EC2-S-C1					
No. of Ships	9	0	0	1	10
GPS Equivalent	3.474	–	–	.386	3.860
Annual Lift Capacity	519,043	–	–	57,671	576,714
EC2-S-C1 (Bulk)					
No. of Ships	1	1	0	2	4
GPS Equivalent	.936	.980	–	.898	2.814
Annual Lift Capacity	139,846	146,420	–	134,168	420,434
T2 (Bulk)					
No. of Ships	2	1	1	0	4
GPS Equivalent	3.669	2.274	2.208	–	8.151
Annual Lift Capacity	548,178	339,754	329,893	–	1,217,825
T2-SE-A1 (Bulk)					
No. of Ships	10	4	0	0	14
GPS Equivalent	19.287	8.835	–	–	28.122
Annual Lift Capacity	2,881,632	1,320,020	–	–	4,201,652
T3-S-A1 (Bulk)					
No. of Ships	0	0	1	0	1
GPS Equivalent	–	–	.849	–	.849
Annual Lift Capacity	–	–	126,847	–	126,847
VC2 (Bulk)					
No. of Ships	1	0	0	0	1
GPS Equivalent	1.402	–	–	–	1.402
Annual Lift Capacity	209,470	–	–	–	209,470

Table B-5 (*continued*)

Ship Type and Item	Foreign Trade	TCMST	Temporarily Inactive	Laid Up	Total
		1966			
VC2-S-AP2					
No. of Ships	1	6	2	0	9
GPS Equivalent	.488	2.928	.976	–	4.392
Annual Lift Capacity	72,911	437,467	145,822	–	656,200
VC2-S-AP3					
No. of Ships	4	24	1	0	29
GPS Equivalent	2.076	12.456	.519	–	15,051
Annual Lift Capacity	310,171	1,861,026	77,543	–	2,248,740
Foreign Construction					
No. of Ships	0	1	0	0	1
GPS Equivalent	–	.122	–	–	.122
Annual Lift Capacity	–	18,228	–	–	18,228
Foreign Construction (bulk)					
No. of Ships	1	0	0	0	1
GPS Equivalent	2,384	–	–	–	2.384
Annual Lift Capacity	356,189	–	–	–	356,189
Tankers (Bulk)					
No. of Ships	3	0	0	0	3
GPS Equivalent	7.374	–	–	–	7.374
Annual Lift Capacity	1,101,735	–	–	–	1,101,735
ZET1 (Bulk)					
No. of Ships	0	1	0	0	1
GPS Equivalent	–	.906	–	–	.906
Annual Lift Capacity	–	135,364	–	–	135,364
Total	59	80	6	5	150
GPS Equivalent	59.143	53.601	5.297	2.129	120.170
Annual Lift Capacity	8,836.437	8,008,419	791,414	318,089	17,954,359

Table B-6

Detailed Data on Fleet Size, GPS Equivalents and Annual Lift Capacity by Ship Type for Subsidized Liners: 1958-1966

Ship Type and Items	1966	1965	1964	1963	1962	1961	1960	1959	1958
C1-A									
No. of Ships	3	3	3	3	3	2	2	3	7
GPS Equivalent	1.302	1.302	1.302	1.302	1.302	0.868	0.868	1.302	3.038
Annual Lift Capacity	194,529	194,529	194,529	194,529	194,529	129,686	129,686	194,529	453,902
C1-B									
No. of Ships	3	3	4	4	4	2	8	8	10
GPS Equivalent	1.275	1.275	1.700	1.700	1.700	0.850	3.400	3.400	4.250
Annual Lift Capacity	190,495	190,495	253,994	253,994	253,994	126,997	507,987	507,987	634,984
C2									
No. of Ships	0	0	0	1	2	2	2	4	4
GPS Equivalent	—	—	—	0.652	1.304	1.304	1.304	2.608	2.608
Annual Lift Capacity	—	—	—	97,414	194,828	194,828	194,828	389,656	389,656
C2-F									
No. of Ships	1	1	1	1	1	1	1	1	1
GPS Equivalent	0.559	0.559	0.559	0.559	0.559	0.559	0.559	0.559	0.559
Annual Lift Capacity	83,519	83,519	83,519	83,519	83,519	83,519	83,519	83,519	83,519

171

Table B-6 (*continued*)

Ship Type and Items	1966	1965	1964	1963	1962	1961	1960	1959	1958
C2-S									
No. of Ships	6	6	6	6	6	2	2	2	2
GPS Equivalent	3.912	3.912	3.912	3.912	3.912	1.304	1.304	1.304	1.304
Annual Lift Capacity	584,484	584,484	584,484	584,484	584,484	194,828	194,828	194,828	194,828
C2-S-A1									
No. of Ships	2	2	2	2	2	2	2	2	4
GPS Equivalent	1.304	1.304	1.304	1.304	1.304	1.304	1.304	1.304	2.608
Annual Lift Capacity	194,828	194,828	194,828	194,828	194,828	194,828	194,828	194,828	389,656
C2-S-DG2									
No. of Ships	0	2	2	0	2	2	2	3	3
GPS Equivalent	–	1.138	1.138	–	1.138	1.138	1.138	1.707	1.707
Annual Lift Capacity	–	170,026	170,026	–	170,026	170,026	170,026	170,026	255,039
C2-SU									
No. of Ships	0	0	0	0	0	0	0	3	3
GPS Equivalent	–	–	–	–	–	–	–	1.743	1.743
Annual Lift Capacity	–	–	–	–	–	–	–	260,418	260,418
C3									
No. of Ships	2	4	5	6	5	5	6	8	10
GPS Equivalent	1.490	2.980	3.725	4.470	3.725	3.725	4.470	5.960	7.450
Annual Lift Capacity	222,618	445,236	556,545	667,854	556,545	556,545	667,854	890,472	1,113,090

(*continued*)

172

Table B-6 (*continued*)

Ship Type and Items	1966	1965	1964	1963	1962	1961	1960	1959	1958
C3-A									
No. of Ships	0	0	1	1	1	1	1	1	1
GPS Equivalent	–	–	0.711	0.711	0.711	0.711	0.711	0.711	0.711
Annual Lift Capacity	–	–	106,229	106,229	106,229	106,229	106,229	106,229	106,229
C3-E									
No. of Ships	1	1	1	1	1	1	3	3	3
GPS Equivalent	0.594	0.594	0.594	0.594	0.594	0.594	1.782	1.782	1.782
Annual Lift Capacity	88,748	88,748	88,748	88,748	88,748	88,748	266,245	266,245	266,245
C3-PC									
No. of Ships	0	0	1	1	1	1	1	3	3
GPS Equivalent	–	–	0.745	0.745	0.745	0.745	0.745	2.235	2.235
Annual Lift Capacity	–	–	111,309	111,309	111,309	111,309	111,309	333,927	333,927
C3-S-BH2									
No. of Ships	6	6	6	6	6	6	6	6	6
GPS Equivalent	4.368	4.368	4.368	4.368	4.368	4.368	4.368	4.368	4.368
Annual Lift Capacity	652,614	652,614	652,614	652,614	652,614	652,614	652,614	652,614	652,614
C3-S-BR1									
No. of Ships	3	3	3	3	3	3	3	3	3
GPS Equivalent	1.572	1.572	1.572	1.572	1.572	1.572	1.572	1.572	1.572
Annual Lift Capacity	234,869	234,869	234,869	234,869	234,869	234,869	234,869	234,869	234,869

Table B-6 (*continued*)

Ship Type and Items	1966	1965	1964	1963	1962	1961	1960	1959	1958
C3-S-33A									
No. of Ships	8	8	8	8	8	7	2	0	0
GPS Equivalent	4.960	4.960	4.960	4.960	4.960	4.340	1.240	–	–
Annual Lift Capacity	741,064	741,064	741,064	741,064	741,064	648,431	741,064	–	–
C3-S-37A									
No. of Ships	9	9	9	9	9	8	5	0	0
GPS Equivalent	6.228	6.228	6.228	6.228	6.228	5.536	3.460	–	–
Annual Lift Capacity	930,513	930,513	930,513	930,513	930,513	827,123	516,952	–	–
C3-S-37B									
No. of Ships	4	4	4	4	3	0	0	0	0
GPS Equivalent	2.760	2.760	2.760	2.760	2.070	–	–	–	–
Annual Lift Capacity	412,366	412,366	412,366	412,366	309,275	–	–	–	–
C3-S-37C									
No. of Ships	8	8	8	7	0	0	0	0	0
GPS Equivalent	5.552	5.552	5.552	4.858	–	–	–	–	–
Annual Lift Capacity	829,513	829,513	829,513	725,824	–	–	–	–	–
C3-S-37D									
No. of Ships	5	5	4	0	0	0	0	0	0
GPS Equivalent	3.510	3.510	2.808	–	–	–	–	–	–
Annual Lift Capacity	524,422	524,422	419,538	–	–	–	–	–	–

(continued)

Table B-6 (*continued*)

Ship Type and Items	1966	1965	1964	1963	1962	1961	1960	1959	1958
C3-S-38A									
No. of Ships	4	4	4	4	4	4	2	0	0
GPS Equivalent	3.080	3.080	3.080	3.080	3.080	3.080	1.540	—	—
Annual Lift Capacity	460,177	460,177	460,177	460,177	460,177	460,177	230,088	—	—
C3-S-43A									
No. of Ships	3	3	3	3	3	3	0	0	0
GPS Equivalent	2.451	2.451	2.451	2.451	2.451	2.451	—	—	—
Annual Lift Capacity	366,199	366,199	366,199	366,199	366,199	366,199	—	—	—
C3-S-45A									
No. of Ships	0	0	0	2	2	2	0	0	0
GPS Equivalent	—	—	—	1.630	1.630	1.630	—	—	—
Annual Lift Capacity	—	—	—	243,535	243,535	243,535	—	—	—
C3-S-46A									
No. of Ships	4	4	4	4	4	2	0	0	0
GPS Equivalent	3.552	3.552	3.552	3.552	3.552	1.776	—	—	—
Annual Lift Capacity	530,697	530,697	530,697	530,697	530,697	265,349	—	—	—
C3-S-46B									
No. of Ships	4	4	4	4	1	0	0	0	0
GPS Equivalent	3.680	3.680	3.680	3.680	0.920	—	—	—	—
Annual Lift Capacity	549,821	549,821	549,821	549,821	137,455	—	—	—	—

175

Table B-6 (*continued*)

Ship Type and Items	1966	1965	1964	1963	1962	1961	1960	1959	1958
C4-S-1A									
No. of Ships	14	14	14	14	14	17	18	19	22
GPS Equivalent	14.896	14.896	14.896	14.896	14.896	18.088	19.152	20.216	24.890
Annual Lift Capacity	2,225,582	2,225,582	2,225,582	2,225,582	2,225,582	2,702,492	2,861,462	3,020,432	3,718,765
C4-S-1F									
No. of Ships	3	3	3	3	3	0	0	0	0
GPS Equivalent	2.808	2.808	2.808	2.808	2.808	—	—	—	—
Annual Lift Capacity	419,538	419,538	419,538	419,538	419,538	—	—	—	—
C4-S-1H									
No. of Ships	4	4	4	4	4	4	4	4	4
GPS Equivalent	3.672	3.672	3.672	3.672	3.672	3.672	3.672	3.672	3.672
Annual Lift Capacity	548,626	548,626	548,626	548,626	548,626	548,626	548,626	548,626	548,626
C4-S-1P									
No. of Ships	4	4	4	4	4	4	4	3	0
GPS Equivalent	4.044	4.044	4.044	4.044	4.044	4.044	4.044	3.033	—
Annual Lift Capacity	604,206	604,206	604,206	604,206	604,206	604,206	604,206	453,154	—
C4-S-1Q									
No. of Ships	2	2	2	2	2	2	0	0	0
GPS Equivalent	1.530	1.530	1.530	1.530	1.530	1.530	—	—	—
Annual Lift Capacity	228,594	228,594	228,594	228,594	228,594	228,594	—	—	—

(*continued*)

Table B-6 (*continued*)

Ship Type and Items	1966	1965	1964	1963	1962	1961	1960	1959	1958
C4-S-1QA									
No. of Ships	3	1	0	0	0	0	0	0	0
GPS Equivalent	3.081	1.027	—	—	—	—	—	—	—
Annual Lift Capacity	460,326	153,412	—	—	—	—	—	—	—
C4-S-1S									
No. of Ships	3	3	3	3	3	0	0	0	0
GPS Equivalent	2.820	2.820	2.820	2.820	2.820	—	—	—	—
Annual Lift Capacity	421,331	421,331	421,331	421,331	421,331	—	—	—	—
C4-S-1SA									
No. of Ships	2	2	1	0	0	0	0	0	0
GPS Equivalent	1.880	1.880	0.940	—	—	—	—	—	—
Annual Lift Capacity	280,887	280,887	140,444	—	—	—	—	—	—
C4-S-1T									
No. of Ships	2	2	2	2	2	0	0	0	0
GPS Equivalent	1.786	1.786	1.786	1.786	1.786	—	—	—	—
Annual Lift Capacity	266,843	266,843	266,843	266,843	266,843	—	—	—	—
C4-S-1U									
No. of Ships	6	6	6	6	5	0	0	0	0
GPS Equivalent	5.934	5.934	5.934	5.934	4.945	—	—	—	—
Annual Lift Capacity	886,587	886,587	886,587	886,587	738,823	—	—	—	—

177

Table B-6 (*continued*)

Ship Type and Items	1966	1965	1964	1963	1962	1961	1960	1959	1958
C4-S-49A									
No. of Ships	4	4	4	3	0	0	0	0	0
GPS Equivalent	2.768	2.768	2.768	2.076	—	—	—	—	—
Annual Lift Capacity	413,561	413,561	413,561	310,171	—	—	—	—	—
C4-S-57A									
No. of Ships	11	11	11	11	3	0	0	0	0
GPS Equivalent	9.878	9.878	9.878	9.878	2.694	—	—	—	—
Annual Lift Capacity	1,475,852	1,475,852	1,475,852	1,475,852	402,505	—	—	—	—
C4-S-58A									
No. of Ships	6	6	6	6	3	0	0	0	0
GPS Equivalent	5.730	5.730	5.730	5.730	2.865	—	—	—	—
Annual Lift Capacity	856,108	856,108	856,108	856,108	428,054	—	—	—	—
C4-S-60A									
No. of Ships	6	6	3	0	0	0	0	0	0
GPS Equivalent	5.844	5.844	2.922	—	—	—	—	—	—
Annual Lift Capacity	873,140	873,140	436,570	—	—	—	—	—	—
C4-S-64A									
No. of Ships	5	5	1	0	0	0	0	0	0
GPS Equivalent	4.790	4.790	0.958	—	—	—	—	—	—
Annual Lift Capacity	715,664	715,664	143,133	—	—	—	—	—	—

(*continued*)

Table B-6 (*continued*)

Shipt Type and Items	1966	1965	1964	1963	1962	1961	1960	1959	1958
C4-S-64B									
No. of Ships	2	0	0	0	0	0	0	0	0
GPS Equivalent	2,164	—	—	—	—	—	—	—	—
Annual Lift Capacity	323,319	—	—	—	—	—	—	—	—
C4-S-65A									
No. of Ships	3	0	0	0	0	0	0	0	0
GPS Equivalent	3,138	—	—	—	—	—	—	—	—
Annual Lift Capacity	468,842	—	—	—	—	—	—	—	—
C4-S-66A									
No. of Ships	6	1	0	0	0	0	0	0	0
GPS Equivalent	6,246	1,041	—	—	—	—	—	—	—
Annual Lift Capacity	933,202	155,534	—	—	—	—	—	—	—
C5-S-77A									
(Containership)									
No. of Ships	2	0	0	0	0	0	0	0	0
GPS Equivalent	3,492	—	—	—	—	—	—	—	—
Annual Lift Capacity	521,733	—	—	—	—	—	—	—	—
P.America									
No. of Ships	0	0	0	1	1	1	1	1	1
GPS Equivalent	—	—	—	0.436	0.436	0.436	0.436	0.436	0.436
Annual Lift Capacity	—	—	—	65,142	65,142	65,142	65,142	65,142	65,142

Table B-6 (*continued*)

Ship Type and Items	1966	1965	1964	1963	1962	1961	1960	1959	1958
P1-S1-DR									
No. of Ships	0	0	2	2	2	2	2	2	4
GPS Equivalent	—	—	0.792	0.792	0.792	0.792	0.792	0.792	1.584
Annual Lift Capacity	—	—	118,331	118,331	118,331	118,331	118,331	118,331	236,662
P2-S1-1K									
No. of Ships	2	2	2	2	2	2	2	2	2
GPS Equivalent	0.664	0.664	0.664	0.664	0.664	0.664	0.664	0.664	0.664
Annual Lift Capacity	99,207	99,207	99,207	9,207	99,207	99,207	99,207	99,207	99,207
P2-S1-1V									
No. of Ships	1	1	1	1	1	1	1	0	0
GPS Equivalent	0.229	0.229	0.229	0.229	0.229	0.229	0.229	—	—
Annual Lift Capacity	34,214	34,214	34,214	34,214	34,214	34,214	34,214	—	—
P2-S2-9A									
No. of Ships	2	2	2	2	2	2	2	2	2
GPS Equivalent	1.038	1.038	1.038	1.038	1.038	1.038	1.038	1.038	1.038
Annual Lift Capacity	155,086	155,086	155,086	155,086	155,086	155,086	155,086	155,086	155,086
P2-S2-11A									
No. of Ships	2	2	2	2	2	2	2	2	2
GPS Equivalent	1.184	1.184	1.184	1.184	1.184	1.184	1.184	1.184	1.184
Annual Lift Capacity	176,899	176,899	176,899	176,899	176,899	176,899	176,899	176,899	176,899

(continued)

Table B-6 (*continued*)

Ship Type and Items	1966	1965	1964	1963	1962	1961	1960	1959	1958
P2-SE2-R3									
No. of Ships	2	2	2	2	2	2	2	2	2
GPS Equivalent	0.460	0.460	0.460	0.460	0.460	0.460	0.460	0.460	0.460
Annual Lift Capacity	68,728	68,728	68,728	68,728	68,728	68,728	68,728	68,728	68,728
P2-S2-R10									
No. of Ships	0	0	0	0	0	1	1	0	0
GPS Equivalent	—	—	—	—	—	0.191	0.191	—	—
Annual Lift Capacity	—	—	—	—	—	28,537	28,537	—	—
P2-S2-R14									
No. of Ships	1	1	1	1	1	0	0	0	0
GPS Equivalent	0.191	0.191	0.191	0.191	0.191	—	—	—	—
Annual Lift Capacity	28,537	28,537	28,537	28,537	28,537	—	—	—	—
P3-S2-DL2									
No. of Ships	2	2	2	2	2	2	2	2	2
GPS Equivalent	0.654	0.654	0.654	0.654	0.654	0.654	0.654	0.654	0.654
Annual Lift Capacity	97,713	97,713	97,713	97,713	97,713	97,713	97,713	97,713	97,713
P6-S4-DS1									
No. of Ships	1	1	1	1	1	1	1	1	1
GPS Equivalent	0.436	0.436	0.436	0.436	0.436	0.436	0.436	0.436	0.436
Annual Lift Capacity	65,142	65,142	65,142	65,142	65,142	65,142	65,142	65,142	65,142

Table B-6 (*continued*)

Ship Type and Items	1966	1965	1964	1963	1962	1961	1960	1959	1958
VC2-S-AP2									
No. of Ships	6	6	6	8	8	5	7	5	5
GPS Equivalent	2,928	2,928	2,928	3,904	3,904	2,440	3,416	2,440	2,440
Annual Lift Capacity	437,467	437,467	437,467	583,289	583,289	364,556	510,378	364,556	364,556
VC2-S-AP3									
No. of Ships	6	6	6	6	6	10	11	15	15
GPS Equivalent	3,114	3,114	3,114	3,114	3,114	5,190	5,709	7.785	7.785
Annual Lift Capacity	465,257	465,257	465,257	465,257	465,257	775,428	852,970	1,163,141	1,163,141
Total-Subsidized Liners									
No. of Ships	322	318	317	317	298	277	278	293	305
GPS Equivalent	230,961	221,336	216,550	214,625	197,061	178,273	174,510	183,353	191,166
Annual Lift Capacity	34,507,419	33,069,338	32,354,303	32,066,693	29,442,492	26,635,413	26,073,189	27,394,404	28,561,730

Table B-7

Detailed Data on Fleet Size, GPS Equivalents and Annual Lift Capacity by Ship Type for Indirectly-Subsidized Liners: 1958-1966

Ship Type and Items	1966	1965	1964	1963	1962	1961	1960	1959	1958
C1-A									
No. of Ships	0	0	0	0	0	1	1	2	0
GPS Equivalent	—	—	—	—	—	0.434	0.434	0,868	—
Annual Lift Capacity	—	—	—	—	—	64,843	64,843	129,686	—
C1-B									
No. of Ships	0	0	0	1	11	16	16	16	15
GPS Equivalent	—	—	—	0.425	4.675	6.800	6.800	6.800	6.375
Annual Lift Capacity	—	—	—	63,498	698,482	1,015,974	1,015,974	1,015,974	952,476
C1-M-AV1									
No. of Ships	1	1	1	1	0	0	0	0	0
GPS Equivalent	0.174	0.174	0.174	0.174	—	—	—	—	—
Annual Lift Capacity	25,997	25,997	25,997	25,997	—	—	—	—	—
C2									
No. of Ships	0	0	1	1	0	0	0	0	0
GPS Equivalent	—	—	0.559	0.559	—	—	—	—	—
Annual Lift Capacity	—	—	83,519	83,519	—	—	—	—	—

Table B-7 (*continued*)

Ship Type and Items	1966	1965	1964	1963	1962	1961	1960	1959	1958
C2 (Containership)									
No. of Ships	5	0	0	0	0	0	0	0	0
GPS Equivalent	4.440	—	—	—	—	—	—	—	—
Annual Lift Capacity	663,372	—	—	—	—	—	—	—	—
C2-F									
No. of Ships	0	0	0	0	0	1	1	1	1
GPS Equivalent	—	—	—	—	—	0.559	0.559	0.559	0.559
Annual Lift Capacity	—	—	—	—	—	83,519	83,519	83,519	83,519
C2-S-AJ1									
No. of Ships	17	16	17	17	10	12	11	6	6
GPS Equivalent	9,503	8,944	9,503	9,503	5.590	6.780	6.149	3,354	3,354
Annual Lift Capacity	1,419,824	1,336,305	1,419,824	1,419,824	835,191	1,002,229	918,710	501,114	501,114
C2-S-B1									
No. of Ships	9	6	10	13	11	12	11	10	9
GPS Equivalent	5.085	3.390	5,650	7,345	6.215	6.780	6.215	5,650	5.085
Annual Lift Capacity	759,740	506,493	844,155	1,097,402	928,571	1,012,986	928,571	844,155	759,740
C2-S-DG2									
No. of Ships	0	0	0	1	1	0	0	0	0
GPS Equivalent	—	—	—	0.569	0.569	—	—	—	—
Annual Lift Capacity	—	—	—	85,013	85,013	—	—	—	—

(*continued*)

184

Table B-7 (*continued*)

Ship Type and Items	1966	1965	1964	1963	1962	1961	1960	1959	1958
C2-S-E1									
No. of Ships	12	12	14	19	19	19	19	19	19
GPS Equivalent	7.056	7.056	8.232	11.172	11.172	11.172	11.172	11.172	11.172
Annual Lift Capacity	1,054,223	1,054,223	1,229,927	1,669,186	1,669,186	1,669,186	1,669,186	1,669,186	1,669,186
C3-S-A2									
No. of Ships	32	32	32	30	29	29	29	25	25
GPS Equivalent	24.640	24.650	24.640	23.100	22.330	22.330	22.330	19.250	19.250
Annual Lift Capacity	3,681,413	3,681,413	3,681,413	3,451,325	3,336,281	3,336,281	3,336,281	2,876,104	2,876,104
C3-S-45A									
No. of Ships	1	0	0	0	0	0	0	0	0
GPS Equivalent	0.815	–	–	–	–	–	–	–	–
Annual Lift Capacity	121,768	–	–	–	–	–	–	–	–
C4 (Containership)									
No. of Ships	6	0	0	0	0	0	0	0	0
GPS Equivalent	7.174	–	–	–	–	–	–	–	–
Annual Lift Capacity	1,071,853	–	–	–	–	–	–	–	–
C4-S-A1									
No. of Ships	6	6	6	0	0	0	0	0	0
GPS Equivalent	4.794	4.794	4.794	–	–	–	–	–	–
Annual Lift Capacity	716,262	716,262	716,262	–	–	–	–	–	–

Table B-7 (*continued*)

Ship Type and Items	1966	1965	1964	1963	1962	1961	1960	1959	1958
C4-S-A3									
No. of Ships	4	2	2	0	0	0	0	0	0
GPS Equivalent	3.196	1.598	1.598	—	—	—	—	—	—
Annual Lift Capacity	477,508	238,754	238,754	—	—	—	—	—	—
C4-S-A4									
No. of Ships	0	0	0	0	0	0	0	0	2
GPS Equivalent	—	—	—	—	—	—	—	—	1.560
Annual Lift Capacity	—	—	—	—	—	—	—	—	233,076
C4-S-B5									
No. of Ships	3	3	3	3	2	2	2	3	3
GPS Equivalent	2.523	2.523	2.523	2.523	1.682	1.682	1.682	2.523	2.523
Annual Lift Capacity	376,956	376,956	376,856	376,956	251,304	251,304	251,304	376,956	376,956
C5-S-AX1									
No. of Ships	2	2	2	2	2	2	2	4	4
GPS Equivalent	1.970	1.970	1.970	1.970	1.970	1.970	1.970	3.940	3.940
Annual Lift Capacity	294,334	294,334	294,334	294,334	294,334	294,334	294,334	588,668	588,668
EC2-S-C1									
No. of Ships	4	4	4	10	11	11	11	12	12
GPS Equivalent	1.544	1.544	1.544	3.860	4.246	4.246	4.246	4.632	4.632
Annual Lift Capacity	230,686	230,686	230,686	576,715	634,386	634,386	634,386	692,058	692,058

(*continued*)

Table B-7 (continued)

Ship Type and Items	1958	1959	1960	1961	1962	1963	1964	1965	1966
R1-S-DH1									
No. of Ships	9	9	9	9	9	9	9	9	9
GPS Equivalent	1.899	1.899	1.899	1.899	1.899	1.899	1.988	1.899	1.899
Annual Lift Capacity	283,726	283,726	283,726	283,726	283,726	283,726	283,726	283,726	283,726
R2-ST-AU1									
No. of Ships	9	9	9	9	9	9	9	9	9
GPS Equivalent	3.600	3.600	3.600	3.600	3.600	3.600	3.600	3.600	3.600
Annual Lift Capacity	537,869	537,869	537,869	537,869	537,869	537,869	537,869	537,869	537,869
T2 (Containership)									
No. of Ships	0	0	0	0	0	0	2	0	1
GPS Equivalent	–	–	–	–	–	–	4.432	–	0.980
Annual Lift Capacity	–	–	–	–	–	–	662,176	–	146,420
VC2-S-AP2									
No. of Ships	13	14	13	14	9	10	10	9	10
GPS Equivalent	6.344	6.832	6.344	6.832	4.392	4.880	4.880	4.392	4.880
Annual Lift Capacity	947,844	1,020,755	947,844	1,020,755	656,200	729,111	729,111	656,200	729,111
VC2-S-AP3									
No. of Ships	4	4	3	3	5	5	5	4	4
GPS Equivalent	2.076	2.076	1.557	1.557	1.557	2.595	2.595	2.076	2.076
Annual Lift Capacity	310,171	310,171	232,628	232,628	232,628	387,714	387,714	310,171	310,171

Table B-7 (*continued*)

Ship Type and Items	1966	1965	1964	1963	1962	1961	1960	1959	1958
VC2-S-AP7									
No. of Ships	0	0	0	0	2	3	3	3	3
GPS Equivalent	—	—	—	—	0.976	1.464	1.464	1.464	1.464
Annual Lift Capacity	—	—	—	—	145,822	218,733	218,733	218,733	218,733
Bulk									
No. of Ships	4	4	4	4	4	4	4	5	5
GPS Equivalent	4.200	4.200	4.200	4.200	4.200	4.200	4.200	5.250	5.250
Annual Lift Capacity	627,514	627,514	627,514	627,514	627,514	627,514	627,514	784,392	784,392
LST (Converted)									
No. of Ships	0	0	0	0	1	1	0	0	0
GPS Equivalent	—	—	—	—	0.111	0.111	—	—	—
Annual Lift Capacity	—	—	—	—	16,584	16,584	—	—	—
TKR (Containership)									
No. of Ships	4	0	0	0	0	0	0	0	0
GPS Equivalent	2,848	—	—	—	—	—	—	—	—
Annual Lift Capacity	425,514	—	—	—	—	—	—	—	—
Total-Nonsubsidized Liners									
No. of Ships	143	119	131	135	133	148	144	142	139
GPS Equivalent	93,397	72,800	82,793	78,374	75,184	82,344	80,621	79,869	79,083
Annual Lift Capacity	13,954,261	10,876,903	12,369,937	11,709,703	11,233,091	12,302,851	12,054,422	11,933,066	11,815,633

Table B-8

Detailed Data on Fleet Size, GPS Equivalents and Annual Lift Capacity by Ship Type for Tramps: 1958-1966

Ship Type and Items	1958	1959	1960	1961	1962	1963	1964	1965	1966
C1-A									
No. of Ships	3	1	1	1	1	0	0	0	0
GPS Equivalent	1.302	0.434	0.434	0.434	0.434	—	—	—	—
Annual Lift Capacity	194,529	64,843	64,843	64,843	64,843	—	—	—	—
C1-B									
No. of Ships	1	0	0	0	0	0	0	1	3
GPS Equivalent	0.425	—	—	—	—	—	—	0.425	1.275
Annual Lift Capacity	63,498	—	—	—	—	—	—	63,498	190,495
C1-M-BTU									
No. of Ships	2	2	2	2	2	2	2	2	0
GPS Equivalent	0.348	0.348	0.348	0.348	0.348	0.348	0.348	0.348	—
Annual Lift Capacity	51,994	51,994	51,994	51,994	51,994	51,994	51,994	51,994	—
C2									
No. of Ships	0	0	0	0	0	1	2	1	1
GPS Equivalent	—	—	—	—	—	0.559	1.118	0.559	0.559
Annual Lift Capacity	—	—	—	—	—	83,519	167,038	83,519	83,519

Table B-8 (*continued*)

Ship Type and Items	1966	1965	1964	1963	1962	1961	1960	1959	1958
C2-S									
No. of Ships	0	0	0	0	0	4	4	4	4
GPS Equivalent	—	—	—	—	—	2.608	2.608	2.608	2.608
Annual Lift Capacity	—	—	—	—	—	389,656	389,656	389,656	389,656
C2-S-AJ1									
No. of Ships	15	12	11	10	6	6	10	13	11
GPS Equivalent	8.385	6.708	6.149	5.590	3.354	3.354	5.590	7.267	6.149
Annual Lift Capacity	1,252,786	1,002,229	918,710	835,191	501,114	501,114	835,191	1,085,748	918,710
C2-S-AJ3									
No. of Ships	0	0	0	0	0	0	0	0	2
GPS Equivalent	—	—	—	—	—	—	—	—	1.164
Annual Lift Capacity	—	—	—	—	—	—	—	—	173,911
C2-S-B1									
No. of Ships	20	18	11	11	10	10	9	9	9
GPS Equivalent	11.300	10.170	6.215	6.215	5.650	5.650	5.085	5.085	5.085
Annual Lift Capacity	1,688,310	1,519,479	928,571	928,571	844,155	844,155	759,740	759,740	759,740
C2-S-DG2									
No. of Ships	0	0	0	2	0	0	0	0	0
GPS Equivalent	—	—	—	1.138	—	—	—	—	—
Annual Lift Capacity	—	—	—	170,026	—	—	—	—	—

(*continued*)

Table B-8 (*continued*)

Ship Type and Items	1966	1965	1964	1963	1962	1961	1960	1959	1958
C3									
No. of Ships	4	4	3	2	4	3	0	0	0
GPS Equivalent	2.980	2.980	2.235	1.490	2.980	2.235	—	—	—
Annual Lift Capacity	445,236	445,236	333,927	222,618	445,236	333,927	—	—	—
C3-S-A2									
No. of Ships	9	8	8	7	8	8	13	12	12
GPS Equivalent	6.930	6.160	6.160	5.390	6.160	6.160	10.010	9.240	9.240
Annual Lift Capacity	1,035,397	920,353	920,353	805,309	920,353	920,353	1,495,574	1,380,530	1,380,530
C4-S-A3									
No. of Ships	0	0	1	0	0	0	0	0	0
GPS Equivalent	—	—	0.799	—	—	—	—	—	—
Annual Lift Capacity	—	—	119,377	—	—	—	—	—	—
C4-S-A3 (Bulk)									
No. of Ships	2	2	1	0	0	0	0	0	0
GPS Equivalent	3.556	3.556	1.769	—	—	—	—	—	—
Annual Lift Capacity	531,295	531,295	264,303	—	—	—	—	—	—
C4-S-A4									
No. of Ships	3	3	3	3	3	3	3	6	6
GPS Equivalent	2.397	2.397	2.397	2.397	2.397	2.397	2.397	4.794	4.794
Annual Lift Capacity	358,131	358,131	358,131	358,131	358,131	358,131	358,131	716,262	716,262

Table B-8 (*continued*)

Ship Type and Items	1966	1965	1964	1963	1962	1961	1960	1959	1958
C4-S-B2									
No. of Ships	1	1	1	1	1	4	0	0	0
GPS Equivalent	0.841	0.841	0.841	0.841	0.841	3.364	—	—	—
Annual Lift Capacity	125,652	125,652	125,652	125,652	125,652	502,609	—	—	—
C4-S-B5									
No. of Ships	0	0	0	0	1	1	1	0	0
GPS Equivalent	—	—	—	—	0.841	0.841	0.841	—	—
Annual Lift Capacity	—	—	—	—	125,652	125,652	125,652	—	—
EC-2									
No. of Ships	7	17	24	31	39	41	61	78	66
GPS Equivalent	2.527	6.137	8.664	11.191	14.079	14.801	22.021	28.158	23.826
Annual Lift Capacity	377,554	916,917	1,294,471	1,672,025	2,103,515	2,211,388	3,290,114	4,207,030	3,559,795
EC-2-AW1									
No. of Ships	0	0	0	0	3	3	3	3	3
GPS Equivalent	—	—	—	—	1.083	1.083	1.083	1.083	1.083
Annual Lift Capacity	—	—	—	—	161,809	161,809	161,809	161,809	161,809
EC-2-SC1									
No. of Ships	4	1	1	1	2	1	0	1	1
GPS Equivalent	1.544	0.386	0.386	0.386	0.772	0.386	—	0.386	0.386
Annual Lift Capacity	230,686	57,671	57,671	57,671	115,343	57,671	—	57,671	57,671

(*continued*)

Table B-8 (*continued*)

Ship Type and Items	1966	1965	1964	1963	1962	1961	1960	1959	1958
EC-2-SC1 (Bulk)									
No. of Ships	3	3	3	3	4	3	2	1	0
GPS Equivalent	2,329	2,329	2,329	2,329	3.265	2,329	1,916	0.980	—
Annual Lift Capacity	347,971	347,971	347,971	347,971	487,817	347,971	286,266	146,420	—
N3-M-A1									
No. of Ships	0	1	1	0	0	0	0	0	0
GPS Equivalent	—	0.100	0.100	—	—	—	—	—	—
Annual Lift Capacity	—	14,941	14,941	—	—	—	—	—	—
P2-N1-MA									
No. of Ships	1	1	0	0	0	0	0	0	0
GPS Equivalent	0.099	0.099	—	—	—	—	—	—	—
Annual Lift Capacity	14,791	14,791	—	—	—	—	—	—	—
P2-S1-IN									
No. of Ships	0	0	0	0	0	0	0	1	1
GPS Equivalent	—	—	—	—	—	—	—	0.229	0.229
Annual Lift Capacity	—	—	—	—	—	—	—	34,214	34,214
SEC-2									
No. of Ships	0	0	0	0	1	1	2	3	4
GPS Equivalent	—	—	—	—	0.351	0.351	0.702	1.053	1.404
Annual Lift Capacity	—	—	—	—	52,442	52,442	104,884	157,327	209,769

Table B-8 (*continued*)

Ship Type and Items	1966	1965	1964	1963	1962	1961	1960	1959	1958
T2-C									
No. of Ships	6	8	11	11	9	8	4	1	0
GPS Equivalent	10.367	16.163	22.169	22.169	17.597	13.229	6.769	2.020	—
Annual Lift Capacity	1,548,913	2,414,882	3,312,226	3,312,226	2,629,133	1,976,518	1,011,343	301,804	—
T2-SE-A1 (Bulk)									
No. of Ships	14	14	12	10	8	6	3	0	0
GPS Equivalent	28.240	28.240	24.183	19.558	15.199	11.009	5.157	—	—
Annual Lift Capacity	4,219,282	4,219,282	3,613,134	2,922,122	2,270,852	1,644,833	770,497	—	—
T3-S-A1 (Bulk)									
No. of Ships	1	1	1	1	1	1	0	0	0
GPS Equivalent	0.849	0.849	0.849	0.849	0.849	0.849	—	—	—
Annual Lift Capacity	126,847	126,847	126,847	126,847	126,847	126,847	—	—	—
VC-2C (Bulk)									
No. of Ships	1	1	3	4	4	2	2	0	0
GPS Equivalent	1.402	1.402	4.206	5.608	5.608	2.804	2.804	—	—
Annual Lift Capacity	209,470	209,470	628,410	837,880	837,880	418,940	418,940	—	—
VC-2-AP2									
No. of Ships	8	6	6	5	8	7	5	6	5
GPS Equivalent	3.904	2.928	2.928	2.440	3.904	3.416	2.440	2.928	2.440
Annual Lift Capacity	583,289	437,467	437,467	364,556	583,289	510,378	364,556	437,467	364,556

(*continued*)

Table B-8 (*continued*)

Ship Type and Items	1966	1965	1964	1963	1962	1961	1960	1959	1958
VC-A-AP3									
No. of Ships	27	26	23	24	21	14	14	13	13
GPS Equivalent	14.013	13.494	11.937	12.456	10.899	7.266	7.266	6.747	6.747
Annual Lift Capacity	2,093,654	2,016,112	1,783,483	1,861,026	1,628,398	1,086,599	1,085,599	1,008,056	1,008,056
VC-2-AP3 (Bulk)									
No. of Ships	1	1	1	1	1	1	0	0	0
GPS Equivalent	0.730	0.730	0.730	0.730	0.730	0.730	–	–	–
Annual Lift Capacity	109,068	109,068	109,068	109,068	109,068	109,068	–	–	–
Bulk									
No. of Ships	1	1	2	2	2	2	1	1	1
GPS Equivalent	2.384	2.384	3.062	3.062	3.062	3.062	0.678	0.678	0.678
Annual Lift Capacity	356,189	356,189	457,487	457,487	457,487	457,487	101,299	101,299	101,299
Freight									
No. of Ships	0	0	1	1	1	1	1	1	1
GPS Equivalent	–	–	0.361	0.361	0.361	0.361	0.361	0.361	0.361
Annual Lift Capacity	–	–	53,936	53,936	53,936	53,936	53,936	53,936	53,936
LST (Converted)									
No. of Ships	0	0	0	1	1	1	0	0	0
GPS Equivalent	–	–	–	0.369	0.369	0.369	–	–	–
Annual Lift Capacity	–	–	–	55,132	55,132	55,132	–	–	–

195

Table B-8 (*continued*)

Ship Type and Items	1966	1965	1964	1963	1962	1961	1960	1959	1958
TKR (Converted)									
No. of Ships	2	2	1	0	0	0	0	0	0
GPS Equivalent	4.318	4.318	1.669	—	—	—	—	—	—
Annual Lift Capacity	645,144	645,144	249,362	—	—	—	—	—	—
Z-ET1									
No. of Ships	0	0	3	3	2	3	2	2	2
GPS Equivalent	—	—	1.098	1.098	0.732	1.098	0.732	0.732	0.732
Annual Lift Capacity	—	—	164,050	164,050	109,367	164,050	109,367	109,367	109,367
Z-ET1 (Bulk)									
No. of Ships	1	1	1	1	1	1	1	1	0
GPS Equivalent	0.906	0.906	0.906	0.906	0.906	0.906	0.906	0.906	—
Annual Lift Capacity	135,364	135,364	135,364	135,364	135,364	135,364	135,364	135,364	—
Total-Tramps									
No. of Ships	135	136	137	138	144	138	144	159	147
GPS Equivalent	111.835	114.609	113.608	107.480	102.771	91.440	80.148	76.037	69.001
Annual Lift Capacity	16,708,443	17,123,502	16,973,944	16,058,372	15,354,809	13,661,867	11,974,755	11,360,537	10,309,302

Appendix C
The Balance of Payments and the U.S. Merchant Marine

The Balance of Payments
and
The U.S. Merchant Marine

A Study
Prepared by

**Harbridge
House
Inc.**

Boston

Washington, D.C.   Encino (Los Angeles)   Toronto   London   Frankfurt am Main   Bonn

HARBRIDGE HOUSE INC

Eleven Arlington Street, Boston, Massachusetts 02116, Telephone (617) 267-6410, Cable: HARBRIDGE BOSTON

17 January 1968

CHARLES D. BAKER
Vice President

Committee of American Steamship Lines
1155 15th Street, N. W.   Suite 1104
Washington, D. C.   20005

Attn: RAdm. Ralph K. James USN (Ret.)

Gentlemen:

We are pleased to present to you the Harbridge House study of the
current impact of the United States merchant marine on the United States balance of payments. This report is one part of our larger study dealing with an
overall evaluation of the economic contribution of the United States merchant
marine to the nation. The report has been prepared as a separate item because
of the significance and timeliness of the issue, and because it is our hope that
it will serve to assist others in putting any analysis and consideration of balance
of payments in what we believe to be the proper context.

The larger study is engaged in analyzing a series of areas--such as
balance of payments, trade expansion, and national security--with regard to
their economic benefits for the nation. It is structured to address these areas
in the context of historical analysis, projection of future impact within the existing maritime environment, and projection of potential impact under various
alternative future policies and programs.

The report presented here is essentially an historical appraisal.
Balance of payments in the context of both the probable and the possible future
will be reported on in other sectional reports to be issued during the progress
of the larger study.

Boston   Washington, D.C.   North Hollywood   Toronto   London   Frankfurt am Main

Committee of American   2   17 January 1968
  Steamship Lines

      This report represents our independent appraisal of the balance of
payments area, and we recognize that the Committee of American Steamship
Lines and/or some of its individual members may disagree with some of the
findings or analysis therein. While the responsibility for the findings and analysis
is ours, we nonetheless wish to express our recognition and appreciation of the
assistance given us by various CASL members in collecting data necessary for
our study.

Sincerely,

CDB/smy

Acknowledgements

This study, "The Balance of Payments and the U.S. Merchant Marine," has been conducted by the professional staff of Harbridge House, Inc. Generous assistance was provided by many government agencies and individuals therein, including: Office of Business Economics, Department of Commerce; Bureau of the Budget; Joint Economic Committee, United States Congress; Maritime Administration, Department of Commerce; Commodity Credit Corporation, Department of Agriculture; Military Sea Transportation Service, Department of the Navy, Agency for International Development, Department of State; Treasury Department; Department of Transportation; Bureau of the Census, Department of Commerce. Although differences of view have existed from time to time between Harbridge House and these individuals, their cooperation in presenting both information and ideas has been generous throughout.

Our study team has been supplemented and greatly aided by the contributions of individual faculty members at Harvard and M.I.T. Specific recognition and appreciation is made to Dr. Eli Shapiro and Dr. Paul W. Cherington of Harvard University and Mr. Robert Rickover of M.I.T., who read and analyzed the draft of this study, and furnished their recommendations.

Charles D. Baker
John B. Schnapp
James R. Barker
Ruth L. Kleinfeld

Table of Contents

List of Tables

Introduction

General

The United States balance of payments is an accounting summary of transactions between U.S. entities and foreign entities. During the ten year period 1957-1966 the nation recorded deficits in its balance of payments totalling approximately $23 billion. Two major factors in these deficits have been American foreign aid programs and overseas military expenditures. Since the magnitude of neither is likely to change radically, the balance of payments role played by other contributants remains crucial. The U.S. Merchant Marine is one of these contributants.

In various research activities Harbridge House has directed its attention to one or another national economic question. Currently, the firm is engaged in an overall assessment of the economic value to the nation of its merchant marine. In the conduct of this project, we are systematically reviewing several areas—such as balance of payments—where the Merchant Marine might provide economic benefit to the nation. This report summarizes the Harbridge House study of the balance of payments impact of the U.S. Merchant Marine.

Purpose

The objective of this balance of payments study is to determine the true impact of the United States Merchant Marine in this area. Earlier attempts at quantifying the balance of payments impact of the merchant marine—and there have been many—were impeded by faulty data and incomplete methodology. Accordingly, we have found it necessary to develop a more complete theoretical framework that could be used as the basis for calculating impact in any given year. This developed methodology and the findings derived therefrom are discussed at length in this report.

This balance of payments analysis is an integral part of the "Study of the Economic Value of the United States Merchant Marine" currently being undertaken by Harbridge House. The measurement of balance of payments impact lends itself to two uses:

i) As one element of the larger study, contributing to it a quantification of one of the major economic benefits (balance of payments) provided by the Merchant Marine;
ii) As an independent study, offering as reliable an assessment of the U.S. Merchant Marine's balance of payments impact as is possible with currently available data.

Organization

This report consists of six parts. This introductory section is Part I. It discusses the purpose and scope of the study and establishes the analytical framework.

Part II summarizes the findings and conclusions of the study as to qualitative and quantitative aspects of the balance of payments impact of the U.S. Merchant Marine.

Part III provides an exposition of the balance of payments framework and its functional relationship to the international operations of the Merchant Marine.

Part IV details the methodology developed and employed in the study to quantify and assess the balance of payments impact. Several aspects of this methodology are newly developed by Harbridge House and, we believe, represent an advance in the technique of analysis in this area.

Part V presents the detailed calculation of the balance of payments impact of the U.S. Merchant Marine for 1957-1966 made in accordance with the methodology described in Part IV. It thus amplifies and expands on the summary findings and conclusions of Part II.

Part VI contains appendices and an annotated bibliography.

Superscribed arabic numerals refer to sources which are listed in Appendix A. Referenced material other than sources appears on the same page as the text reference.

Harbridge House Approach

Sources of Balance of Payments Contribution

The international ocean shipping operations of the U.S. Merchant Marine* are reflected in the transportation sector of the balance of payments. Therefore, we consider the balance of payments impact of U.S. merchant shipping as the amount of loss that would be sustained by the *transportation sector* of the U.S. balance of payments if the shipping services provided by the U.S.-fleet were performed instead by another fleet.

In many types of economic analysis, balance of payments impact is characterized only as receipts of foreign currency reflected in the balance of payments accounts. However, in assessing the balance of payments importance of the Merchant Marine in the context of alternative sources of transportation, it is equally important to consider the services it provides to U.S. customers. These avoid additional payments of dollars to foreign shipping operators. Therefore, throughout this study we consider balance of payments impact of the U.S. Merchant Marine as the sum of *two* elements:

i) Net improvement in U.S. foreign exchange position, consisting of revenue from foreign nationals;

---

*Cabotage and Great Lakes shipping are not considered part of international operations and are not included in this study.

ii) Dollar retention, consisting of revenue from U.S. nationals that would otherwise be paid out to foreign vessel operators.

Although the latter element does not appear in published balance of payments reports, it is essential to consider if the true balance of payments impact of the Merchant Marine is to be assessed.

Alternatives to the U.S. Fleet

If we are to measure the loss that would be sustained by the transportation sector of the balance of payments if shipping services currently provided by U.S. vessels were performed instead by a foreign fleet, we must take into account the several alternative (foreign) fleets that might be substituted in place of the U.S. Merchant Marine. Therefore we measure the change in balance of payments associated with the employment of each of the alternatives in lieu of U.S. vessels. The three principal alternatives are:

i) Flags of convenience shipping—vessels manned by foreign citizens and registered abroad but beneficially owned by U.S. citizens and chartered back to U.S. vessel operators; these ships are usually deemed by the Navy Department to be under effective U.S. control through agreements covering transfer in national emergencies; PANLIBHON is a frequent term of reference for such vessels because most of them are registered in Panama, Liberia, or Honduras.
ii) Foreign-owned charter shipping—vessels not only manned by foreign citizens and registered abroad but also owned by foreign nationals; they may be chartered to U.S. operators for a single voyage or for longer periods.
iii) Foreign-owned and -operated shipping—vessels that are manned, registered, owned, and operated by foreigners.

The balance of payments impact of the U.S. fleet can vary depending upon which of these alternatives were to supply the services that the U.S. fleet currently renders.

Ideally we would wish to make our analysis on the basis of an entirely U.S.-owned, -operated, and -citizen-manned fleet. This can be done with data available for the year 1964 and later and such is our approach. For the full decade—1957-1966—data limitations confine the analysis to an assessment in terms of a "mixed" U.S. fleet (that is, one containing some chartered foreign-flag vessels along with the U.S.-flag ships).

Some Baselines in the Analysis

Implicit in our approach is the assumption that transferring transportation services from a U.S. fleet to any other vessels would have no effect on the volume or the mode of transportation of U.S. foreign trade and passenger services. Thus in our study we do not purport to derive the net loss in *total* balance of payments that the U.S. would suffer if all of its merchant shipping operations passed to other fleets but only the effect on the transportation sector of the balance of payments. The *total* effect might be considerably lower than our calculation of the balance of payments impact of the fleet if the transfer to an alternative fleet stimulated substantial increases in the export of U.S. products; on the other hand, it might be even higher if the U.S.-flag fleet is, of itself, responsible for the promotion of much U.S. export activity. However, this relates to a separate issue: the impact of the U.S. Merchant Marine on the volume of U.S. world trade. This issue is treated in a separate study.

We have also adopted the assumption made by the Office of Business Economics that the *importer* pays ocean freight charges. This is valid even for shipments quoted as C and F, CIF, Delivered Free or FOB Freight Paid. In many shipments effected under these terms, the exporter employs one of these forms of quotation only in order to control the movement of the goods. Even when he appears to absorb the ocean freight charges, they are not reduced and such apparent absorptions are more properly viewed as price concessions on the goods, themselves. (Analytically, the net effect in our calculation of impact is the same even if the exporter *does* absorb freight costs, but using the assumption simplifies procedure.)

Vessel Revenue

In calculating the balance of payments impact of the U.S. fleet on the basis of a transfer to alternative fleets, we deal with "vessel revenue," the *transportation* portion of gross revenues—those amounts relating to the ship and the services it provides. Port charges, the amounts included in gross revenues which are paid out by the ship for port services, are subtracted because we are only concerned with the effects of using U.S. *vessels* as compared with foreign *vessels.* The port charges at both ends of a voyage will be paid by the same party—the consignee— and received by the same party—the port concerned—irrespective of the carrier. Thus, the only part of the gross revenue that has balance of payments impact here is the portion of total revenue attributable to the vessel and *its* services.

The reasons can be demonstrated schematically. As an example, we can look from the U.S. balance of payments point of view at the effect of a shift in the carrying of a U.S. export or a U.S. import from a U.S. vessel to a foreign vessel. In this example we assume port charges abroad of 20, port charges in the U.S. of 30, vessel revenue of 50, and gross shipping revenue of 100.

In both instances, the difference in the transportation sector of the U.S. balance of payments between effecting the carrying on a U.S. vessel and on a foreign vessel is 50, the exact portion of gross revenue relating to the ship and its services. When viewing exports, this difference is one of improvement in the

213

Table C-1

Balance of Payments Impact Calculation

	Gross Revenue	Port Charges Abroad	Port Charges U.S.	Net*	Impact†
	(1)	(2)	(3)	(4)	(5)
Export Shipping					
I. U.S. Vessel	+100	(20)	‡	+80	+50
II. Foreign Vessel	‡	‡	+30	+30	–
Import Shipping					
I. U.S. Vessel	‡	(20)	‡	(20)	+50
II. Foreign Vessel	(100)	‡	+30	(70)	–

*Col. (4) = sum of col. (1), (2), and (3).   ‡ Does not enter balance of payments accounting.

†Col. (5) = [I. Col. 4] − [II. Col 4].

U.S. foreign exchange position; when viewing imports, it is in the amount of dollars that would otherwise be paid out to foreign entities or, as we identify it, in dollar retention.

The relationship may be expressed as the equation:

$$B = R - (PC_a + PC_{us})$$

B = balance of payments impact
R = gross shipping revenue
PC_a = port charges payable abroad
PC_{us} = port charges payable in the U.S.

Summary

We deal with balance of payments impact as a sum of foreign exchange receipts and domestic dollars conserved. We determine the net differential in the U.S. balance of payments if the services provided by the U.S. fleet were transferred to each of the alternative fleets. These fleets are: flags of convenience vessels, foreign-owned vessels chartered to U.S. operators, and foreign-owned and -operated vessels.

Summary of Findings
and Conclusions

The principal findings and conclusions of this study are summarized below. In some cases, when appropriate, we have included brief amplifying comments. These findings and conclusions are discussed in detail in Parts IV and V where supporting analysis is presented.

The Balance of Payments Impact of the
U.S. Merchant Fleet

The transportation sector of the U.S. balance of payments would have suffered a loss of approximately $2.2 billion for the three-year period 1964-1966 if the shipping services performed by the U.S. flag fleet—only those vessels of U.S. registry that are citizen owned and operated—had been performed instead by foreign owned and operated vessels; a loss of such magnitude, even if stimulating some additional demand for U.S. goods, would very probably have had severe economic repercussions.

The *apparent* balance of payments impact of foreign flag vessels under charter to U.S. operators during the same period was a net deficit of $0.4 billion; this implies that the operators of these chartered vessels pay out more in port charges and charter fees than they recover in revenue benefits from the hauling performed by the vessels. This seems highly unlikely and the apparent deficit is probably traceable to incomplete or erroneous reporting.

For the ten-year period 1957-1966 the balance of payments impact of all U.S. merchant shipping operations (including U.S. operated chartered vessels) was a net gain of $5.7 billion. If the circumstances generating the apparent negative impact of chartered vessels in the years 1964-1966 held equally true during the ten-year period, it is likely that the balance of payments impact of an entirely U.S.-flag fleet during that period was $7.3 billion.

During the three-year period 1964-1966, liner service contributed 85 percent, or $1.9 billion, of the total balance of payments impact of the U.S.-flag merchant fleet.

If the services provided by the U.S. registered vessels were transferred to chartered foreign-flag vessels—even to those flags of convenience ships beneficially owned by U.S. entities—the balance of payments loss would be as great or nearly as great as if the services were transferred to foreign owned and operated vessels.

Percentages of Gross Shipping Revenue
Creating Balance of Payments Impact

Of each dollar of non-defense gross revenue received, U.S.-operated vessels contribute 42 cents to the balance of payments; this figure is substantially higher than the estimate of 30 cents that has been used by some in earlier analyses of this question.

U.S. liner service produces a net gain in balance of payments of 50 cents for each dollar of non-defense revenue received, and a net gain of 75 cents for each dollar of defense FIO revenue; these high gain figures are caused principally by the comparatively high value per ton of cargo carried by U.S. liners.

U.S. nonliner service produces a gross gain in balance of payments of 25 cents for each dollar of non-defense revenue received and 50 cents for each dollar of defense FIO revenue. For U.S. flag nonliners, net gain is synonymous with gross gain. For U.S. charters of foreign flags, charter payments must be deducted to establish net gain.

Government Support and Balance of Payments Impact

The ratio of the balance of payments impact of U.S. subsidized liners to the operating differential subsidy received by them in the years 1964-1966 ranged from 2:1 to 3:1. While it is recognized that balance of payments contribution alone by no means provides an adequate measure of the effectiveness of the subsidy, these ratios have been developed in this study to verify or correct past computations.

The apparent ratio of the balance of payments impact of most non-subsidized U.S. liners and U.S. nonliners to the current rate differentials they receive on government sponsored carrying is significantly less than 2:1. The ratio of balance of payments impact to differential varies inversely with the magnitude of the differential.

Government Sponsored Carrying and the
Balance of Payments

Preferential carrying of government sponsored cargo by U.S.-flag vessels in the three-year period 1964-1966 contributed approximately $1.3 billion to the balance of payments; this is slightly more than half of the total balance of payments impact of the U.S. merchant fleet.

Changes in preferential carrying policies designed to enhance the *total* U.S. balance of payments appear to offer relatively little potential for doing so; proposals that recipients of U.S. international aid finance all transportation costs on vessels of their choice in order to reduce grants seem impractical because of the economic weakness of the recipient nations.

Context of the Study

The U.S. Balance of Payments

The balance of payments is an accounting framework designed to relate transactions between the U.S. government and its citizens and foreign governments and their citizens. Its principal components are:

—receipts for exports of goods and services;
—receipts through repayments on government loans;
—receipts of foreign capital other than liquid funds;
—payments for imports of goods and services;
—payments in the form of private remittances;
—payments in the form of private capital outflow;
—payments for government pensions and other transfers;
—payments in the form of government grants and capital outflow.

The greatest gross value is associated with the exchange of goods and services, including transportation. The balance in the accounts listed, before compensating movements of gold and liquid dollar assets, is the balance of payments of the U.S.

Recent History

During the latest ten years for which data are available—1957 to 1966—the U.S. recorded an annual deficit in its balance of payments in all but one year, and a total ten year deficit of approximately $23 billion.[1] In short, the outflow of payments exceeded the inflow of receipts by that amount.

The annual deficits were greatest in 1959 and 1960 when they reached $3,870 million and $3,881 million respectively. Subsequently, the balance of payments improved considerably and in 1966 the deficit reported was $1,213 million. However, all indications suggest that the deficit for 1967 will be considerably larger, perhaps approaching the 1959-1960 level.

During the same ten-year period the U.S. experienced substantial trade surpluses. The excess by value of merchandise exports over merchandise imports, excluding military grants and expenditures, varied from 6.3 percent to 45.8 percent with no major discernible trend or pattern.[2] Peaks were apparent in 1957, 1961, and 1964; troughs in 1959 and 1966.

In the face of a positive balance of trade, the U.S. balance of payments deficits are traceable to other factors, the principal ones being military expenditures and government grants. There is no current evidence of a major change in the overall trends of these two classes of expenditure. Therefore, the future balance of payments position of the U.S. will be determined to a great extent by the degree to which favorable balances for goods and services can be maintained or augmented.

Critical Aspects

Foreign governments and individuals who accumulate dollar reserves may determine whether they prefer to hold them as liquid dollar assets or convert any portion of these assets to gold. Thus an unfavorable U.S. balance of payments provides foreign governments and nationals with an option, which, if exercised, bears directly on our gold supply. During the ten-year period 1957 to 1966, the net drain on U.S. Treasury gold stock was $8.3 billion, reducing this stock at the close of 1966 to approximately $13 billion.[3]

The U.S. Treasury is required by statute to maintain a minimum gold stock equal to 25 percent of the value of the Federal Reserve notes in circulation. At present, this value is approximately $40 billion, requiring a gold reserve of $10 billion.[4]

Any further substantial depletion of gold stock might cause elimination of the statutory minimum so as to permit use of the entire federal gold stock for external support of the dollar. This measure might possibly weaken confidence in the dollar and generate increased conversion of foreign-held liquid dollar assets to gold. Of greater significance is the likelihood that it might also force the government to enact the sort of Draconian measures that have been employed by other countries confronted by similar crises. These include:

—restrictions on imports;
—restrictions on foreign travel;
—currency controls;
—reductions of overseas military programs;
—reductions of foreign aid programs;
—limitations on capital available for foreign and, perhaps, domestic investment;
—devaluation.

The Merchant Marine in the Balance of Payments

The United States Merchant Marine not only carries a significant portion of the exports and imports which exert such a strong influence on the U.S. balance of payments but, as an industry, the Merchant Marine is in itself a major source of foreign exchange. For example, in 1965, gross shipping revenues received from foreign sources totalled $680 million.[5] Only six major export categories exceeded it. These were:

Machinery -	$6,820 million
Transportation equipment -	$3,196 million
Metals and manufactures -	$1,735 million

Wheat - $1,185 million
Chemical elements and compounds - $970 million
Corn - $830 million.[6]

These revenues for services provided to foreigners are reflected in the balance of payments as receipts. Expenditures made in foreign countries by U.S. vessels and their operators in the extension of these services give rise to payments. These expenditures, called port charges, include fuel purchased, stores, repairs, stevedoring, harbor fees, agents' commissions and advances of wages to crew members paid in foreign ports.[7] Payments made by U.S. entities to foreign shipping operators exert a negative effect on our balance of payments while the port charges paid by these operators in the U.S. have a positive effect.

The Composition of the U.S.-Operated Fleet

The vessels that compose the U.S. operated Merchant Marine differ in their national status. The three principal classifications into which these vessels fall are:

i) U.S.-flag vessels that are registered under the U.S.-flag and are owned, operated, and manned by U.S. citizens;
ii) Flag of convenience (or flag of necessity) vessels which are registered under foreign flags and are foreign manned but are beneficially owned by U.S. entities; those included under the general heading of "U.S.-operated Merchant Marine" are chartered to U.S. operators which may be the beneficial owners or third parties;
iii) Chartered foreign-owned vessels which are owned and manned by foreign nationals and chartered to U.S. operators.

The U.S. Merchant Marine also involves three broad types of services—liner, nonliner, and cabotage.

i) Liner service is composed of vessels that normally maintain scheduled berth service and carry predominantly breakbulk rather than loose bulk (such as ores and agricultural commodities) cargoes. U.S. liner service includes both subsidized and non-subsidized operators. Virtually all passenger service as such is performed by liner operators.
ii) Nonliner service is composed of two types of vessels: tramps, which may carry breakbulk cargoes on unfixed schedules but are more commonly dry bulk carriers of ores and grains; and tankers, which normally carry liquid bulk cargoes although many are also suitable for carrying dry bulk as well.
iii) Cabotage service involves domestic coastal and lake carrying and, under federal law, is reserved for U.S.-flag vessels.

Since cabotage is an entirely domestic service, its impact is not taken into account in this study. Nevertheless, if foreign vessels were allowed to enter domestic service, it is clear that the balance of payments would be affected negatively to the extent of foreign participation.

Government Regulation and Maritime Policy

Government policy determines to a great extent the size, composition, and even vessel characteristics of the U.S. merchant fleet. In short, the U.S. government has a good deal of influence in the posture of the U.S. Merchant Marine. Because the posture of the fleet greatly bears on the fleet's balance of payments impact, it is desirable at this point to consider briefly the nature of government regulation.

The most important guidelines to government policy are embodied in two forms of legislation, the Merchant Marine Act of 1936[8] and the cargo preference programs.[9]

i) The Merchant Marine Act of 1936 - This law establishes two basic subsidy programs. The first, designed to sustain a U.S. shipbuilding and repair industry, equalizes the cost to U.S. ship operators of acquiring vessels from U.S. yards or from foreign yards. Vessel designs must meet government criteria, most of which are based upon usefulness in national emergencies. The second program, called the operating differential subsidy, was planned to establish parity between U.S. vessel operating costs and those of foreign vessels. These usually differ markedly, principally because of wage scale variances. This subsidy has been paid only to liner operators sailing U.S. built ships flying the U.S. flag, employing only U.S. citizens as crew members and maintaining approved regular schedule frequencies over key trade routes. Not all U.S. liner operators have applied for and been awarded operating differential subsidies, and no operating differential subsidies are currently paid to nonliner operators.

ii) Cargo preference programs - These were established by statutes and pertain to the carrying of government sponsored cargo. The statutes specify, for example, that *all* cargo lifted by the Department of Defense in other than its own vessels must be carried in U.S.-flag ships (if capacity is available) at rates negotiated between the Military Sea Transportation Service (MSTS) and individual operators or groups of operators. (In our measurement of the merchant fleet's balance of payments impact we take into account the services it provides to the Department of Defense since these services might presumably be purchased from foreigners; notwithstanding the legislation on the books, some defense carrying *is* being done on foreign-flag vessels.)

Similarly a minimum of 50 percent by tonnage of the shipments made under programs of the State Department's Agency for International Development must be carried by U.S. flag vessels (if capacity is available) at contracted rates. A parallel regulation applies to the Agriculture Department's Food for Peace Program enacted under Public Law 480.

Other federal agencies such as the Post Office and the Export-Import Bank must also give preference to U.S.-flag shipping.

Because of the nature of this legislation and the manner in which it has been enforced, the current U.S.-flag Merchant Marine is predominantly a liner fleet. Nonliners flying the U.S. flag tend to be outdated vessels heavily dependent on government-sponsored cargo. Most carrying of U.S. commercial bulk cargo, either dry or liquid, is performed by foreign-operated nonliners or by foreign-registered nonliners that have been chartered to U.S. operators. Therefore, it would be logical to expect that liner service would exert a predominant influence in the balance of payments contribution of the total U.S. fleet.

Methodology

Introduction

This section of the study presents the method Harbridge House has developed and employed to calculate the balance of payments impact of the U.S. Merchant Marine. In describing the method, the elements of data used in the calculations are also defined.

Method of Quantification

As the total balance of payments impact of U.S. shipping services is derived from two sources—net improvement in foreign exchange position and net dollar retention—analysis has been structured to reflect each source separately. The components of each source are given in Table 2.

Table C-2

Components of Balance of Payment Impact

I. *Net Improvement in U.S. Foreign Exchange Position*

  −revenues from AID cargoes
  −revenues from P.L. 480 (Food for Peace) cargoes
  −revenues from commercial and other government sponsored nondefense cargoes (U.S. exports)
  −revenues from cargoes carried between foreign countries
  −passenger revenues from foreign citizens
  −charter fees received
  LESS:
  −charter fees paid
  −port charges paid abroad

II. *Net Dollar Retention*

  −revenues from commercial and government sponsored non-defense cargoes (U.S. imports)
  −passenger revenues from U.S. citizens
  −Department of Defense (DOD) payments for shipping contract and berth terms
  −DOD payments for time and voyage charters
  −DOD payments for other services
  LESS:
  −estimated domestic port charges paid on non-defense carrying
  −estimated DOD port charges

Notes to Table C-2

1. Revenues from AID cargoes—These are portions of loans or grants made to AID recipients to cover ocean freight services performed by U.S. operators under the minimum 50 percent tonnage stipulation by which AID sponsored cargoes are apportioned. In effect, these amounts increase *payments* in the balance of payments account for U.S. government grants and increase *receipts* in the transportation account.

2. Revenues from Public Law 480 cargoes—These are revenues paid by recipients of Food for Peace commodities or are grants given them by the U.S. for transportation performed by U.S.-flag vessels under the 50 percent minimum tonnage stipulation specified in Public Law 664. Under Titles I and IV of Public Law 480, the revenues are based upon international bulk shipping rates. Since these international rates are lower in nonliner services than the rates that can be quoted by U.S.-flag operators, the Department of Agriculture pays a differential to the operator based on the difference between the contract rate and the international rate. This differential represents a direct revenue subsidy and is thus *not* included in balance of payments calculations.

3. Revenues from commercial and other government sponsored non-defense cargoes (U.S. exports)—As previously specified, we assume that the importer ultimately pays transportation charges no matter what terms of quotation may be employed. Other government cargoes include shipments made by the Post Office and those under Export-Import Bank financing. In 1964, the last year for which data was available, these accounted for slightly over 18 percent of this total.[1] No revenues from shipments carried for the Department of Defense are included here.

4. Revenues from cargoes carried between foreign countries—Commonly called foreign-to-foreign revenues, these are receipts from foreigners for carrying of cargo loaded in one foreign port for discharge in another foreign port.

5. Passengers revenues from foreign citizens—All fares paid to U.S. operators by foreign citizens for either inbound, outbound, or port-to-port transportation are included in this category.

6. Charter fees received—These may be revenues received by owners of U.S.-flag vessels for chartering these vessels to foreign operators. They may also be revenues received by U.S. charterers of foreign-flag vessels for rechartering the vessels to foreign operators.

7. Charter fees paid—These are payments made by U.S. citizens or companies for chartering foreign-flag vessels. Many such payments are made by U.S. companies that are beneficial owners of the vessels to their own overseas subsidiaries in whose names the ships are registered.

8. Port charges paid abroad—The definition of the expenditure items included in "port charges" has been given in the previous section. The expenditures made by vessels under U.S. operation in foreign ports do not necessarily bear any direct relationship to export freight receipts from foreigners. Amounts paid by vessels in foreign ports are related both to their outbound carrying revenues, a published balance of payments items, as well as to their inbound carrying which is a retention item. In fact, a vessel carrying only inbound and traveling the outbound leg in ballast will sustain port charges related to cargo-loading as well as port use without generating any foreign exchange revenues. The Maritime Administration states that more than 90 percent of the use of chartered vessels of foreign registry under effective U.S. control is of this sort.[2]

An additional factor which tends to exaggerate the apparent relationship of port charges paid by U.S. operated vessels to their published balance of payments receipts is the influence of certain Department of Defense carrying. The cargoes carried for the Department of Defense under berth terms create additional port charges, particularly those related to unloading, but they generate no foreign-exchange revenues.

9. Revenues from commercial and government sponsored non-defense cargoes (U.S. imports)—These are payments made by U.S. persons or entities for transportation services provided by U.S.-operated vessels.

10. Passenger revenues from U.S. citizens—All fares paid by U.S. citizens to U.S.-operated vessels are included in this category.

11. Department of Defense payments for shipping contract and berth terms—Both of these headings generally refer to shipments effected for the Department of Defense involving less than full shiploads. Under shipping contract terms the space will have been previously contracted, usually at specially negotiated tariffs; under berth terms DOD cargo is shipped much like any other commercial cargo.

12. DOD payments for time and voyage charters—Both terms relate to payments made by the Department of Defense to owners of U.S. registered vessels for charter rights. Time charters cover stated periods of time and voyage charters generally cover individual crossings.

13. DOD payments for other services—The components of this category are general agency agreements and contract operations. A general agency agreement is an accord between the Military Sea Transportation Service (MSTS) and a merchant shipping company, under which the company agrees to man a government-owned vessel for a stated period of time in exchange for a fee. A contract operation is basically similar but refers to Navy Department tankers rather than dry-cargo vessels. In both instances, it is assumed that U.S. ship operators provide services which Department of Defense would otherwise have to purchase from foreigners in periods of emergency. These are the only periods in which substantial expenditures of this kind are made.

14. Estimated domestic port charges paid on non-defense carrying—This is an estimate of the port charges that would be received by the U.S. from foreign ship operators if the non-defense freight and passenger services currently provided by U.S. vessels were provided by foreign vessels. In this respect it reflects again the fact that transferring revenues from ships operated by one country to ships operated by another creates an impact on their respective balances of payments only to the extent of the portion of that revenue pertaining to the ship and the services it provides.

15. Estimated DOD port charges—These port charges are estimated separately because, according to MSTS, most cargo shipped under Department of Defense bills of lading is carried on an FIO (free in and out) basis. Since the Department of Defense thus undertakes nearly all cargo handling, the port charges associated with these shipments are considerably lower than in normal cargo shipments and represent a lower percentage of revenue.

The Method and the Role of Port Charges

Gross revenues received by U.S. vessels from both foreign and U.S. sources are not the proper measure of balance of payments impact. Only the portion of gross revenues affected by the transfer determine impact; that portion may be termed vessel revenue, that is, the revenue relating to the ship and its services. Thus $B = VR$, where B = impact; VR = vessel revenue.

Accurate measurement of vessel revenue is critical because if vessel revenue is a small percentage of gross shipping revenues, a shift of cargo from a U.S. vessel to a foreign-flag vessel would entail a slight loss to the U.S. balance of payments in terms of the gross revenues involved. On the other hand, if vessel revenue is a relatively large percentage of revenues, such a shift to foreign-flag vessels will result in a large share of gross revenues showing up as a loss to the balance of payments.

Because vessel revenue is not a reported figure, we have expressed the calculation of impact as

$$B = R - (PC_a + PC_{us})$$

B	=	balance of payments impact
R	=	gross shipping revenue
PC_a	=	port charges payable abroad
PC_{us}	=	port charges payable in the U.S.

However, not all port charges are reported, so that estimates are required. We have employed a highly detailed estimating procedure designed to produce the most reliable estimate of port charges.

Calculation of Port Charges

All of the port charge totals of U.S. vessels required for a quantification of balance of payments impact are not reported by the Office of Business Economics. On non-defense carrying, data is available on port charges paid abroad but *not* on port charges paid in the U.S. On defense carrying, only a small portion of total port charges are reported at all. Therefore, a need exists for careful calculation of total port charges.

Definition of Port Charges

The definitive description of the elements included in port charges is the one provided to ocean carriers and according to which they report this information. This definition is given under "Special Instructions" in Department of Commerce form BE-30.[3] It is:

. . . all expenses in foreign countries, such as fuel, stores, repairs, stevedoring, harbor fees, agents' commissions, and so forth, in connection with both passenger and freight operations whether inbound, outbound, or on voyages between foreign ports. Include advances incurred in foreign countries but paid for in the United States, that is, fuel laden abroad for which payment is made to oil companies in the United States . . . Include foreign expenses incurred by respondent for own account on cargoes carried for U.S. Department of Defense responsibility. Do not include hull and machinery protection and indemnity and other insurance premiums paid to foreign insurers directly or through his domestic agents . . . If a vessel is chartered from a U.S. resident, expenses abroad paid directly by respondent should be included in this item. The U.S. resident from whom the vessel is chartered should report separately expenses incurred abroad which are paid directly by him.

Maritime Administration Position Paper

In November 1966, Dr. Peter Schumaier, a distinguished economist then in the Office of Program Planning of the Maritime Administration, prepared an estimating procedure for Maritime Administration calculation of the percentages of revenues paid out in port charges.[4] As his basic sources of information Dr. Schumaier employed the Ernst and Ernst study,[5] the reports of costs submitted by the subsidized lines for 1965 on the Administration's MA-172 forms[6] and the summary reports provided to him by the Office of Business Economics.[7] Among the conclusions he reaches are the following:

i) The percentage of port charges to gross revenues is higher on short hauls than on long hauls. He states, "The evidence from this source [the Ernst and Ernst study] indicates that about half of liner ocean freight costs are associated with the ship and the other half with the loading and unloading functions in the port.[8]

ii) The MA-172 reports reveal that for the subsidized lines the percentages of freight revenues and passenger revenues paid out in port charges is roughly equal.

iii) The MA-172 reports indicate that in 1965 the fourteen subsidized lines realized aggregate revenues of $699 million and paid out $296 million in voyage expense (another term for port charges).[9] He points out, however, that the reporting lines carry large volumes of Department of Defense cargo. "When account is taken of MSTS shipments," he comments, "the percentage of voyage costs to commercial revenue would be much higher than the 42 percent of *all* voyage costs to all revenue [emphasis supplied]."[10]

iv) Cargo expense (stevedoring) accounts for approximately two thirds of total voyage expense (that is, port charges) in liner service according to the MA-172 data.[11]

He concludes his review of the available information by stating, "There is no way to determine the exact breakdown of port expenditures to total ocean freight receipts and payments because of the round voyage character of port expenditures and because MSTS transportation is a non-balance of payments item while port expenditures abroad for unloading MSTS cargo may be a balance of payments item if foreign labor is employed in the unloading."[12]

In order to construct a methodology suitable for estimating percentages of total revenue attributable to total port charges, Dr. Schumaier points out that the operating differential subsidy assumes that port charges will be approximately the same for both U.S. and foreign operators on the same ocean freight earning volume. Based upon this, Dr. Schumaier develops a method for calculating percentage of port charges to revenues. It is:

$$\left(\frac{\text{U.S. Vessel Port Charges Abroad}}{\text{Total U.S. Vessel Non-Defense Trade Revenue}}\right) + \left(\frac{\text{Foreign Vessel Port Charges U.S.}}{\text{Total Foreign Vessel U.S. Trade Revenue}}\right) = \begin{array}{l}\% \text{ Total Port} \\ \text{Charges to Total} \\ \text{Revenues}\end{array}$$

By applying this method to data he presents for total shipping services in 1964 and 1965 as well as to data for its three components—liner, tramp, and tanker—he derives the following percentages of port charges to revenues:[13]

	1965	1964
All U.S. services	69%	74%
U.S. Liner service alone	70%	74%
U.S. Tramp service alone	72%	88%
U.S. Tanker service alone	60%	56%

As a result of this analysis, Dr. Schumaier concludes his paper with the following comment: "On the basis of the Balance of Payments Division figures, it is recommended that we assume a 30 percent [of revenues] net gain in balance of payments from using U.S. versus foreign flag ships . . ."[14]

Analysis of Position Paper and Conclusions

Detailed review of both the methodology devised in the Maritime Administration position paper and the calculations it presents have indicated to us that its conclusions are mistaken. This is due to:

i) omission of certain revenue elements;
ii) use of other revenue data that was later revised;
iii) intermixing U.S.- and foreign-flag liner data without recognition of the significant differences in the characteristics of their carrying.

Although the calculations in the Maritime Administration paper present total port charges in both numerators, they omit one component of total revenues against which these port charges have been levied. This is passenger revenue to and from the U.S.

Furthermore, apparently since the calculations in the Maritime Administration position paper were made, the Office of Business Economics has updated both the revenue and port charges data applicable to the United States vessel portion of the calculation. Taking the information for all services published in the 1966 Statistical Abstract of the United States[15] and the OBE estimates[16] for liner service which concord with it, the calculation would appear as it does in Table C-3.

Calculation of Liner Port Charges

Although the totals estimated for port charges attributable to U.S. liner service cannot be verified and may for 1965 be understated,[a] it appears that the inclusion of passenger revenues in Dr. Schumaier's calculations alters significantly the net gain in balance of payments from using U.S. versus foreign flag ships, particularly in the liner segment. Rather than a 30 percent net gain in balance of payments from using U.S. versus foreign-flag ships, the calculation now

---

[a]Liner revenues for 1965 and 1966 are estimated from data provided by the OBE[17] to be approximately the same percentage of total U.S. shipping revenues. In 1966 the port charges paid abroad by U.S. liners is two-thirds of total port charges paid abroad by all U.S. vessels; the data presented by Dr. Schumaier for 1964 shows the same relationship. Liner port charges abroad for 1965, however, as a percentage of total U.S. port charges paid abroad is only slightly above half; if they were two-thirds of total U.S. port charges paid abroad as they were in the preceding and succeeding year, the final percentage calculated for port charges to total revenues would be nearer 60 percent than the 55.3 percent shown.

Table C-3

**Maritime Administration Calculation of
Ocean Freight Revenues and Port Charges
of U.S. and Foreign Ships in U.S. Trade
Including Passenger Revenue and
Updated with Final Published Data and
Final Estimates (Dollars in Millions)**

	All Services		Liner Services	
	1965	*1964*	*1965*	*1964*
Revenues U.S. Operators:				
U.S. Exports	519	599	393	488
U.S. Imports	375	380	215	230
Foreign-to-Foreign	152	158	53	66
Passenger	80	103	80	103
Total	1,126	1,240	741	887
Port Charges Abroad	281	317	150*	204*
% Port Charges to Revenue	25.0	25.6	20.2	23.0
Revenues Foreign Operators:				
U.S. Exports	1,271	1,242	609	619
U.S. Imports	1,083	958	446	397
Passenger	300	305	300	305
Total	2,654	2,505	1,355	1,321
Port Charges U.S.	1,032	956	475	455
% Port Charges to Revenue	38.9	38.2	35.1	34.4
% Port Charges to Total Revenues	63.9	63.8	55.3	57.4

*Estimates provided by OBE to Maritime
Administration; impossible to determine if
should be updated or not due to changes in
personnel and methods. Liner share of total
U.S. port expenditures in 1966 is two-thirds.

reveals more than 35 percent gain for all services and approximately 45 percent gain in the liner service.

A more significant source of error is the fact that the Maritime Administration methodology treats foreign shipping operations statistically as if they were entirely comparable to U.S. shipping operations in the percentage of their revenues paid out in port charges. Reference to the value-tonnage reports issued annually by the Maritime Administration[18] indicates they are not.

Two factors stand out prominently in this report. First, liner carrying represents a much greater share of total cargo value carried by U.S. vessels than by foreign-flag vessels. Second, the average value per ton of cargo carried in U.S. liners is considerably higher than that of cargo carried in foreign-flag liners, more than 50 percent higher in 1966. Both factors can be expected to affect the level of port charges to total revenues.

Ocean freight rate making at times is an involved process involving a number of different factors. Nevertheless, it is generally observable that break-bulk cargo tariffs in liner service are based to a greater extent on the *value* of a commodity than dry or liquid bulk tariffs are. In other words, if there are two commodities of equal tonnage or cubage, the more valuable of the two is likely to carry a higher rate. Cargo handling, however, as Dr. Schumaier observed, accounts for approximately two-thirds of total port charges in liner service. Also, cargo handling costs relate principally to the weight or cubage of the cargo rather than to its value.

This leads to the logical conclusion that a liner carrying higher value cargo will pay out a lower percentage of its revenues in port charges than a liner carrying cargo of inferior value per ton. When the differential in value per ton is great, as it is here, the difference in the percentage of port charges to revenue will also be great.

Supporting this conclusion is the fact cited in the Maritime Administration paper that the MA-172 reports submitted by the subsidized U.S. lines in 1965 reveal voyage expense (that is, port charges) totalling only 42.3 percent of revenues.[19] Nevertheless, the contention is valid that this percentage is artificially low because of the influence of FIO Department of Defense cargo carried by U.S. liners.

In order to calculate the percentage applicable to the non-FIO cargo, we assume that the 42.3 percent reported by the subsidized U.S. operators is equally applicable to the non-subsidized liner operators who produce between 35 and 40 percent of total U.S. liner revenues. Although no comparable reporting by non-subsidized liner operators is available, there appears to be no vast difference between the efficiency of their operations and those of the subsidized liners, at least as measured by profit retained from revenues. In the combined condensed income accounts published by the Maritime Administration for 1965,[20] the subsidized lines showed a net profit before taxes from shipping operations of 6.6 percent compared to 5.2 percent for the non-subsidized lines.

Table C-4

**Value per Ton in Dollars of U.S.
Exports and Imports Carried by
U.S.-Flag and Foreign-Flag Vessels
(Dollars in Millions)**

	1966	1965	1964
Liner Service			
U.S.-Flag	655	553	493
Foreign-Flag	431	418	396
Nonliner Service			
U.S.-Flag	44	51	52
Foreign-Flag	40	38	36
Tanker Service			
U.S.-Flag	34	37	37
Foreign-Flag	23	24	22
Liner % of Total Value			
U.S.-Flag	91.4%	89.9%	90.3%
Foreign-Flag	60.1%	64.3%	64.3%

The calculation we have employed to estimate the percentage of non-FIO cargo revenue consumed by port charges is illustrated in Table 5. It indicates that by removing the influence of the FIO cargo revenue for 1965, we find that port charges account for approximately 47 percent of non-FIO gross revenues. Similar calculations based upon 1966 data also indicate that U.S. liners pay out no more than 50 percent of their non-FIO cargo revenues in port charges.

A further general confirmation of this level of port charges to revenues for U.S. liner service may be drawn from the Ernst and Ernst study. One of its basic conclusions is that, "Typically from 60 to over 85 percent of unit shipping cost is incurred in port (cargo handling, port costs, vessel costs) with costs in

Table C-5

Calculation of Ratio of U.S. Liner Port
Charges to Revenue for Non-FIO Cargoes

1965 Data (Dollars in Millions)

Freight Revenue Outbound	393
Foreign-to-Foreign Revenue	53
Passenger Revenue	80
Freight Revenue Inbound	215
Department of Defense – Shipping Contract and Berth Terms	202*
Department of Defense – Time and Voyage Charters	33†
Department of Defense – Other	2
Total Revenue	978
Voyage Cost (Port Charges) – 42.3% of Total Revenue	414
FIO Cargo Revenue	184‡
Non-Voyage Cost Revenue	2
Normal Cargo Revenue	792

x = % Port Charges of Non-FIO Revenue

y = Estimated revenue on FIO cargo if it *had* included factor for cost of cargo handling.§

$$y - y\left(\frac{2x}{3}\right) = 184$$

$$y\left(\frac{x}{3}\right) + 792x = 414$$
$$x = 46.96\%$$
$$y = 268.9$$

*According to detailed Maritime Administration studies for 1964 confirmed orally by MSTS, *all* shipping contract and berth terms revenues are for liner service.

† Division of charter revenue among different types of services is not normally reported by MSTS; quarterly reports list only number of dry cargo and tanker vessels chartered. Figure is 1965 extrapolation drawn from data in Maritime Administration study of 1964 operations and tested for other years.

‡ According to MSTS and confirmed by Marad study of 1964 operations, approximately 75 percent of revenue under shipping contract and berth terms is shipping contract (FIO) and all cargo usually handled on chartered vessels is FIO.

§This assumes that MSTS will not pay the same tariff for shipping a cargo that it loads and unloads as it would if the vessel undertook these tasks; it also assumes that MSTS would be likely to negotiate rates that would be reduced by the value of cargo handling which both the reports of the subsidized carriers and the Ernst and Ernst study shows as two-thirds of port charges; 184, then, the actual revenue paid by MSTS on FIO cargo, would be theoretically calculated by letting "y" represent revenues including cargo handling and subtracting $y\left(\frac{2}{3}\right)(x)$, "x" being normal percentage of port charges to revenue.

U.S. ports two to three times greater than those in foreign ports."[21] The term "cost incurred in port" is meant to include port charges plus vessel cost (wages, insurance, repairs, stores consumed in port, fuel consumed in port and depreciation). The data presented in Table C-6 shows Ernst and Ernst estimates of *vessel* cost per day in port for different types of U.S. liner vessels and average port charges for the same vessels during visits to various ports.[22] The sum of vessel cost per day in port and port charges would be "cost incurred in port."

Assuming the *highest* percentage of cost set forth by Ernst and Ernst for "cost incurred in port"—85 percent—and the lower vessel cost per day in port for each vessel type as well as the costliest port shown for each type, port charges as a percentage of total cost are never far above 50 percent except for the C2 vessels. Employing any combination of data *other than the most adverse* set forth by Ernst and Ernst, the percentage of total cost paid out as port charges is well below 50 percent.

We therefore conclude that carrying of non-FIO cargo in the U.S. liner service produces a *50 cent* net gain in balance of payments for each dollar of revenue received.

Calculation of U.S. Operated Nonliner Port Charges

As we have demonstrated, the methodology employed by the Maritime Administration for calculating the relationship between port charges and revenues is not appropriate to U.S. liner operations. Nevertheless, it has a great deal of logical validity when applied to nonliner service for the following reasons:

i) In bulk carrying, commodity value has little if any influence on tariffs charged.
ii) Although U.S.-flag nonliners receive preferentially high revenues on most of the government sponsored cargoes they carry, the majority of the non-liners under U.S. operation are chartered foreign-flag vessels which realize their revenues at international tariff levels. According to the Maritime Administration, those chartered vessels alone that are under effective U.S. control carried approximately five times as much U.S. bulk cargo imports and exports as U.S.-flag vessels in 1960 and 1963.[23]
iii) In some of the preference rate carrying done by U.S.-flag nonliners, the difference between international rates and the preference rates are paid to the vessel operators as differentials and these differentials do not appear as revenues in balance of payments reports. This is true of carrying under Titles I and IV of Public Law 480.

Although little detailed information is available on the subject, it is very likely that the relationships between port charges and revenues in nonliner service will be quite different from liner service. Cargo handling, for example, should represent a lower proportion of total port charges because of the nature

Table C-6

**Comparison of U.S.-Flag Liners Vessel
Cost Per Day in Port and Typical Port
Charges Per Visit**

	C2	Old C3	New C3	New C4
	Trade Routes 5-7-8-9	*Trade Route 24*	*Trade Route 12*	*(Mariner) Trade Route 29*
Vessel Cost/Day in Port With Subsidy	$1,690	$2,139	$3,098	$3,777
Vessel Cost/Day in Port– No Subsidy	3,149	3,659	5,572	7,632
Port Charges:				
New York	5,718		5,766	
Philiadelphia	2,866		3,467	
Baltimore	2,003		2,059	
Bremen	2,187			
Hamburg	2,799			3,152
Los Angeles		3,799		4,682
San Francisco		4,334		
Santos		1,352	1,315	
Montevideo		786	1,162	
Buenos Aires		2,059	2,575	
Manila				1,073
Hong Kong				600
Kobe				1,630
Yokohama				1,412

of the highly mechanized equipment employed with bulk commodities. Furthermore, a large part of the carrying by U.S.-operated nonliners—both U.S.-flag vessels and foreign-flag chartered vessels—is one way carrying. Most U.S.-flag bulk carriers are loaded on only the outbound leg because of their dependence on preference cargo and because nearly all of this is outbound cargo. The foreign-flag bulk carriers under charter to U.S. operators make most of *their* outbound sailings in ballast. According to the Maritime Administration, 92 percent of these vessels (or at least of those considered to be under effective U.S. control) sail loaded only inbound.[24] Estimates of the percentage of port charges to revenues on non-defense carrying in U.S. trade for nonliners are calculated in Table C-7 by subtracting liner service data from the all service data in Table C-3 on page 228.

It appears that in the carrying of non-FIO cargo the nonliners under U.S. operation—including U.S.-flag nonliners and chartered foreign-flag vessels—produce a *25 cent* gain in balance of payments for each dollar of revenue received. In the case of the chartered foreign-flag vessels, their balance of payments contribution must be reduced by the payments of charter fees to the foreign ship owners.

It should be pointed out, however, that this estimate is not as well documented as our liner estimate and is thus not so precise. Data provided by the Office of Business Economics for nonliner revenues and port charges is extrapolated from fairly limited reporting. If, for example, the revenues or revenue benefits provided by foreign flag nonliners chartered to U.S. operators were greatly underestimated in OBE data, the real balance of payments gain would be somewhat *higher* than 25 cents. On the other hand, the use of some preference revenues in making the calculation tends to inflate slightly the estimate of balance of payments gain per dollar of revenue.

Calculation of Total U.S.-Operated
Fleet Port Charges

In order to calculate port charge to revenue ratio for *total* U.S. operated merchant shipping service, the two previously calculated ratios can be applied to all *non-Department of Defense* revenues for the past three years as we have done in Table C-8.

We therefore assume that for total U.S. operated merchant shipping service there is a balance of payments gain of 42 cents for each dollar of non-FIO revenue received.

Estimated Port Charges on Department
of Defense FIO Carrying

The Department of Defense operating through the Military Sea Transportation Service (MSTS) assumes cargo handling responsibility for most defense shipments effected on U.S. vessels and pays rates that have been scaled downward

Table C-7

**Calculation of Port Charges as a
Percentage of Non-Defense Revenues
of U.S. and Foreign Nonliners in the
U.S. Trade (Dollars in Millions)**

	1965	1964
Revenues U.S. Operators:		
U.S. Exports	126	111
U.S. Imports	160	150
Foreign-to-Foreign	99	92
Passenger	–	–
Total	385	353
Port Charges Abroad	131	113
% Port Charges to Revenue	34.0	32.0
Revenues Foreign Operators:		
U.S. Exports	662	623
U.S. Imports	637	561
Passenger	–	–
Total	1,299	1,184
Port Charges U.S.	557	501
% Port Charges to Revenue	42.9	42.3
% Port Charges to Total Revenues	76.9	74.3

accordingly. In liner service, cargo handling represents approximately two-thirds of port charges. Removing that component lowers the ratio of port charges to revenue and concurrently increases the percentage of total FIO (free in and out) revenue contributed to the balance of payments. This is demonstrated in Table C-9. We therefore conclude that in carrying FIO cargo for the Department of Defense, U.S. liner service produces a *75 cent* net gain in balance of payments for each dollar of revenue received.

Similar calculations for U.S. nonliner carrying of FIO cargo show a *50 cent* net gain in balance of payments for each dollar of revenue received. However, if cargo handling of bulk cargoes does represent appreciably less than two-thirds of total port charges, the balance of payments gain may be somewhat less. For example, if cargo handling accounted for half of bulk cargo port charges instead of two-thirds, the gain in balance of payments would be 40 rather than 50 cents.

Table C-8

**Calculation of Estimated Percentage of
Port Charges to Revenues:
All U.S. Operated Shipping Services
(Dollars in Millions)**

	1966	1965	1964
U.S.-Operated Liner			
Revenues – Export	490	454	565
– Import	368	287	322
Total	858	741	887
Estimated Port Charges (50%)	429	371	444
U.S.-Operated Nonliner			
Revenues – Export	201	225	203
– Import	200	160	150
Total	401	385	353
Estimated Port Charges (75%)	301	289	265
Total Revenue	1,259	1,126	1,240
Total Port Charges	730	660	709
% Total Port Charges to Total Revenue	58.0%	58.6%	57.0%

Table C-9

**Example Calculation of Balance of
Payments Gain in Liner Carrying of
Defense FIO Cargoes**

I.   Gross revenue, non-DOD, including cargo handling costs = 100

II. Port charges associated with above revenue (estimated 50%) = 50

III. Cargo handling charges (estimated $2/3$ of II) = 33

IV. FIO revenue, which is gross revenue less cargo handling (I-III) = 67

V.   FIO port charges, which are normal port charges less cargo handling (II-III) = 17

VI. FIO balance of payments impact as percent of FIO revenue $(1.00 - V/IV)$ = 75%

Analysis of Impact

This section, containing detailed calculations of the balance of payments impact of U.S. merchant shipping services, presents a series of four different estimates:

i) All U.S.-operated shipping services—including chartered vessels—for the ten year period 1957-1966, compared with foreign-owned and -operated shipping;

ii) U.S. liner services for the three-year period 1964-1966, compared with foreign-owned and -operated liners;

iii) U.S. nonliner services for the three-year period 1964-1966, compared with foreign-owned and -operated nonliners;

iv) All U.S.-*flag* shipping services—liner and nonliner—for the three-year period 1964-1966, compared with foreign-owned and -operated services.

Also included are estimates of the extent to which the impacts calculated would differ if comparison were made with *chartered* vessels rather than *foreign operated* vessels.

The section also offers some general observations on the relationship of balance of payments impact to sums expended on national support programs.

Calculation of Balance of Payments Impact

All U.S.-Operated Shipping Services

Table C-10 presents a summary of the calculations employed in deriving the balance of payments impact of U.S. operated merchant shipping services—including U.S.-flag vessels and chartered foreign-flag vessels—for the period 1957-1966.

Included in the totals listed for Estimated Foreign and Domestic DOD Port Charges is an amount relating to time and voyage charters. By including a factor for estimated port charges relating to these Department of Defense time and voyage charters, we assume that the charter fees are roughly equivalent to the cost of contracting cargo space aboard the same vessels. This assumption may err in either of two directions. The Department of Defense may use the vessels very intensively and thus obtain a greater amount of carrying than it would by spending the same amount of money for cargo space under shipping contract. On the other hand, it may employ the vessels relatively unintensively for strategic purposes and thus obtain less cargo carrying than it would by investing the same funds in shipping contracts. Nevertheless, for the purpose of this study it seems more appropriate to make the assumption that charter fees are indeed roughly

238

Table C-10

Balance of Payments Impact of U.S. Merchant Shipping Operations, All Services: 1957-1966 (Dollars in Millions)

Item	1966	1965	1964	1963	1962	1961	1960	1959	1958	1957
Foreign Exchange Contribution	157	172	220	188	221	175	250	222	253	495
Gross Revenue	702	688	777	711	676	596	591	526	591	862
Export Freight Receipts	542	519	599	538	479	424	428	359	429	639
AID Cargoes	89	88	91	83	67	47	43	53	49	56
P. L. 480 Cargoes	84	148	159	136	122	110	79	68	68	78
Commercial Cargoes and Other Gov't Sponsored	369	283	349	319	290	267	306	238	312	505
Freight Between Foreign Countries	139	152	158	154	177	155	136	140	130	179
Passenger Fares – Foreign Citizens	10	8	11	10	10	9	19	20	24	24
Charter Fees Received	11	9	9	9	10	8	8	7	8	20
Less Port Charges Abroad (non-DOD)	294	281	317	288	260	231	167	155	170	203
Less Charter Fees Paid	251	235	240	235	195	190	174	149	168	164
Dollar Retention Contribution	779	405	395	380	354	291	258	330	304	194
Gross Revenue	1,215	777	797	756	725	616	679	732	718	751
Non-DOD	568	447	472	442	422	370	430	443	424	469
Import Freight Receipts	500	375	380	340	339	290	346	358	336	391
Passenger Fares – U.S. Citizens	68	72	92	102	83	80	84	85	88	78
DOD*	647	330	325	314	303	246	249	289	294	282
Shipping Contract and Berth Terms	262	202	205	203	189	153	163	180	175	178
Time and Voyage Charters	261	90	89	83	84	62	54	63	42	37
Other	124	38	31	28	30	31	32	46	77	67
Less Estimated Domestic Port Charges (non-DOD)	436	372	402	376	371	325	421	402	414	557
Less Estimated Foreign and Domestic DOD Port Charges	163	91	92	89	85	67	68 / 137†	76 / 131†	68 / 136†	67 / 172†
Total Balance of Payments Impact	773	486	523	479	490	399	577	607	625	794

*Fiscal-year data.

† Adjustment for lower level of port charges 1957-1960.

Notes To Table C-10

1. Commercial Cargoes and Other Government Sponsored—This total is calculated by taking the balance of payments amount for export freight revenues and subtracting revenues from AID and P.L. 480 cargoes. The last year for which data was published on "other government" (principally Export-Import Bank and Post Office carrying) was 1964[1] when it represented approximately 18 percent of the total amount recorded in this line.
2. Import Freight Receipts—These are estimates compiled by the Office of Business Economics and, until 1960, published in its Balance of Payments Statistical Supplement. In 1964 approximately 3 percent were nondefense government sponsored cargoes.[2]
3. Passenger Fares, U.S. Citizens—These are estimates prepared by the Office of Business Economics which have been reduced here by the amounts reported by MSTS for military passenger service which is reported by it under "Shipping Contract and Berth Terms."
4. Shipping Contract and Berth Terms—Of these amounts, the MSTS reports that approximately 25 percent are berth terms (generally handled FAS) and 75 percent are under shipping contract (generally handled FIO). These percentages correspond also to the detailed analysis of defense shipping made by the Maritime Administration for fiscal 1964.
5. Time and Voyage Charters—According to MSTS, cargo shipped on chartered vessels is almost invariably handled on an FIO basis.
6. Estimated Port Expenditures in the U.S. on Nondefense Cargo—This figure is an estimate of the port charges paid by U.S. operated vessels in U.S. ports. It is derived by applying 58 percent (see previous section) to all nondefense revenues and then subtracting from the product the amount of port charges paid abroad (a published balance of payments item).
7. Estimated Port Expenditures on Department of Defense Cargo—If these shipping services were performed by foreign vessels, the U.S. balance of payments retention would suffer. It would not suffer by the gross revenues lost but rather by a smaller amount. This amount would be the difference between these revenues and the total port charges that would be paid by these foreign vessels to U.S. ports *plus* savings of port charges currently paid to foreign ports by the U.S. vessels doing this hauling. The following factors shape the way in which this estimate is calculated:

   —according to MSTS and the Maritime Administration[3] all of the shipping contract and berth terms revenue is paid out to liner operators;
   —according to the same sources, 25 percent of the total is under berth terms;
   —the remaining 75 percent of the revenues are under shipping contract in which the usual terms are FIO;
   —according to the Ernst and Ernst study, roughly two-thirds of port charges are associated with cargo handling; on Department of Defense FIO shipments the vessel has no cargo handling responsibility.

   The estimate, then, is derived by totalling the following elements:

   (i) 25 percent of the amount of shipping contract and berth terms revenue times 50 percent, the percentage of U.S. *liner* revenue paid out in total port charges;
   (ii) 75 percent of the amount of shipping contract and berth terms revenue times 25 percent (see comments in previous section) to approximate the percentage of U.S. *liner* revenue paid out in port charges on FIO carrying;

(iii) total time and voyage charter revenue times 31.4 percent to approximate the percentage of *all* U.S. shipping services revenues paid out in port charges on FIO carrying.[a]

It should be pointed out that the way in which the Office of Business Economics collects and reports port charges has obliged us to introduce a relationship in our own Tables 10, 12, and 13 that is somewhat deceptive as to the proportion of these port charges that are paid abroad and in the United States. U.S. vessels undertaking carrying for the Department of Defense must include the port charges abroad associated with this carrying among all other port charges paid abroad. Therefore, the amounts published by the OBE for port charges abroad and which we show in our tables as "Port Charges Abroad (non-DOD)" actually do include some port charges related to DOD carrying. Although the *total* of our "Port Charges Abroad (non-DOD)" and "Estimated Domestic Port Charges (non-DOD)" represents an accurate estimate of non-DOD port charges, the distribution of the charges between those paid abroad and those paid in the U.S. is likely to be incorrect. In truth, the amounts paid abroad on non-DOD carrying are probably lower and the amounts paid in the U.S. are correspondingly higher.

Supplement To Table C-10

The total balance of payments impact for the ten-year period 1957-1966, derived by summing the annual impacts presented in Table 10, amounts to approximately $6 billion. However, Table 10 does not reflect any adjustments in the calculations for the fact that the operations of foreign flag nonliner vessels under charter to U.S. operators were included. As the detailed discussion on pages 49 to 51 points out, the balance of payments impact of the foreign flag vessels under charter to U.S. operators would appear to be negative; this indicates that transferring chartered operations to foreign flag, foreign operated vessels would *improve* the U.S. balance of payments. This illogical result is believed to be more apparent than real, and probably stems from incomplete or erroneous reporting of charter fees and/or the revenue benefits associated with charter operations. Accordingly, we have estimated the impact of U.S. merchant shipping operations exclusive of such charters, that is, the impact of an entirely U.S. *flag* fleet for the years 1957-1966.

The following table summarizes our estimate of the balance of payments impact of the U.S. flag fleet. It incorporates the appropriate adjustments to eliminate the effect of the U.S. operated foreign flag vessels. The adjustments were determined as follows:

(i) *For the years 1964-1966* an increase in impact of $0.4 billion as calculated in Table 15, based on sufficient data available for that period to permit segregating the effect of the charter vessels;

(ii) *For the years 1957-1963* an increase in impact of $1.1 billion, derived from regression analysis. Statistical analysis indicated that this is as precise an estimate as can be made with the limited data available for the earlier period.

The total balance of payments impact of a U.S. flag fleet is therefore estimated to be approximately $7.3 billion.

---

[a]$1 = normal tariff including cargo handling

$1 - (2/3) (.58) =$ normal tariff discounted by value of cargo handling $= .614$

$\dfrac{.58 \, (1/3)}{.614} =$ one third of normal port charge applied to the discounted tariff $= 31.4\%$

Table C-10 (Adjusted)

**Estimated Balance of Payments Impact
of U.S.-Flag Merchant Shipping: 1957-
1966 (Dollars in Millions)**

	1966	1965	1964	1963	1962
I. U.S.-Operated Fleet (U.S.-flag vessels and chartered foreign vessels)	773	486	523	479	490
II. Adjustment to eliminate chartered foreign vessels	141	146	157	152	169
III. U.S.-Flag Fleet	914	632	680	631	659

	1961	1960	1959	1958	1957
I. U.S.-Operated Fleet (U.S.-flag vessels and chartered foreign vessels)	399	577	607	625	794
II. Adjustment to eliminate chartered foreign vessels	152	138	141	133	171
III. U.S.-Flag Fleet	551	715	748	758	965

equivalent to the cost of contracting space on the same vessels.

Another element that appears to merit analysis is the sharp increase in the percentages of revenues paid out in port charges after 1960, both in the U.S. and abroad. These are summarized in Table C-11.

These sharp differences may be attributable to changes in reporting methods and/or to actual cost structure changes. Nevertheless, they indicate that assuming 58 percent of revenues for port charges during the period 1957-1960 would seem to be unreasonably high. In order to calculate an adjustment, it can be observed from Table C-10 that over the past three years approximately 40 percent of the estimated port charges paid by U.S. operated vessels were in foreign ports and 60 percent in U.S. ports. During the period 1957-1960 the port charges paid by U.S. operated vessels abroad represented one-third less of their revenue than after 1960; during the same period, the percentage of revenue paid by foreign vessels to U.S. ports was about 10 percent less than in succeeding years and this same percentage is probably equally applicable to U.S. vessels in U.S. ports. Applying these to the aforementioned approximate division of port charges—60 percent in the U.S. and 40 percent abroad—it appears that 46 percent of revenues for port charges would be a more reasonable estimate for these years than 58 percent.

The special adjusting entries recorded in Table C-10 were calculated by employing 46 percent as the base percentage and recalculating estimated port charges for both nondefense and defense carrying.

From our analysis we conclude that if all of the merchant shipping services performed by vessels under U.S. operation had been performed by foreign operators of foreign flag vessels, the transportation sector of the U.S. balance of payments would have sustained a loss of approximately $6 billion over the ten-year period. A loss of such magnitude in the balance of payments would have caused severe economic repercussions even if it had stimulated some additional demand for U.S. goods or other U.S. services. If any substantial portion of the loss had been converted to additional demand for gold it might have led to any of the restrictive measures previously described.

U.S. Liner Services

In the years prior to 1964 insufficient data precludes any possibility of refining the balance of payments impact calculations by type of service. Commencing in that year, however, changes in reporting procedures permit calculation to be made of impact by type of service. This is particularly valuable for liner service in that it is a service in which chartering is a negligible factor. Therefore, the estimates of balance of payments impact of U.S.-operated liner service closely approach being estimates of the impact of an entirely U.S.-registered and -manned service.

The calculations for U.S. operated liner service for 1964 to 1966 are presented in Table C-12.

Over the three-year period analyzed, U.S.-operated liner service generated a balance of payments impact of nearly $1.9 billion.

U.S.-Operated Nonliner Service, 1964-1966

The balance of payments impact calculations for U.S.-operated nonliner shipping (U.S.-flag vessels and chartered foreign-flag vessels) for 1964 to 1966 are presented in Table C-13.

The apparent negative impact of nonliner service requires further analysis. The two major components of this service are:

i) U.S.-registered vessels which depend heavily on government-sponsored cargo for their revenues;
ii) Foreign-flag vessels chartered to U.S. operators which do not carry government-sponsored cargo.

The first component — U.S.-flag vessels carrying principally government-sponsored cargo—exerts a positive impact. Only if gross revenues did not equal or exceed port charges could it exert a negative impact. According to Maritime Administration reports, operators of U.S.-flag nonliners earn a profit; this indicates that revenues cover all costs, including port charges. Therefore, by applying the finding that all nonliners provide 25 cents of positive balance of payments impact for each dollar of nondefense revenue and an estimated 50 cents for each dollar of defense revenue, and attributing *only* the government sponsored nonliner revenue to the U.S.-flag nonliners, we derive the U.S.-flag nonliner estimate shown in Table C-14.

The derived negative impact of chartered nonliners implies that U.S. operators of chartered vessels pay out more in charter fees and port charges than they recover in revenue benefits from the vessels they operate. This is unlikely. We cannot identify the specific causes of this paradox due to the limitations in reporting by the operators.

U.S.-Flag Services, 1964-1966

If we attribute *only* the government sponsored nonliner carrying to the U.S.-flag nonliner service, the balance of payments impact for an entirely U.S.-flag fleet (citizen-owned, -operated, and -manned) for 1964-1966 would be that presented in Table C-15.

As is readily apparent, the balance of payments impact of the entirely U.S.-flag fleet is approximately 25 percent higher than that of the mixed fleet.

Table C-11

Percentages of Revenues Paid Out as
Port Charges: 1957-1966
(Dollars in Millions)

	U.S. Operators Non-Defense Revenues	Port Charges Abroad	Port Charges as Percent of Revenues
1966	1,259	294	23.4
1965	1,126	281	25.0
1964	1,240	317	25.6
1963	1,144	288	25.2
1962	1,088	260	23.9
1961	958	231	24.1
1960	1,013	167	16.5
1959	962	155	16.1
1958	1,007	170	16.9
1957	1,311	203	15.5

	Foreign Operators U.S. Trade Revenues	Port Charges U.S.	Port Charges as Percent of Revenues
1965	2,654	1,032	38.9
1964	2,505	956	38.2
1960	2,145	746	34.8
1959	2,032	698	34.3
1958	2,027	726	35.8
1957	2,423	798	32.9

Note: In the foreign operators tabulations, the years 1966, 1963, 1962, and 1961 have been omitted because of incomplete data.

Source: *Statistical Abstract of the United States.*

Table C-12

**Balance of Payments Impact of U.S.
Merchant Shipping Operations, Liner
Services: 1964-1966 (Dollars in Millions)**

Item	1966	1965	1964
Foreign Exchange Contribution	281	294	352
Gross Revenue	490	454	565
Export Freight Receipts	422	393	488
AID Cargoes	77	73	78
P. L. 480 Cargoes	39	57	79
Commercial Cargoes and Other Gov't Sponsored	306	263	331
Freight Between Foreign Countries	58	53	66
Passenger Fares – Foreign Citizens	10	8	11
Charter Fees Received	–	–	–
Less Port Charges Abroad (non-DOD)	196	150	204
Less Charter Fees Paid	13	10	9
Dollar Retention Contribution	619	303	305
Gross Revenue	852	524	545
Non-DOD	368	287	322
Import Freight Receipts	300	215	230
Passenger Fares – U.S. Citizens	68	72	92
DOD*	484	237	223
Shipping Contract and Berth Terms	262	202	205
Time and Voyage Charters	139	33	15
Other	83	2	3
Less Estimated Domestic Port Charges (non-DOD)	233	221	240
Less Estimated Foreign and Domestic DOD Port Charges	117	71	68
Total Balance of Payments Impact	783	526	589

*Fiscal-year data.

(continued)

Notes To Table C-12

1. AID Cargoes—In its annual reports AID separates its payments to United States shipping operators by type of service.
2. P.L. 480 Cargoes—The total for 1964 derives from a detailed internal study performed by the Maritime Administration; their total has been expanded slightly on a pro rata basis because their analysis was based upon preliminary statistics rather than the final ones published by the Department of Agriculture. The 1966 figure is an estimate of the Office of Business Economics. The 1965 figure is an estimate prepared by applying the same percentage, Title by Title, reported by the Maritime Administration for liner service in 1964 to 1965.
3. Commercial Cargoes and Other Government Sponsored—This is the difference between total export freight receipts as estimated by the Office of Business Economics and the sum of AID and P.L. 480 revenues.
4. Freight Between Foreign Countries—These are estimates made by the Office of Business Economics.
5. Passenger Fares, Foreign Citizens—This is a published balance of payments item.
6. Charter Payments—These are estimated by the Office of Business Economics.
7. Port Expenditures Abroad—The 1966 figure is an estimate by the Office of Business Economics; the 1965 and 1964 figures are those stated in the study of port charges made by the Office of Program Planning of the Maritime Administration.[4] (Although, as previously mentioned, the 1965 estimate may be too low, our estimate of port expenditures in U.S. ports would compensate to some extent by being too high).
8. Import Freight Receipts—These are estimates made by the Office of Business Economics.
9. Passenger Fares, U.S. Citizens—These are estimates of the Office of Business Economics from which the amounts reported by the MSTS for military passengers have been deducted.
10. Department of Defense Shipping Contract and Berth Terms—MSTS reports that all expenditures of this sort are for liner service, a contention confirmed by the Maritime Administration in its study of 1964 payments.[5]
11. Department of Defense Time and Voyage Charters—MSTS does not separate revenues paid for liner charters and for tanker charters. It does report number of vessels of each type chartered.[6] Factors of approximately $3.3 million per non-liner chartered and approximately $1 million per liner chartered produce totals that correlate closely with actual expenditures over the past six years and these amounts have been adopted.

(continued)

Notes to Table C-12 (*continued*)
Estimate Of Revenues Paid by MSTS
for Liner and Non-Liner Chartering
1961-1966

Fiscal Year	Cargo Vessels Chartered	Tankers Chartered	Theoretical Expenditure ($ Million)	Actual Reported Expenditure ($ Million)
1966	139	38	$264	$261
1965	33	16	86	90
1964	15	20	81	89
1963	15	22	88	83
1962	14	22	87	84
1961	11	16	64	62

Tanker – $3.3 Million
Cargo – 1.0 Million

12. Department of Defense Other—On the basis of information provided by MSTS it is assumed that all general agency agreements for the operation of Reserve Fleet vessels are made with liner operators and that no agreements for contracts operation of naval tankers are made with liner operators.
13. Estimated Port Expenditures—These are calculated in the same way as previously explained for all shipping operations, the only difference being that 50 percent is used as the basis for estimating port charges in U.S. liner service.

Note on the Impact of U.S. Operated
Chartered Vessels

If the available data for the balance of payments impact of U.S.-operated chartered vessels were more complete, it is likely that the operation of these vessels would reflect no more than a minor positive impact. For balance of payments purposes the only long run difference between chartering a foreign-flag vessel and shipping on the same vessel under foreign operation is the amount of operator's profit that would accrue to the charterer. Other sources of impact would have the same effect whether the foreign vessel were chartered or not. The U.S. merchant shipping industry consistently records profits *before taxes* in the range of 5 to 8 percent of revenues; since these percentages include both owner *and* operator profits, the favorable balance of payments impact from operator profit to be expected if the charter data were complete would probably not be substantial.

Table C-13

**Balance of Payments Impact of U.S.
Merchant Shipping Operations,
Nonliner Services: 1964-1966
(Dollars in Millions)**

Item	1966	1965	1964
Foreign Exchange Contribution	(124)	(122)	(132)
Gross Revenue	212	234	212
Export Freight Receipts	120	126	111
AID Cargoes	12	15	13
P. L. 480 Cargoes	45	91	80
Commercial Cargoes and Other Gov't Sponsored	63	20	18
Freight Between Foreign Countries	81	99	92
Passenger Fares – Foreign Citizens	–	–	–
Charter Fees Received	11	9	9
Less Port Charges Abroad (non-DOD)	98	131	113
Less Charter Fees Paid	238	225	231
Dollar Retention Contribution	160	102	90
Gross Revenue	363	253	252
Non-DOD	200	160	150
Import Freight Receipts	200	160	150
Passenger Fares – U.S. Citizens	–	–	–
DOD*	163	93	102
Shipping Contract and Berth Terms	–	–	–
Time and Voyage Charters	122	57	74
Other	41	36	28
Less Estimated Domestic Port Charges (non-DOD)	203	151	162
Less Estimated Foreign and Domestic DOD Port Charges	46	20	24
Total Balance of Payments Impact	(10)	(40)	(66)

*Fiscal-year data.

Table C-14

**Balance of Payments Impact by Types
of Nonliner Service (Dollars in Millions)**

Type of Service	1966	1965	1964
U.S.-Flag Nonliners	131	106	91
U.S.-Chartered Nonliners	(141)	(146)	(157)

Table C-15

**Estimated Balance of Payments Impact
of U.S.-Flag Merchant Fleet: 1964-1966
(Dollars in Millions)**

	1966	1965	1964
U.S.-Flag Liners	783	526	589
U.S.-Flag Nonliners	131	106	91
Total U.S.-Flag Fleet	914	632	680
Total U.S.-Operated Fleet (U.S.-flag vessels and chartered vessels)	773	486	523

Therefore, if we were to measure the loss to the transportation section of the U.S. balance of payments if the service now furnished by the U.S.-flag fleet were performed instead by chartered foreign-flag vessels, this loss would not differ greatly from the loss we have calculated in comparison with foreign-owned and -operated vessels.

Analysis of the Relationship Between Balance of Payments Impact of the Merchant Marine and Government Support: Subsidized U.S. Liner Service and the Operating Differential Subsidy. The operating differential subsidy is designed to serve many purposes, such as strengthening the competitive position of a national merchant marine, promoting U.S. exports, providing employment for U.S. seamen, and assuring sealift capacity for defense needs as well as improving U.S. balance of payments. Thus, any pairing of costs and benefits that does not assess *all* costs and *all* benefits is an analytical tool of limited usefulness. Despite this limitation, frequent comparisons have been made between balance of payments benefit provided by U.S. subsidized liner service and operating differential subsidy costs. Recognizing that such comparisons exist (most of which appeared to have been drawn from faulty data), it may be of some interest to examine the relationship that can be drawn from this study.

During the three years for which estimates have been produced on the balance of payments impact of U.S. *liner* service, the net operating differential subsidies for the same periods were:

	Balance of Payments Impact – All U.S. Liner Service (Dollars in Millions)	Net Operating Differential Subsidy[7] (Dollars in Millions)
1966	783	189.0*
1965	526	190.9
1964	589	207.6

*$94.5 million for 6 months annualized.

To these subsidies should be added any P.L. 480 differentials received by liner operators. These differentials totalled $9 million in 1964 and have been considerably lower in succeeding years. If we take into account the fact that the subsidized liners earn approximately 65 percent of U.S. liner revenues and thus generate approximately 65 percent of liner balance of payments impact, it can be seen that during the three year period studied, the ratio of balance of payments impact to operating differential subsidy varied in the range of 2:1 to 3:1.

Table C-16

**Ratio of Balance of Payments Impact
to Differentials Paid on P. L. 480 (Titles
I and IV) Carryings: 1964**

	Nonsubsidized Liners	Nonliners
I. International Tariff Levels	100	100
II. Differential (not reported as balance of payments revenue)	80	100
III. Port Charges	50 (50% of I)	75 (75% of I)
IV. Balance of Payments Impact (I-III)	50	25
V. Ratio of Impact to Differential (IV:II)	0.675:1	0.25:1

Analysis of the Relationship between Balance of Payments Impact of the Merchant Marine and Government Support: Nonsubsidized U.S. Liners and U.S. Flag Nonliners. For nonsubsidized U.S. liners and U.S. flag nonliners, the preference rates developed for government sponsored carrying represent an important form of support. One typical example is the grain carrying executed under Public Law 480, the Food for Peace program. In 1964, a year for which detailed analyses were prepared of the differentials paid under Titles I and IV of this law, these differentials represented an increment of 80 percent above international rates to nonsubsidized U.S. liners and 100 percent above international rates to U.S. nonliners. As Table C-16 illustrates, when the differential paid is this high and when vessels depend predominantly upon this type of carrying, the balance of payments impact associated with each dollar of support is relatively low considering the magnitude of the subsidy.

Analysis of Proposals to Alter Cargo Preference Regulations. The amount of balance of payments impact attributable to the carrying of government sponsored cargo on U.S. flag vessels during the past three years has been:

	1966	*1965*	*1964*	*Total*
	Dollars in Millions			
U.S.-Flag Liners	452	254	263	969
U.S.-Flag Nonliners	131	106	91	328
Total	583	360	354	1,297

Proposals have been set forth by some that steps be taken to release the shipping capacity—particularly the liner capacity—now being occupied by this government sponsored cargo, if this can be accomplished without balance of payments loss. Should this be done, it is contended that all or part of the released capacity could be dedicated to additional commercial cargo, thus benefiting the *total* U.S. balance of payments (as distinguished from solely the transportation sector). The theoretical effect of this proposal is illustrated in Table C-17.

Since the implementation of such a proposal would largely affect three types of government sponsored carrying — AID, Public Law 480 and Department of Defense — we can best appraise its desirability by analyzing each type of carrying separately.

(1) *Preference carrying of AID cargo* — AID grants and loans generally include amounts to cover transportation of the goods acquired. By regulation, 50 percent of the tonnage must be carried in U.S. flag ships. If the U.S. removed this requirement, it is certain that all of the AID carrying conducted by nonliner vessels would be transferred to foreign flag nonliners because of the lower rates they offer. Even though U.S. liners do not normally receive preference rates but rather carry government sponsored cargo at international liner rates, it is probable that instead of more than 50 percent of the AID tonnage continuing to move on U.S. liners, the percentage would probably fall to the same 22 percent of export liner tonnage currently moved by U.S. liners.

In essence, then, if the U.S. continued to include financing of transportation in its AID grants *without* preference for U.S. vessels, nearly all of the funds granted for transportation would represent a balance of payments loss. Under present regulations, the revenues from the AID cargo carried on U.S. ships becomes a receipt in the transportation sector of the balance of payments. In other words, there is no net balance of payments loss on the revenue received by U.S. ships but rather an internal transfer involving a *payment* for transportation in the government grants account and a compensating *receipt* in the transportation account.

If the recipient countries could entirely finance from their own resources the ocean transportation cost of the AID goods they receive so that no grants for transportation would be needed, the *total* U.S. balance of payments would benefit to the extent of any additional revenues that might be earned from the vacated ship space. This effect was illustrated in Table C-17. However, of the six countries which receive 85 percent of AID cargo by tonnage[8] — Vietnam, India, Korea, Pakistan, Tunisia and Brazil — only Brazil has any substantial merchant fleet, and all of the countries experience severe balance of payments difficulties which make them extremely dependent on foreign aid. The prospect that they might easily be able to finance this carrying without any grants to cover its cost appears unlikely.

If they cannot finance the carrying, a removal of preference would have a strongly negative effect on the U.S. balance of payments.

Table C-17

**Theoretical Effect on Total Balance of
Payments Created by Requiring Aid
Recipients to Finance Transportation**

	Under Present Conditions	Without Additional Commercial Revenue	With Some Additional Commercial Revenue
Foreign Assistance – Goods	(100)	(100)	(100)
Transportation	(10)		
Revenues of U.S. Merchant Marine	10	–	1
Net Balance of Payments	(100)	(100)	(99)

(2) *Preference carrying of Public Law 480 cargo* – Each of the four titles of Public Law 480 deals with ocean freight payments somewhat differently. These are:

– *Title I, Sales for Foreign Currencies:* The Commodity Credit Corporation receives foreign currencies in payment for the export market value of the commodities *and* their ocean transportation cost at international rates. It then arranges for transportation, at least half of which by tonnage must be performed in U.S.-flag vessels. The CCC converts the foreign currencies to dollars, and any differentials between the rates charged by the U.S. vessels and international rates are paid directly by the CCC to the vessel operators. Of the foreign currency acquired under this program, about one quarter is dedicated to direct U.S. uses and the remainder employed for grants, defense subsidies, and loans to the foreign country.[9]

– *Title II, Disaster Relief:* Under this title emergency commodity assistance may be given in cases of famine or other severe emergency and all shipping costs for these commodities is financed by the U.S.[10]

– *Title III, Donations to Needy Persons and Barter:* These distributions are grants and their shipment is financed entirely by the U.S.[11]

– *Title IV, Sales on Long Term Dollar Credits:* The credits provided for the purchase of U.S. Agricultural commodities include applicable ocean transportation costs[12] at international rate levels. The recipient country uses part of its credit to pay the U.S. vessel at international bulk carrying rate levels and, as in Title I, the Commodity Credit Corporation pays the vessel operator a differential for the difference between international rates and the rates charged by U.S. carriers.

Under Titles II and III, the requirement that at least 50 percent of the tonnage must be carried by U.S.-flag vessels clearly provides balance of payments conservation of the transportation portion of the grant.

Superficially it would appear that the application of preference to Title I shipments requires the Commodity Credit Corporation to pay large differentials (historically they have been about equal in magnitude to the dollar value of the foreign currency received)[13] so that the vessel operators can be assured of receiving revenues from the foreign food recipients. In other words, it appears to require one dollar of differential (not a balance of payments item) for each dollar of balance of payments revenue.

In reality, however, the foreign currencies received are not channeled into the economy as normal revenues would be. All of these currencies are dedicated to U.S. government expenditures in the same country and 75 percent of these expenditures are additional aid grants of one kind or another. In large part, then, Title I is really a *grant* program like Titles II and III for which the U.S. is contributing nearly all costs. Therefore, the preference awarded to U.S. shipping represents a means of conserving for the U.S. balance of payments at least the transportation revenues that are paid to U.S. vessels.

The maintenance of preference on Title IV shipments is somewhat more open to question since the loans granted will presumably be repaid by their foreign recipients. It therefore appears again that the Commodity Credit Corporation must pay one dollar in differential in order to permit U.S. vessel operators to receive one dollar in balance of payments revenue. Nevertheless, the credits under Title IV are long term credits and repayments under them will have no immediate effect on balance of payments. On the other hand, the cargo preference requirement does, at least, provide some short-term balance of payments relief.

(3) *Preference carrying of Department of Defense cargo* – Obviously if the Department of Defense were able to undertake a greater share of its carrying in its own vessels, this would release the large amount of cargo capacity it currently employs without affecting the retention of funds. In other words, the Defense Department's own sealift capacity would retain the same amounts currently retained by the privately owned merchant marine. Whether this is possible is more properly a consideration of defense strategy and budgetary considerations than of balance of payments analysis. Naturally one of the crucial aspects of the question is whether a military transport fleet would permit the rapid build-up of shipping services provided by the use of privately owned vessels and whether trained crews could readily be provided.

In summary, it appears clear that the present cargo preference regulations, as applied to AID and Public Law 480 carrying, *do* exert a favorable effect on the U.S. balance of payments that would be lost if recipient nations were permitted to move the goods received on vessels of their own choice with U.S. financing of the shipping costs. As for the possibility that these recipient nations might be able to finance this transportation to any great extent by themselves, this is extremely unlikely.

Even if recipients of aid were able to finance shipment, the opportunity of obtaining additional commercial revenue from the released space appears severely limited at best. The international trade of the U.S. is not presently constrained by lack of shipping availability. Thus an assumption of increased U.S. exports by reason of increased lift available is questionable unless the ships "made available" were of far greater effectiveness (for example, speed) than the lift now available to U.S. exporters in certain areas. As for increasing the U.S. Merchant Marine's share of total carrying of U.S. commercial trade, this would seem equally doubtful. Most of the vessel space made available by the removal of preference cargo would be on older vessels which are at a competitive disadvantage with foreign flag vessels.

The proposed expansion of the Department of Defense's own sealift capability involves the consideration of many aspects of military and economic policy. This will be the subject of extended analysis elsewhere.

Appendix C-A

U.S. International Shipping Operations in Context: Selected Statistics (Dollars in Millions)

	1966	1965	1964	1963	1962	1961	1960	1959	1958	1957
I. Total Balance of Payments										
Annual Balance	(1,213)	(1,377)	(2,798)	(2,670)	(2,203)	(2,370)	(3,881)	(3,870)	(3,365)	578
II. Balance of Trade Data										
Exports of Merchandise	29,180	26,276	25,288	22,069	20,604	19,936	19,489	16,282	16,264	19,390
Imports of Merchandise	25,507	21,492	18,619	16,992	16,173	14,507	14,732	15,310	12,952	13,291
Balance of Trade	3,673	4,784	6,669	5,077	4,431	5,429	4,757	972	3,312	6,099
III. Gold Flow										
Annual Increase or Drain	(430)	(1,547)	(36)	(392)	(833)	(820)	(1,669)	(1,041)	(2,294)	772
IV. Published International Ocean Transportation Balance of Payments										
Receipts	1,856	1,720	1,733	1,581	1,468	1,331	1,337	1,224	1,317	1,660
Export Freight Earnings	542	519	599	538	479	424	428	359	429	639
Shipments between Foreign Countries	139	152	158	154	177	155	136	140	130	179
Passenger Fares	10	8	11	10	10	9	19	20	24	24
Port Expenditures	1,154	1,032	956	870	792	735	746	698	726	798
Charter Hire	11	9	9	9	10	8	8	7	8	20
Payments	1,932	1,809	1,730	1,636	1,517	1,382	1,333	1,299	1,247	1,217
Import Freight Payments	1,187	1,083	958	888	833	746	780	812	743	717
Passenger Fares	200	210	215	225	229	215	212	183	166	133
Port Expenditures	294	281	317	288	260	231	167	155	170	203
Charter Hire	251	235	240	235	195	190	174	149	168	164
Balance on Account	(76)	(89)	3	(55)	(49)	(51)	4	(75)	70	443

Source: *Statistical Abstract of the United States.*

Note: Parentheses indicate negative.

Appendix C-B
Sources of Data

1. *Office of Business Economics, Department of Commerce* – This agency has the responsibility for compiling and reporting official balance of payments data which is published quarterly in the Federal Reserve Bulletin, in the Annual Statistical Abstract of the United States and in the Department of Commerce's own Balance of Payments Statistical Supplement. In the collection of data, particularly that relating to receipts and payments of foreign operators, the Office of Business Economics is often forced to extrapolate from incomplete reporting and only in recent years has begun to receive relatively complete reporting from many United States vessel operators. These problems were discussed by the Bernstein Committee in its report on balance of payments statistics made to the Bureau of the Budget. The OBE also prepares rough estimates of non-published balance of payments retention items such as inbound freight revenues of United States ocean carriers as well as dissections of total revenues by type of service. Both Dr. Walter Lederer, chief of the balance of payments division, and Mr. Gordon Smith, who prepares the transportation section, emphasized that although these estimates are the best ones possible, given the paucity of reliable reporting, they cannot be considered extremely accurate in any sense.

2. *Joint Economic Committee, Congress of the United States* – During hearings held from April through June of 1965 on discriminatory ocean freight rates and on balance of payments statistics, this committee received testimony from many people, both inside and outside of the federal government, which has been published along with its report on the former subject. In the latter part of 1965, the committee also published a report to it prepared by the Maritime Administration on the importance to the United States fleet of government-generated cargo.

3. *The Maritime Administration* – A crucial document in any study of the balance of payments impact of United States shipping operations is the paper produced by Dr. Peter Schumaier in November 1966 while he was in the Office of Program Planning of the Maritime Administration. It deals with determination of the percentages of freight and passenger revenues which is attributable to port charges. Other reports issued by the Maritime Administration and containing pertinent information are its annual value and tonnage reports, often published in the Survey of Current Business, its tonnage reports on governmental non-defense shipments, the Administration's annual reports, and special papers dealing with the world's merchant fleets, patterns of U.S. trade, foreign-registered ships under effective United States control, and participation of foreign ships in U.S. oceanborne trade.

4. *Commodity Credit Corporation, Department of Agriculture* – This agency publishes an annual report detailing ocean transportation payments made under the four titles of Public Law 480 (the Food for Peace Program. The report shows both the payments made by foreign governments to United States shipping operators and the freight differentials covered by the Department.

5. *Agency for International Development, Department of State* – AID's Office of Material Resources of the Resources Transportation Division publishes annually a cargo preference report outlining shipments made during the previous

fiscal year by tonnage. Mr. Clinton Watson was kind enough to provide parallel information expressed in revenue terms.

6. *Military Sea Transportation Service, Department of the Navy* – In its quarterly report, MSTS provides data on its payments to private firms for different forms of shipping service.

7. *Department of Commerce* – In 1966, Ernst and Ernst was contracted by the Department to prepare a study of unit shipping costs in United States liners from different ports and over different trade routes. Much of the information collected in this investigation is germane to the influence of port charges on the balance of payments impact of United States shipping revenues.

8. *Treasury Department* – The monthly Treasury Bulletin contains reports on gold transactions of the United States.

9. *Department of Transportation* – Captain Ira Dye and Dr. Peter Schumaier were particularly helpful (in discussing aspects of the subject being studied) and provided access to extremely detailed information compiled on 1964 Public Law 480 shipments and on 1964 Department of Defense shipping activities. Similarly detailed information is not compiled for any other year.

One of the major difficulties confronting anyone seeking to quantify the balance of payments impact of United States shipping services in any but a highly superficial manner is the lack of cohesive information. Many governmental agencies are interested in discrete aspects of the subject and may maintain detailed data on these aspects. However, the data do not usually fit together, largely because no single agency has a comprehensive interest in the subject as a whole.

Apart from the inexactness of critical published data, unpublished data provided by the Office of Business Economics must be considered much less reliable than its published data due to the difficulties encountered by that agency in collecting information from foreign operators. These affect the division of revenues and port charges by different types of shipping service—liner, tramp, and tanker.

Furthermore, all data published by the Office of Business Economics on merchant shipping operations are organized by nationality of ship *operator*. For example, once the charter of a foreign-registered vessel has been arranged by a U.S. operator, the balance of payments accounts will record the charter fee as a payment but subsequently and throughout the term of the charter all receipts and port charges accruing to that vessel are treated in the same way as those of U.S.-registered vessels. On the other hand, data prepared by the Maritime Administration and the Bureau of the Census are classified exclusively by flag of registry.

Also complicating attempts to correlate information received from different sources are conflicts in terminology. Many agencies, such as the Office of Business Economics and the Agency for International Development classify shipping services in three groupings—liner, tramp, and tanker. Basically a tramp is a vessel much like a liner but merely one that follows no fixed routing. Today a more indicative and useful classification breakdown would be breakbulk (including liners and tramps); dry bulk cargo; and tanker, but no agency is yet employing this nomenclature. In some Maritime Administration reports, "tramp" has been replaced by the terms "irregular" and "non-liner."

Moreover, data prepared by most sources are on a calendar-year basis but all reports published by the MSTS and AID are on a fiscal-year basis. For simplification in this study, this MSTS and AID data has been treated as if the fiscal year coincided with the calendar year.

There is also occasional variation from the term "port charges" as defined by the Office of Business Economics for the forms BE-29 and BE-30 provided to foreign and United States operators for the reporting of raw data. The Ernst and Ernst study employs the term "port expense" which includes all of the elements of port charges plus vessel cost in port, a factor composed of personnel cost, insurance, repairs and maintenance, stores, fuel, general and administrative expense and depreciation.

Until 1964 not even rough estimates of revenues and port charges by type of shipping service were prepared, thereby rendering it impossible to approximate the balance of payments impact of the different types of service for periods prior to 1964. It should also be recognized that data reporting, at least by United States operators, has grown considerably more complete in the past few years and estimates made for the period 1964 to 1966 are more reliable than those based upon data of the previous years. The information available for 1964 is more complete and detailed than for any other year, largely because of the pressure exerted by the hearings held by the Joint Economic Committee under the direction of Senator Paul Douglas.

Because of the influence of Department of Defense shipping operations on balance of payments impact, particularly during those periods when these operations involve private operators to an unusually high degree, it would be extremely valuable if the Military Sea Transportation Service were to separate in their reporting the following elements:

i) Revenues paid to the different types of services—liner, dry bulk, and tanker.
ii) Revenues paid under berth terms (since these usually entail cargo handling paid for by the ship operator, thus increasing the percentage of revenues applicable to port charges) and the revenues paid under shipping contract (since these are usually cargoes handled on an FIO basis with relatively small percentages of the revenues applicable to port charges).
iii) Revenues paid to the different types of services for chartering, whether it be time or voyage chartering; at present the MSTS quarterly reports indicate the numbers of the different types of vessels chartered by tanker and non-tanker and provide only a total amount for all chartering costs.

Appendix D
Detailed Description
of Cost Assumptions

Vessel and Voyage Expense for "Old" Ships

In order to derive expense data that would be more applicable to the ship types present in the 1968 fleet and remaining in the fleet in 1976, it was necessary to use the information submitted to the Maritime Administration by the subsidized liners on Form 3002 of the MA-172 Schedule.[1] Since the most recent year for which it was possible to secure these data was 1967, a decision to use 1966 and 1967 information was made, both to ensure that the 1967 figures were fairly typical and also to enable us to figure the rate of increase in costs between the two years.

The dollar amounts (and other pertinent data such as freight payable tons, voyage days at sea, etc.) for the revenue and expense detail were tabulated by ship type — those used in the Profile Performance Report (C-1; C-2; Old C-3; New C-3; Old C-4; New C-4[a], C-5 Containership; Victory; Passenger; Cargo and Passenger (as well as Time Charter and Non-subsidized). It should be noted that in a few cases where the reported data covered several ship types it was necessary to allocate the revenue and expense data; this was done on the basis of freight payable tons.[b]

Examination of the 1966 and 1967 ratios (to total vessel operating revenue and to freight payable tons) indicated that the 1967 data were relevant, and these were used in the subsequent calculations. For purposes of estimating the 1976 expense levels for the 1968 ships remaining in the fleet, the 1967 aggregate dollar amounts for vessel expense were used to compute dollar costs per ship for the following ship types — New C-3; New C-4; C-5 Containership. Similarly, the aggregate dollar amounts for the voyage expense items were used to compute cost per freight payable ton.

It was assumed that all vessel-expense-per-ship items, except fuel, and all voyage-expense-per-measurement-ton accounts would be increased 5% per annum between 1967 and 1976. (Note that the increase in total voyage expense per measurement ton between 1966 and 1967 for the ship types remaining in the 1976 fleet was over 14%.) Then the 1976 expense estimates for the above three ship types were weighted by their estimated lift capacities to derive average expense ratios to be used in the *pro forma* profit and loss statements.

Vessel and Voyage Expense for "New" Ships

To establish estimates for the 1976 costs of operating the new containerships entering the fleet in 1968 and subsequent years proved much more difficult.

---

[a]The data for the C-4 Containerships were tabulated separately, but later combined with the New C-4's since they closely resembled that category (and actually represented ore carriers which had been converted to containerships).

[b]The term freight payable tons is used interchangeably with measurement tons in this appendix.

Table D-1

**1967 Vessel Expense for Ship Types
Remaining in Fleet (Dollars per Ship)**

	C-3	C-4	Converted Containership
Wages and Subsistence	$ 676,844	$ 792,606	$ 631,156
Stores	38,060	49,614	192,196
Fuel	157,263	216,111	184,042
Repairs and Maintenance	102,946	119,423	412,847
Insurance	164,189	171,370	260,695
All Other Vessel Expense	7,717	17,963	13,030
Total Vessel Expense	$1,147,019	$1,367,087	$1,693,966

The following assumptions were made regarding the vessel-expense-per-ship figures (based on 1967 data and then compounded 5% per annum, except for fuel):

i) *Wages and subsistence* would amount to 80% of that for the new C-4's in the 1967 fleet (1967: $650,000; 1976: $1,008,400).

ii) *Stores* were estimated at twice the 1967 figure for the new C-4, roughly one-half the figure for the converted containership (1967: $100,000; 1976: $155,100).

iii) *Fuel expense* per ship was assumed to equal $400,000 on a 1967 basis (and was not increased for 1976), as per the following: the breakbulk GPS ship travels 5.6 round trips with a round-trip distance of 13,500 miles, or 75,600 miles per 175-day year, plus 175 days in port; the containership GPS ship was assumed to travel 11 round trips with a round-trip distance of 13,500 miles, or 148,500 miles in 280 days at sea, plus 70 days in port. Since the containership will travel almost twice as many miles per year, fuel cost was assumed to be almost twice the new C-4 cost.

iv) *Repairs, insurance and all other vessel expense* were estimated at $135,000, $300,000 and $25,000, respectively, for 1967 and written up to $209,400, $465,400, and $38,800 for 1976.

Table D-2

**1967 Voyage Expense for Ship Types
Remaining in Fleet (Dollars per
Measurement Ton Carried)**

	C-3	C-4	Converted Containership
Port Expense:			
Agency Fees and Commissions	$ 1.50	$ 0.99	$ 1.08
Wharfage and Dockage	1.03	1.06	0.39
Other Port Expense	1.77	1.42	2.03
Subtotal − Port Expense	$ 4.30	$ 3.47	$ 3.50
Cargo Expense:			
Stevedoring	$ 7.34	$ 7.99	$ 7.44
Other Cargo Expense	3.24	4.83	3.94
Subtotal − Cargo Expense	$10.58	$12.82	$11.38
Other Voyage Expense	1.19	2.01	1.98
Total Voyage Expense	$16.07	$18.30	$16.86

v) *The assumed 1967 total vessel expense* per new containership totals to $1,610,000[c]; the 1976 figure is estimated at $2,277,100.

The estimated containership figures for voyage expense were based roughly on the American President Line data − (adjusted back to 1967, rounded, and then increased 5% per annum, except for stevedoring.)

i) *Base-year stevedoring costs* were estimated at $3.00 per ton, (based on American Mail Lines and U.S. Lines data) and other cargo expense was taken at $3.25 (based on APL data). For 1976, it was assumed that one-half of the

___

[c]It should be noted that the estimated **total** expense figure for 1967 compares closely with that estimated for Delta.

Table D-3

**Estimated 1976 Vessel Expense per
Ship for Ships Entering 1976 Fleet
Prior to 1968**

				Weighted Averages	
	C-3	C-4	Converted Containership	*Alternatives A and B**	*Alternatives C and D†*
Wages and Sub-sistence	$1,050,000	$1,229,600	$ 979,100	$1,144,700	$1,128,700
Stores	59,000	77,000	298,200	101,600	132,500
Fuel	157,300	216,100	184,000	195,000	196,400
Repairs and Maintenance	159,700	185,300	640,500	239,200	301,600
Insurance	254,700	265,800	404,400	281,300	300,600
All Other Vessel Expense	12,000	27,900	20,200	22,300	22,800
Total Vessel Expense	$1,692,700	$2,001,700	$2,526,400	$1,984,100	$2,082,600

*As Is and Increased Funding.   †Extended Benefits and Foreign Build.

stevedoring cost and other cargo expense would increase 5% per annum while the remainder of the stevedoring expense would not increase at all. Thus, the cargo expense figures used for 1976 amounted to $8.90 per ton.[d]

ii) The 1967 APL figure for *port expense* of $1.65 was increased to $2.65 to include agency fees, while the base APL figure of $0.10 for all other voyage expense was increased $0.50 for canal tolls and $0.45 for brokerage expense, giving a 1967 base figure of $3.70 per ton for port and other voyage expense, or a 1976 figure of $5.75 per ton carried.

---

[d]Note that for bulk shipments on containerships a cargo expense figure of $5.20 per ton was used.

Table D-4

**Estimated 1976 Voyage Expense per
Measurement Ton for Ships Entering
1976 Fleet Prior to 1968**

				Weighted Averages	
	C-3	C-4	Converted Containership	*Alternatives A and B**	*Alternatives C and D†*
Cargo Expense	$ 6.70	$ 5.40	$ 5.45	$ 5.75	$ 5.65
Stevedoring & Port Exp.	16.40	19.90	17.65	18.60	18.60
Other Voyage Expense	1.85	3.10	3.05	2.75	2.85
Total Voyage Expense	$24.95	$28.40	$26.15	$27.10	$27.10

Note: For bulk shipments a cargo-handling
expense figure of $5.20 per ton was used
($0.15 for stevedoring costs and $5.05 for
other cargo expense).

*As Is and Increased Funding.

† Extended Benefits and Foreign Build.

iii) Thus, 1976 *per-ton cost figures* for containership voyage expenses are:

	General Cargo	Bulk
Stevedoring and Other Cargo Expense	$ 8.90	$ 5.20
Port and Other Voyage Expense	5.75	5.75
Total Voyage Expense	$14.65	$10.95

**Distribution of Cargo Between "Old" and "New"
Ships**

Having established expense rates for 1976, it was then necessary to make
assumptions regarding the distribution of cargoes between the "old" ships (those
having entered the 1976 fleet prior to 1968 — i.e., principally C-3's, C-4's and
converted containerships) and the "new" ships (the containerships entering the
fleet in 1968 and subsequent years). It was hypothesized that the cargo would
be allocated in proportion to the available lift capacity. Thus, Table D-5 presents
the lift capacities under the respective construction programs, and the percentages
of "old" ship capacity used in estimating the tonnage distribution under the
various program and rate assumptions. (See Table D-6 for tonnage distribution
data.)

Table D-5

Estimated Capacity: 1976
(Measurement Tons in Thousands)

	"Old" Ships	"New" Ships	Total Fleet	Capacity of "Old" Ships as % of Total Capacity
As Is				
Subsidized	19,286	33,430	52,716	36.58%
Other	10,550	14,961	25,511	
Total	29,836	48,391	78,227	
Increased Funding				
Subsidized	19,286	80,544	99,830	19.32%
Other	10,550	14,961	25,511	
Total	29,836	95,505	125,341	
Extended Benefits/ Foreign Build				
Subsidized	19,286	119,245	138,531	
Other	10,550	14,961	25,511	
Total	29,836	134,206	164,042	18.19%

Note: The capacity figures used here do not agree with those presented in Chapter III Tables 3-2 and 3-3, since these are apportioned as of the end of 1967 instead of 1968.

Table D-6

**Estimated Cargo Distribution Between
"Old" and "New" Ships for Alternative
Contruction Programs and Specified
Market Shares: 1976 (Measurement Tons
in Thousands)**

Commercial General Cargo Market Share	General Cargo Carried in:			Bulk Cargo Carried in:			Total Cargo
	"Old" Ships	"New" Ships	Subtotal	"Old" Ships	"New" Ships	Subtotal	
As Is							
15.92%	18,392	31,886	50,278	892	1,546	2,438	52,716
14	16,514	28,630	45,144	892	1,546	2,438	47,582
12	14,560	25,242	39,802	892	1,546	2,438	42,240
10	12,605	21,855	34,460	892	1,546	2,438	36,898
9	11,628	20,161	31,789	892	1,546	2,438	34,227
8	10,651	18,467	29,118	892	1,546	2,438	31,556
7	9,674	16,773	26,447	892	1,546	2,438	28,885
6	8,697	15,079	23,776	892	1,546	2,438	26,214
4	6,743	11,691	18,434	892	1,546	2,438	20,872
3	5,766	9,997	15,763	892	1,546	2,438	18,201
Increased Funding							
33.56%	18,816	78,576	97,392	471	1,967	2,438	99,830
30	16,978	70,902	87,880	471	1,967	2,438	90,318
25	14,398	60,127	74,525	471	1,967	2,438	76,963
20	11,818	49,352	61,170	471	1,967	2,438	63,608
15	9,238	38,577	47,815	471	1,967	2,438	50,253
12	7,690	32,112	39,802	471	1,967	2,438	42,240
11	7,174	29,957	37,131	471	1,967	2,438	39,569
9	6,142	25,647	31,789	471	1,967	2,438	34,227
8	5,626	23,492	29,118	471	1,967	2,438	31,556
7	5,110	21,337	26,447	471	1,967	2,438	28,885
Extended Benefits/ Foreign Build							
52.2%	27,637	124,297	151,934	2,202	9,906	12,108	164,042
40	21,708	97,632	119,340	2,202	9,906	12,108	131,448
30	16,849	75,781	92,630	2,202	9,906	12,108	104,738
25	14,420	64,855	79,275	2,202	9,906	12,108	91,383
20	11,991	53,929	65,920	2,202	9,906	12,108	78,028
18	11,019	49,559	60,578	2,202	9,906	12,108	72,686
16	10,047	45,189	55,236	2,202	9,906	12,108	67,344
15	9,562	43,003	52,565	2,202	9,906	12,108	64,673
14	9,076	40,818	49,894	2,202	9,906	12,108	62,002

Other Deductions

Operating Differential Subsidy

Having derived total vessel and total voyage expense, or total terminated voyage expense, it was next necessary to estimate the 1976 operating differential subsidy for the various options. Based on the 1967 experience, it was assumed that ODS would amount to 65% of the expenditures for wages (including payroll taxes, contributions to welfare plans and subsistence).

Depreciation

To derive the depreciation figure, figures were estimated for the existing (1967) subsidized liner fleet, as shown in Table D-7.

Since the table gives an estimate of $44,100,000 for 1967 depreciation compared to a figure of $44,200,000 reported on Schedule 3001 as depreciation on floating equipment and other ship property, these estimated rates were applied to the pre-1968 ships remaining in the 1976 fleet, giving 1976 depreciation costs for the subsidized liners of $20,850,000, and for all ships remaining of $31,130,000.

To estimate 1976 depreciation for the containerships entering the fleet between the beginning of 1968 and the end of 1976, assumptions were made as shown in Table D-8.

It was further assumed: that the ships would have a 20-year life; that they would enter the fleet at a steady pace so that one-half the annual depreciation cost could be charged the first year, etc. (see Table D-9 for depreciation worksheet); and, based on the 1967 figures, that vessel depreciation would represent about 85% of total depreciation and amortization expense.

Container Leasing

It was assumed: that all containers would be leased; that two sets (2,400) per ship would be sufficient; and that 1976 leasing costs would amount to $400 per container.

Administration and General

Based on the 1967 relationship, 1976 administrative and general costs were estimated at 12% of total vessel operating revenue.

Table D-7

Estimated Annual Depreciation of "Old" Ships

Ship Type	Estimated Annual Depreciation*	No. of Ships in 1967 Subsidized Fleet†
C-1	$ 25,000	4
C-2	49,000	73
Old C-3	125,000	65
New C-3	140,000	40
Old C-4	135,000	27
New C-4	150,000	61
C-5 (converted)	200,000	2
Passenger (Conv.)	400,000	25
P-2 or P-3	600,000	2
P-6	2,200,000	1
Victory	10,000	9
Total		309

*Per ship.
†Estimated from Form 3002 schedules.

Table D-8

Assumptions for Estimating Depreciation on "New" Ships

	As Is	Increased Funding	Extended Benefits/ Foreign Build
No. of New Ships	62	146	226
Cost per Ship (to Owners)	$ 9,450,000	$ 9,450,000	216 @ $ 9,450,000
			8 @ $33,000,000
			2 @ $20,000,000
Total Cost	$585,900,000	$1,379,700,000	$2,345,200,000
Less Residual Value (17%)	99,603,000	234,549,000	398,684,000
Total	$486,297,000	$1,145,151,000	$1,946,516,000

Mortgage Interest

"Old Ships." The following assumptions were used:

i) Down payments of 25% are required for subsidized liners and 12.5% for nonsubsidized ships.
ii) The gross construction costs per ship to the owner were:

	Subsidized Liners	Indirectly- Subsidized Liner/Tramp
C-3	$3,500,000	$7,000,000
C-4	3,750,000	7,500,000
Converted Containership	2,000,000	4,000,000

iii) Average age of the ships in 1976 would be 15 years.
iv) Mortgage interest rate averages 5%.

Based on the above, 1976 mortgage interest for the "old" ships in the subsidized fleet would be $5,100,000 and for all "old" vessels, $9,800,000.

Table D-9

**Depreciation Computations for "New"
Ships for Alternative Construction Programs:
1976 (Dollar Amounts in Thousands)**

	No. of Ships	Cumulative Gross Value	Cumulative Residual Value	Annual Depreciation	Net Value at End of Period
As Is					
1968	7	$ 66,150	$ 54,904.5	$ 1,373	
1969	7	132,000	109,809.0	4,118	
1970	7	198,450	164,713.5	6,863	
1971	7	264,600	219,618.0	9,608	
1972	7	330,750	274,522.5	12,354	
1973	7	396,900	329,427.0	15,099	
1974	7	463,050	384,331.5	17,844	
1975	7	529,200	439,236.0	20,589	
1976	6	585,900	486,297.0	23,139	
Total	62			$110,987, or $111,000	$ 474,900
Increased Funding					
1968	7	$ 66,150	$ 54,904.5	$ 1,373	
1969	17	226,800	188,244.0	6,079	
1970	17	387,450	321,583.5	12,746	
1971	18	557,550	462,766.5	19,609	
1972	17	718,200	596,106.0	26,472	
1973	17	878,850	729,445.5	33,139	
1974	18	1,048,950	870,628.5	40,002	
1975	17	1,209,600	1,003,968.0	46,865	
1976	18	1,379,700	1,145,151.0	53,728	
Total	146			$240,013, or $240,000	$1,139,687
Extended Benefits/ Foreign Build					
1968	8	$ 75,600	$ 62,748	$ 1,569	
1969	26				
	10	625,300	518,999	14,544	
1970	26	871,000	722,930	31,048	
1971	26	1,116,700	926,686	41,245	
1972	26	1,362,400	1,130,792	51,433	
1973	26	1,608,100	1,334,723	61,638	
1974	26	1,853,800	1,538,654	71,834	
1975	26	2,099,500	1,742,585	82,031	
1976	26	2,345,200	1,946,516	92,228	
Total	226			$447,570 or $447,600	$1,897,600

Table D-10

**1976 Mortgage Interest Payments on
"New" Ships (Dollars in Thousands)**

	As Is	Increased Funding	Extended Benefits/ Foreign Build
Cost per Ship to Owners	$9,450	$9,450	216 @ $ 9,450 8 @ $33,000 2 @ $20,000

	As Is		Increased Funding		Extended Benefits/ Foreign Build	
Year	No. of Ships	Net Costs	No. of Ships	Net Costs	No. of Ships	Net Costs
1968	7	$ 49,612	7	$ 49,612	8	$ 56,700
1969	7	49,612	17	120,487	36	450,275
1970	7	49,612	17	120,487	26	184,275
1971	7	49,612	18	127,575	26	184,275
1972	7	49,612	17	120,487	26	184,275
1973	7	49,612	17	120,487	26	184,275
1974	7	49,612	18	127,575	26	184,275
1975	7	49,612	17	120,487	26	184,275
1976	6	42,525	18	127,575	26	184,275
Total	62	$439,421	146	$1,034,772	226	$1,796,900
1976 Interest Payments		$ 24,100		$ 58,200		$ 96,400

"New Ships." Assuming a 7% interest rate, 20-year mortgages, with semi-annual payments, and 25% down payment for all ships, Table D-10 shows how mortgage interest was derived for the "new" ships.

Other Income

Other nonoperating income was assumed to increase 5% per annum from the 1967 level.

Appendix E
Estimated Return
on Investment

The following tables present a range of estimated return on investment for each of the fleet sizes as they vary their participation in the commercial general cargo market. The method of calculating revenue for the fleet is explained in Chapter 4, p. 79, and the expense calculations are presented in Appendix D.

The lower limit of each table is the market share at which the fleet will break even in 1976. The upper limit is the market share at which the fleet will be operating at 100% capacity. These figures are an aggregate of many types of ships, some of which will provide a higher return on investment than is indicated while others will not offer high returns even when the fleet is achieving market shares close to maximum capacity.

Table E-1

Estimated Return on Investment Data for Subsidized Segment Based on As Is Construction Program and Specified Market Shares: 1976 (Dollar in Thousands)

	Market Share of Commercial General Cargo					
	15.92%	14%	12%	10%	9%	8%
Total Revenue	$2,273,565	$2,066,575	$1,847,020	$1,626,222	$1,513,386	$1,402,349
Total Vessel Expense	$ 409,033	$ 409,033	$ 409,033	$ 409,033	$ 409,033	$ 409,033
Total Voyage Expense	994,702	896,108	793,520	690,920	639,626	588,333
Total Terminated Voyage Expense	$1,403,735	$1,305,141	$1,202,553	$1,099,953	$1,048,659	$ 997,366
Terminated Voyage Profit or Loss	$ 869,830	$ 761,434	$ 644,467	$ 526,269	$ 464,727	$ 404,983
Operating Differential Subsidy	141,100	141,100	141,100	141,100	141,100	141,100
Net Terminated Voyage Profit or Loss	$1,010,930	$ 902,534	$ 785,567	$ 667,369	$ 605,827	$ 546,083
Other Deductions:						
Depreciation	$ 51,750	$ 51,750	$ 51,750	$ 51,750	$ 51,750	$ 51,750
Container Leasing	59,520	59,520	59,520	59,520	59,520	59,520
Administrative and General	272,830	247,990	221,640	195,150	181,610	168,280
Other Deductions (including interest)	500	500	500	500	500	500
Subtotal	$ 384,600	$ 359,760	$ 333,410	$ 306,920	$ 293,380	$ 280,050
Earnings before Federal Income Taxes	$ 626,330	$ 542,774	$ 452,157	$ 360,449	$ 312,447	$ 266,033
Federal Income Taxes	125,266	108,555	90,431	72,090	62,489	53,207
Earnings after Federal Income Taxes	$ 501,064	$ 434,219	$ 361,726	$ 288,359	$ 249,958	$ 212,826
Additions to Stockholders' Investment	$1,417,955	$1,275,589	$1,116,692	$ 949,662	$ 858,941	$ 768,568
Stockholders' Investment at End of Year	2,384,859	2,242,493	2,083,596	1,916,566	1,825,845	1,735,472
Return on Investment	21.0%	19.4%	17.4%	15.0%	13.7%	12.3%

Table E-1 (*continued*)

Market Share of Commercial General Cargo

	7%	6.7%	6%	4%	3%	2.84%
Total Revenue	$1,288,037	$1,254,373	$1,173,574	$ 939,540	$ 819,362	$ 799,992
Total Vessel Expense	$ 409,033	$ 409,033	$ 409,033	$ 409,033	$ 409,033	$ 409,033
Total Voyage Expense	537,039	521,656	485,745	383,157	331,864	323,666
Total Terminated Voyage Expense	$ 946,072	$ 930,689	$ 894,778	$ 792,190	$ 740,897	$ 732,699
Terminated Voyage Profit or Loss	$ 341,965	$ 323,684	$ 278,796	$ 147,350	$ 78,465	$ 67,293
Operating Differential Subsidy	141,100	141,100	141,100	141,100	141,100	141,100
Net Terminated Voyage Profit or Loss	$ 483,065	$ 464,784	$ 419,896	$ 288,450	$ 219,565	$ 208,393
Other Deductions:						
Depreciation	$ 51,750	$ 51,750	$ 51,750	$ 51,750	$ 51,750	$ 51,750
Container Leasing	59,520	59,520	59,520	59,520	59,520	59,520
Administrative and General	154,560	150,520	140,830	112,740	98,320	96,000
Other Deductions (including interest)	500	500	500	500	500	500
Subtotal	$ 266,330	$ 262,290	$ 252,600	$ 224,510	$ 210,090	$ 207,770
Earnings before Federal Income Taxes	$ 216,735	$ 202,494	$ 167,296	$ 63,940	$ 9,475	$ 623
Federal Income Taxes	43,347	40,499	33,459	12,788	1,895	125
Earnings after Federal Income Taxes	$ 173,388	$ 161,995	$ 133,837	$ 51,152	$ 7,580	$ 498
Additions to Stockholders' Investment	$ 668,766	$ 639,050	$ 563,524	$ 312,413	$ 120,887	$ 47,726
Stockholders' Investment at End of Year	1,635,670	1,605,954	1,530,428	1,279,317	1,087,791	1,014,630
Return on Investment	10.6%	10.1%	8.7%	4.0%	0.7%	0.0%

Table E-2

Estimated Return on Investment Data for Subsidized Segment Based on Increased Funding Construction Program and Specified Market Shares: 1976 (Dollar in Thousands)

Market Share of Commercial General Cargo

	33.56%	30%	25%	20%	15%
Total Revenue	$4,134,185	$3,764,560	$3,238,523	$2,710,073	$2,173,445
Total Vessel Expense	$ 600,310	$ 600,310	$ 600,310	$ 600,310	$ 600,310
Total Voyage Expense	1,689,044	1,526,809	1,299,038	1,071,266	843,495
Total Terminated Voyage Expense	$2,289,354	$2,127,119	$1,899,348	$1,671,576	$1,443,805
Terminated Voyage Profit or Loss	$1,844,831	$1,637,441	$1,339,175	$1,038,497	$ 729,640
Operating Differential Subsidy	196,100	196,100	196,100	196,100	196,100
Net Terminated Voyage Profit or Loss	$2,040,931	$1,833,541	$1,535,275	$1,234,597	$ 925,740
Other Deductions:					
Depreciation	$ 87,740	$ 87,740	$ 87,740	$ 87,740	$ 87,740
Container Leasing	140,160	140,160	140,160	140,160	140,160
Administrative and General	496,100	451,750	388,620	325,210	260,813
Other Deductions (including interest)	34,600	34,600	34,600	34,600	34,600
Subtotal	$ 758,600	$ 714,250	$ 651,120	$ 587,710	$ 523,313
Earnings before Federal Income Taxes	$1,282,331	$1,119,291	$ 884,155	$ 646,887	$ 402,427
Federal Income Taxes	256,466	223,858	176,831	129,377	80,485
Earnings after Federal Income Taxes	$1,025,865	$ 895,433	$ 707,324	$ 517,510	$ 321,942
Additions to Stockholders' Investment	$2,451,390	$2,204,627	$1,838,542	$1,452,436	$1,027,000
Stockholders' Investment at End of Year	3,418,294	3,171,531	2,805,446	2,419,340	1,993,904
Return on Investment	30.0%	28.2%	25.2%	21.4%	16.1%

Table E-2 (*continued*)

	Market Share of Commercial General Cargo				
	12%	*11%*	*9%*	*8%*	*7.22%*
Total Revenue	$1,847,020	$1,735,987	$1,513,386	$1,402,349	$1,313,598
Total Vessel Expense	$ 600,310	$ 600,310	$ 600,310	$ 600,310	$ 600,310
Total Voyage Expense	706,831	661,276	570,168	524,614	489,080
Total Terminated Voyage Expense	$1,307,141	$1,261,586	$1,170,478	$1,124,924	$1,089,390
Terminated Voyage Profit or Loss	$ 539,879	$ 474,401	$ 342,908	$ 277,425	$ 224,201
Operating Differential Subsidy	196,100	196,100	196,100	196,100	196,100
Net Terminated Voyage Profit or Loss	$ 735,979	$ 670,501	$ 539,008	$ 473,525	$ 420,301
Other Deductions:					
Depreciation	$ 87,740	$ 87,740	$ 87,740	$ 87,740	$ 87,740
Container Leasing	140,160	140,160	140,160	140,160	140,160
Administrative and General	221,640	208,320	181,610	168,280	157,630
Other Deductions (including interest)	34,600	34,600	34,600	34,600	34,600
Subtotal	$ 484,140	$ 470,820	$ 444,110	$ 430,780	$ 420,130
Earnings before Federal Income Taxes	$ 251,839	$ 199,681	$ 94,898	$ 42,745	$ 171
Federal Income Taxes	50,368	39,936	18,980	8,549	34
Earnings after Federal Income Taxes	$ 201,471	$ 159,745	$ 75,918	$ 34,196	$ 137
Additions to Stockholders' Investment	$ 740,250	$ 633,144	$ 394,478	$ 249,538	$ 34,432
Stockholders' Investment at End of Year	1,707,154	1,600,048	1,361,382	1,216,442	1,001,336
Return on Investment	11.8%	10.0%	5.6%	2.8%	0.0%

Table E-3

Estimated Return on Investment Data for U.S-Flag Fleet Based on Extended Benefits Construction Program And Specified Market Shares: 1976 (Dollar in Thousands)

Market Share of Commercial General Cargo

	52.2%	40%	30%	25%	20%
Total Revenue	$6,406,897	$5,152,138	$4,116,013	$3,594,595	$3,070,127
Total Vessel Expense	$ 926,702	$ 926,702	$ 926,702	$ 926,702	$ 926,702
Total Voyage Expense	2,708,581	2,157,234	1,705,438	1,479,546	1,253,654
Total Terminated Voyage Expense	$3,635,283	$3,083,936	$2,632,140	$2,406,248	$2,180,356
Terminated Voyage Profit or Loss	$2,771,614	$2,068,202	$1,483,873	$1,188,347	$ 889,771
Operating Differential Subsidy	240,000	240,000	240,000	240,000	240,000
Net Terminated Voyage Profit or Loss	$3,011,614	$2,308,202	$1,723,873	$1,428,347	$1,129,771
Other Deductions:					
Depreciation	$ 145,100	$ 145,100	$ 145,100	$ 145,100	$ 145,100
Container Leasing	216,960	216,960	216,960	216,960	216,960
Administrative and General	768,830	618,260	493,920	431,350	368,420
Other Deductions (including interest)	77,500	77,500	77,500	77,500	77,500
Subtotal	$1,208,390	$1,057,820	$ 933,480	$ 870,910	$ 807,980
Earnings before Federal Income Taxes	$1,803,224	$1,250,382	$ 790,393	$ 557,437	$ 321,791
Federal Income Taxes	360,645	250,076	158,079	111,487	64,358
Earnings after Federal Income Taxes	$1,442,579	$1,000,306	$ 632,314	$ 445,950	$ 257,433
Additions to Stockholders' Investment	$3,824,014	$2,908,001	$2,088,331	$1,638,737	$1,139,382
Stockholders' Investment at End of Year	5,124,014	4,208,001	3,388,331	2,938,737	2,439,382
Return on Investment	28.2%	23.8%	18.7%	15.2%	10.6%

Table E-3 (*continued*)

Market Share of Commercial General Cargo

	19.5%	18%	16%	15%	14%	13.38%
Total Revenue	$3,016,270	$2,858,266	$2,644,578	$2,537,124	$2,430,481	$2,364,947
Total Vessel Expense	$ 926,702	$ 926,702	$ 926,702	$ 926,702	$ 926,702	$ 926,702
Total Voyage Expense	1,231,071	1,163,292	1,072,931	1,027,763	982,581	954,561
Total Terminated Voyage Expense	$2,157,773	$2,089,994	$1,999,633	$1,954,465	$1,909,283	$1,881,263
Terminated Voyage Profit or Loss	$ 858,497	$ 768,272	$ 644,945	$ 582,659	$ 521,198	$ 483,684
Operating Differential Subsidy	240,000	240,000	240,000	240,000	240,000	240,000
Net Terminated Voyage Profit or Loss	$1,098,497	$1,008,272	$ 884,945	$ 822,659	$ 761,198	$ 723,684
Other Deductions:						
Depreciation	$ 145,100	$ 145,100	$ 145,100	$ 145,100	$ 145,100	
Container Leasing	216,960	216,960	216,960	216,960	216,960	
Administrative and General	361,950	342,990	317,350	304,450	291,660	
Other Deductions (including interest)	77,500	77,500	77,500	77,500	77,500	$ 283,790
Subtotal	$ 810,510	$ 782,550	$ 756,910	$ 744,010	$ 731,220	$ 723,350
Earnings before Federal Income Taxes	$ 296,987	$ 225,722	$ 128,035	$ 78,649	$ 29,978	$ 334
Federal Income Taxes	59,397	45,144	25,607	15,730	5,996	67
Earnings after Federal Income Taxes	$ 237,590	$ 180,578	$ 102,428	$ 62,919	$ 23,982	267
Additions to Stockholders' Investment	$1,082,596	$ 912,418	$ 653,189	$ 500,561	$ 312,801	$ 74,021
Stockholders' Investment at End of Year	2,382,596	2,212,418	1,953,189	1,800,561	1,612,801	1,374,021
Return on Investment	10.0%	8.2%	5.2%	3.5%	1.5%	0.0%

279

Bibliography

Selected Bibliography

All Agencies (Except Department of Defense) Summary of P.L. 664 Exports and Imports (Washington, D.C.: U.S. Department of Commerce, Maritime Administration, Office of Maritime Promotion, Division of Cargo Promotion).

The Balance of Payments Statistics of the United States, A Review and Appraisal, Report of the Review Committee for Balance of Payments Statistics to the Bureau of the Budget, April 1965, pp. 3-5.

Brewer, Stanley H. and de Coster, Don T. *The Nature of Air Cargo Costs* (Seattle: University of Washington, Graduate School of Business, 1967).

Cargo Preference Report, Fiscal Year 1966, July 1, 1965-June 30, 1966 (Washington, D.C.: U.S. Department of State, Agency for International Development, Office of Procurement, Resources Transportation Division).

Changing Patterns in U.S. Trade and Shipping Capacity (Washington, D.C.: U.S. Department of Commerce, Maritime Administration, Office of Statistics, December 1964).

Clones, Angelos J. and McKay, Gary C. "Transportation Transactions in the U.S. Balance of Payments," *Survey of Current Business,* August 1963 (Washington, D.C.: U.S. Department of Commerce).

Committee of American Steamship Lines. *Combined Financial Statement of Lines Holding Operating-Differential Subsidy Contracts Under the Provision of the Merchant Marine Act* (Washington, D.C.: 1958-1967).

Ernst and Ernst. *Review of Merchant Fleet Replacement* (Washington, D.C.: August 1965).

_____. *Selected Commodity Unit Costs for Oceanborne Shipments via Common Carriers (Berth Liner) U.S. Department of Commerce* (Washington, D.C.: n.d.).

Ferguson, Allen R., et al. *The Economic Value of the United States Merchant Marine* (Evanston, Ill.: Northwestern University, Transportation Center, 1961).

Food for Peace, Nineteenth Annual Report on Public Law 480 (Washington, D.C.: House Doc. No. 294-88/2, 1964), pp. 20-21.

Form BE-29, *Foreign Carriers' Ocean Freight Revenues and Expenses in the United States* (Washington, D.C.: U.S. Department of Commerce, Office of Business Economics).

Form BE-30, *Quarterly Report Ocean Freight Revenues and Expenses United States Carriers,* (Washington, D.C.: U.S. Department of Commerce, Office of Business Economics, Balance of Payments Division).

Form MA-172, Schedule 3002, *Vessel Operating Statement* (Washington, D.C.: U.S. Department of Commerce, Maritime Administration, 1958-1968).

Form MA-578, *Voyage Report* (Washington, D.C.: U.S. Department of Commerce, Maritime Administration, 1966-1968).

Gilbert, Jerome. *Foreign Trade at the Port of New York* (New York: Port of New York Authority, 1969).

Gold Reserve Act of January 30, 1934.

The Impact of Government-Generated Cargo on the U.S.-Flag Foreign Trade Fleet for Calendar Year 1964: A Study Presented to the Subcommittee on Federal Procurement and Regulation of the Joint Economic Committee, Congress of the United States (Washington, D.C.: U.S. Department of Commerce, Office of Business Economics).

Lawrence, Samuel. *The U.S. Merchant Marine: Policies and Politics* (Washington, D.C.: The Brookings Institution, 1965).

Litton Systems, Inc. *Ocean Shipping: Demand and Technology Forecast* (Culver City, Calif.: 1968).

Maritime Resources for Security and Trade (Washington, D.C.: U.S. Department of Commerce, Maritime Evaluation Committee, 1963).

Merchant Marine Act, 1936 (49 Stat. 1985, approved June 29, 1936).

The Merchant Marine in National Defense and Trade: A Policy and a Program (Washington, D.C.: U.S. Interagency Maritime Task Force, October 1965).

MSTS Form 4280/6B (rev. 12/68), *Shipping Container Agreement Schedule of Rates* (Washington, D.C.: U.S. Department of the Navy, Military Sea Transportation Service, 1966-1970).

MSTS Quarterly Financial Statistical Report, Code No. MSTS 7700-2, Parts 1 and 2 (Washington, D.C.: U.S. Department of the Navy, Military Sea Transportation Service).

Military Transportation Act, enacted April 28, 1904, amended August 30, 1956.

National Academy of Sciences/National Research Council, Maritime Transportation Conference. *Inland and Maritime Transportation of Unitized Cargo* (Washington, D.C.: 1963).

_____. *Maritime Transportation of Unitized Cargo* (Washington, D.C.: 1959).

Norwegian Shipping News, "Time Charter Index," 2A, 1970, pp. 159-160.

Participation of Merchant Ships, by Flag of Registry, in the Commercial Ocean-borne Foreign Trade of the United States, by Type of Service (Washington, D.C.: U.S. Department of Commerce, Maritime Administration, Office of Statistics, Division of Cargo Data, Reports Branch, 16 August 1965).

Public Law 664 (The Cargo Preference Act), enacted 26 August 1954, amended 31 September 1961.

Schumaier, Peter. *The Contribution of Earnings of U.S. Flag Ships to the Balance of Payments* (Washington, D.C.: U.S. Department of Commerce, Maritime Administration, Office of Program Planning, July 1965).

_____. *Shipping and the U.S. Balance of Payments: Estimating Procedures for Determining Ship Rental and Port Expenditure Portions of Ocean Freight Receipts and Payments for Computations* (Washington, D.C.: U.S. Department of Commerce, Maritime Administration, Office of Program Planning, November 1966).

Sealift Requirement Study (Washington, D.C.: U.S. Department of the Navy, Office of the Chief of Naval Operations, Long-Range Objectives Group, 20 February 1967).

George G. Sharp, Inc. *Final Report: Projection of Ocean Freight Rates* (New York: 9 January 1967).

Ship Exchange Report Status May 1969 (Washington, D.C.: U.S. Department of Commerce, Maritime Administration, Office of Government Aid, 1969).

Ships Registered Under the Liberian, Panamanian, and Hondurian Flags Deemed by the Navy Department to be Under Effective U.S. Control as of March 31, 1967 (Washington, D.C.: U.S. Department of Commerce, Maritime Administration, Division of Trade Studies, Office of Maritime Promotions, 12 June 1967).

A Statistical Analysis of the World's Merchant Fleets, Showing Age, Size, Speed, and Draft by Frequency Groupings as of December 31, 1964, (Washington, D.C.: U.S. Department of Commerce, Maritime Administration, 1965).

Tamagna, Frank M. and Bowles, W. Donald, *The Contribution of the American Maritime Industry to the United States Balance of Payments,* prepared for the Committee of American Steamship Lines, September 1960.

Total Ocean Transportation Payments Financed by CC from Inception of the Program Through December 31, 1966, (P.L. 480) (Washington, D.C.: U.S. Department of Agriculture, Commodity Credit Corporation, February 15, 1967).

U.S. Bureau of the Census. *Statistical Abstract of the United States, 1966, 1967, 1968* (Washington, D.C.: 1966-1968).

U.S. Congress, House. HR 13940, *A Bill to Amend the Merchant Marine Act of 1936*, 90th Cong., 1st Sess., introduced November 1967.

――. HR 15424, *Merchant Marine. Maritime Programs.* 21st Cong., 1st Sess, introduced 23 December 1969.

U.S. Congress, House, Committee on Armed Services, Special Subcommittee on Seapower. *Status of Naval Ships.* 90th Cong., 2nd Sess., 8 October 1968. 91st Cong., 1st Sess., 22-23, 28-30 January 1969.

U.S. Congress, House, Committee on Merchant Marine and Fisheries. *Testimony of the AFL-CIO Maritime Committee on HR 13940.* 90th Cong., 2nd Sess., 7 May 1968.

U.S. Congress, Senate. *Hearings on Department of Agriculture,* Part III. 91st Cong., 1st Sess., pp. 1719-1721.

――. S 2650, *A Bill to Amend the Merchant Marine Act. 1936.* 90th Cong., 1st Sess., introduced November 1967.

――. S 3287, *Shipping. Merchant Marine Act.* 91st Cong., 1st Sess., introduced 22 December 1969.

U.S. Department of Commerce, Maritime Administration. *Annual Reports.* (Washington, D.C.: Government Printing Office, 1958-1968).

U.S. Department of the Navy, Military Sea Transportation Service. *Fiscal Reports* (Washington, D.C.: 1958-1969).

Value and Tonnage of Commercial Cargo Carried in United States Oceanborne Foreign Trade (Washington, D.C.: U.S. Department of Commerce, Maritime Administration, Office of Maritime Promotion, Division of Trade Studies, 1964-1966).

Vessel Inventory Report (Washington, D.C.: U.S. Department of Commerce, Maritime Administration, Office of Trade Promotion, 1958-1968).

Notes

Notes

Notes to Chapter 2

1. The most important of the basic studies are Allen Ferguson, et al., *The Economic Value of the United States* (Evanston, Ill: Transportation Center, Northwestern University, 1961) hereafter cited as Ferguson, *Economic Value*, and Samuel Lawrence, *The U. S. Merchant Marine: Policies and Politics* (Washington, D. C.: The Brookings Institution, 1965). The first of these is a painstaking study of the U. S. subsidized liner industry, conducted just before the economics of ocean shipping was transformed by the advent of containerization. Sharply critical of the liner industry for its commercial failures, this book has been influential in shaping attitudes toward the Merchant Marine since its publication.

Our study departs from this earlier work in two major ways. First, the authors of the Northwestern study reject balance of payments and national security calculations as legitimate benefits, insisting that, at best, these are by-products of any fleet, however maintained, and that the real test of subsidy is its effect on the commercial operation of the fleet. Our view of the Merchant Marine is far broader; we are not involved in efforts to prove the effectiveness or ineffectiveness of one segment over another. As we indicate in Chapter 3, the whole industry receives subsidy of one sort or another; moreover, these subsidies are provided in part to stimulate exactly the benefits which the Northwestern study excludes from its calculations. Second, any quarrels we might have with the methodology of the Northwestern study are rendered superfluous by its obsolescence. This book has studied an industry which no longer exists. Containerization has altered the economics, and the economic value, of the U. S. Merchant Marine from the days of 1961.

Samuel Lawrence's perceptive book discusses the institutions associated with the U. S. Merchant Marine, thereby narrowing the focus to the subsidized industry and the administration of the subsidy program. Concentrating as it does on the mechanisms of subsidy, this book provides little aid in making an economic assessment of industry performance. In this respect, we are closer to the Northwestern study. Lawrence, too, is outdated by the advent of containerization; ours is the first comprehensive study of the Merchant Marine which takes this revolution into account.

There are two major works by the National Academy of Sciences/National Research Council, Maritime Transportation Conference which treat containerization: *Maritime Transportation of Unitized Cargo*, (Washington, D. C.: 1959), publication 745, and *Inland and Maritime Transportation of Unitized Cargo* (Washington, D. C.: 1963), publication 1135. These studies will be cited as NAS,

Unitized Cargo, 1959 and 1963, respectively. Both studies are definitive treatments of the advantages of containerization in the movement of cargo. However, these studies confine themselves to the operational efficiencies of the system, while our study extends the analysis to include the potential for national benefits from the new systems.

2. *Value and Tonnage of Commercial Cargo Carried in United States Oceanborne Foreign Trade* (Washington, D. C.: U. S. Department of Commerce, Maritime Administration, Office of Maritime Promotion, Division of Trade Studies) is one example.

3. Form MA 578, *Voyage Report* (Washington, D. C.: U. S. Department of Commerce, Maritime Administration, 1966-1968).

4. Calculated from Schedule 3002, Vessel Operating Statement, 1960-1966 (Washington, D. C.: U. S. Department of Commerce, Maritime Administration). Hereafter cited as Marad, Schedule 3002, with the date.

Notes to Chapter 3

1. We do recognize that a positive cost/benefit ratio does not necessarily justify an expenditure. As the Northwestern study points out, there may be other ways of obtaining the same kinds of benefits at a lower cost. For example, direct programs for increasing U. S. exports might have been a more effective method for righting the balance of payments deficits. There is also an alternative of seeking other benefits entirely; spending the money from the subsidies of American seamen and American shipyards on food programs for malnourished Americans might return a higher ratio of benefits to costs.

The problem with this approach, particularly for assessing the past, is that it is fruitlessly speculative. A methodology for comparing "what-was" with all the "might-have-beens" is fraught with opportunities for loading the analysis either unfavorably or favorably. We have eschewed this approach in favor of a straightforward assessment of the actual costs and actual benefits. We have compared this ratio informally with other government investments and have found, for example, that it is more favorable than ones used to justify projects of the Army Corps of Engineers.

2. Ferguson, *Economic Value*, p. 45.

3. An average of figures from U. S. Senate, *Hearings on Department of Agriculture Appropriations*, Part III, 91st Cong., 1st Sess., pp. 1719-1721; the U. S. Congress, Joint Economic Committee, "The Impact of Government-Generated Cargo in the U.S.-Flag Foreign Trade for Calendar Year 1964," (printout), 89th Cong., 1st Sess.; Letter of Maritime Administration of November 19, 1965, Title III, Part A.

4. (Washington, D. C.: Department of Commerce, Maritime Administration, Office of Trade Promotion).

5. (Washington, D. C.: Department of Commerce, Maritime Administration, Office of Government Aid). Hereafter cited as Marad, *Status of Fleet*, with dates.

291

6. Ernst & Ernst, *Selected Commodity Costs for Oceanborne Shipments Via Common Carrier* (Washington, D. C., n. d.). Hereafter cited as Ernst & Ernst, *Oceanborne Shipments.*

7. Marad, *Status of Fleet*, 31 December 1968.

8. *Value and Tonnage of Commercial Cargo Carried in United States Ocean-borne Foreign Trade* (Washington, D. C.: Department of Commerce, Maritime Administration, Office of Maritime Promotion, Division of Trade Studies, 1964).

9. This section condenses the previously published analysis of balance of payments benefits, *The Balance of Payment and the U. S. Merchant Marine* (Boston: Harbridge House, 1967). The full publication, which presents the complete methodology and computations used to derive the figures used in this section, is reprinted in Appendix C.

10. U. S. Congress, House, Committee on Armed Services, Special Subcommittee on Seapower, *Status of Naval Ships,* 90th Cong., 2nd Sess., Oct. 8, 1968, p. 138-139.

11. Ferguson, et al., Economic Value, p. 142.

12. Calculated from MSTS Form 4280/6B (Rev 12/68), *Shipping/Container Agreement Schedule of Rates* (Washington, D. C.: Department of the Navy, Military Sea Transportation Service, 1966-1970).

Notes to Chapter 4

1. (Culver City, Calif., 1968). Hereafter cited as Litton, *Ocean Shipping.*

2. (Washington, D. C.; October 1965). Hereafter cited as Interagency Task Force, *Policy and Program.*

3. (Washington, D. C.: Department of the Navy, Office of the Chief of Naval Operations, Long Range Objectives Group, 20 February 1967). Hereafter cited as Navy, *Sealift.*

4. Litton, *Ocean Shipping*, pp. 2-38, 2-39, 2-51, 2-65.

5. Navy, *Sealift,* Table II-2, p. II-8, and Interagency Task Force, *Policy and Program,* Exhibit 1.

6. *Ibid.*

7. Stanley H. Brewer and Don T. deCoster, *The Nature of Air Cargo Costs* (Seattle: Graduate School of Business Administration, University of Washington, 1967), p. 6.

8. U. S. Bureau of the Census, *Statistical Abstract of the United States: 1968* (Washington, D. C.: Government Printing Office, 1968).

9. (49 Stat. 1985, approved June 29, 1936).

10. H. R. 13940, *A Bill to Amend the Merchant Marine Act, 1936,* 90th Cong., 1st Sess., and S. 2650, *A Bill to Amend the Merchant Marine Act, 1936,* 90th Cong., 1st Sess.

11. Interagency Task Force, Policy and Program.

12. *Maritime Resource for Security and Trade* (Washington, D. C.: January 1963).

13. U. S. House, Committee on Merchant Marine and Fisheries, *Testimony of the AFL CIO Maritime Committee on HR 13940,* 90th Cong., 2nd Sess., 7 May 1968.

14. HR 15424, *Merchant Marine-Maritime Programs,* 91st Cong., 1st Sess., 23 December 1969. S3287, *Shipping-Merchant Marine Act-Amendment,* 91st Cong., 1st Sess., 22 December 1969.

15. The dates of construction of each ship in the 1968 fleet, as well as the design designation and the dates of conversion (if any), were available from the Marad printout, *Status of Fleet,* 31 December 1968, plus information secured from the Office of Trade Promotion.

Notes to Chapter 5

1. NAS-NRC, *Unitized Cargo,* 1963, p. 39.

Notes to Appendix A

1. Jerome Gilbert, *Foreign Trade at Port of New York* (New York: Port of New York Authority, 1969).

Notes to Appendix B

1. Ernst & Ernst, *Oceanborne Shipping.*

Notes to Appendix C

Part III

1. Balance of payments statistics in this report are taken from the *Statistical Abstract of the United States, 1966* (Washington, D. C.: U. S. Bureau of the Census, 1966), except as otherwise noted. Cited hereafter as Statistical Abstract.

2. By calculation.

3. *Statistical Abstract.*

4. Gold Reserve Act of January 30, 1934; *Treasury Bulletin May 1967* (Washington: U. S. Treasury Department, Office of the Secretary, May, 1967), p. 30.

5. *Statistical Abstract.*

6. *Ibid.*

7. *Form BE-30, Quarterly Report Ocean Freight Revenues and Expenses United States Carriers* U. S. Department of Commerce, Office of Business Economics, Balance of Payments Division (one page form). Cited hereafter as Form BE-30.

8. Merchant Marine Act, 1936 (49 Stat. 1985, approved June 29, 1936).

9. Military Transportation Act, enacted April 28, 1904, amended August 10,

1956; Public Law 664 (The Cargo Preference Act), enacted August 26, 1954, amended September 31, 1961.

Part IV

1. *The Impact of Government-Generated Cargo on the U. S.-Flag Foreign Trade Fleet for Calendar Year 1964: A Study Presented to the Subcommittee on Federal Procurement and Regulation of the Joint Economic Committee, Congress of the United States* (Washington: U. S. Department of Commerce, Office of Business Economics). Cited hereafter as Government Generated Cargo.

2. *Changing Patterns in U. S. Trade and Shipping Capacity* (Washington: U. S. Department of Commerce, Maritime Administration, Office of Statistics, December 1964), p. 12. Cited hereafter as Changing Patterns.

3. *Form BE-30.*

4. C. Peter Schumaier, *Shipping and the U. S. Balance of Payments: Estimating Procedures for Determining Ship Rental and Port Expenditure Portions of Ocean Freight Receipts and Payments for Computations* (Washington: Office of Program Planning, Maritime Administration, November 1966). Cited hereafter as Shipping.

5. Ernst and Ernst, *Selected Commodity Unit Costs for Oceanborne Shipments via Common Carriers (Berth Liner)* U.S. Department of Commerce (Washington: n. d.). Cited hereafter as Commodity Unit Costs.

6. Form MA-172, U. S. Department of Commerce, Maritime Administration.

7. *Shipping*, p. 1.

8. *Ibid.*, p. 3.

9. *Ibid.*, p. 4.

10. *Ibid.*

11. *Ibid.*

12. *Ibid.*, p. 5.

13. *Ibid.*, p. 6

14. *Ibid.*, p. 7.

15. *Statistical Abstract*, p. 599.

16. Estimates furnished at an interview by Gordon Smith, Balance of Payments Section, Office of Business Economics, U. S. Department of Commerce, June 26, 1967.

17. See the reports for calendar year 1964, 1965, and 1966 entitled *Value and Tonnage of Commercial Cargo Carried in United States Oceanborne Foreign Trade* (Washington: U. S. Department of Commerce, Maritime Administration, Office of Maritime Promotion, Division of Trade Studies, 1964, 1965, 1966).

18. *Shipping*, p. 4.

19. *1966 Annual Report of the Maritime Administration,* (Washington: U. S. Department of Commerce, Maritime Administration), p. 101. Cited hereafter as MARAD.

20. *Commodity Unit Costs*, p. 8.

21. *Ibid.*

22. *Ibid.*, pp. 55, 56, 64, 65.
23. *Changing Patterns,* Table 8, p. 21.
24. *Ibid.*, p. 12.

Part V

1. *Government-Generated Cargo.*
2. *Ibid.*
3. *Ibid.,* unpublished documentation.
4. *Shipping.*
5. *Government-Generated Cargo,* unpublished documentation.
6. *M. S. T. S. Quarterly Financial Statistical Report,* Code No. M. S. T. S. 7700-2, Parts 1 and 2 (Washington: Department of the Navy, Military Sea Transportation Service).
7. *MARAD,* p. 99.
8. Cargo Preference Report, Fiscal Year 1966, July 1, 1965 – June 30, 1966 (Washington: Agency for International Development, Office of Procurement, Resources Transportation Division).
9. *Food for Peace, Nineteenth Annual Report on Public Law 480* (Washington: House Document No. 294-88/2, 1964), pp. 20-21.
10. *Ibid.*, p. 61.
11. *Ibid.*, p. 77.
12. *Ibid.*, p. 82.
13. *Total Ocean Transportation Payments Financed by CC From Inception of the Program Through December 31, 1966* (P. L. 480) (Washington: United States Department of Agriculture, Commodity Credit Corporation, February 15, 1967).

Notes to Appendix D

1. Marad, Schedule 3002. Approval to use the material from these statements filed with the Maritime Administration was secured from all 14 subsidized shipping companies.

Glossary

Glossary

AID cargo – Cargo shipped under the foreign aid programs of the Agency for International Development of the Department of State; these programs employ both grants and loans.

balance of payments – An accounting framework for registering transactions between the United States government and its citizens with foreign governments and foreign citizens; if out flows exceed inflows, the balance of payments is said to be negative and unfavorable. This report uses the term balance of payments in a broader way, including dollar retention as well as dollar receipts in the balance.

balance of trade – The difference between the values of total exports of goods and services and total imports of goods and services; if the value of a country's exports exceeds the value of its imports, its balance of trade is said to be positive and favorable.

bare boat charter – Hire of a vessel without a crew.

bilateralism – A policy which requires that trade between two nations be carried in ships bearing the flag of one of the trading partners. *Cf.* third-flag fleets.

breakbulk – Packaged cargo that must be stowed aboard a ship. *Cf.* dry bulk, container.

C and F – Export quotation terms under which the price quoted by the exporter includes the cost of ocean transportation to the port of destination.

cabotage – Coastal maritime transportation within one country restricted to vessels of domestic registry.

Capital Reserve Fund – A tax-deferred fund in which directly-subsidized firms are required to deposit funds to finance ship replacement.

cargo preference – An indirect subsidy program which reserves government-impelled cargo for U.S.-flag vessels only if their rates are competitive with world rates.

charter fees – Payments for the hire of a vessel; payment is made by the operator to the owner.

CIF – Cost of insurance and freight. Export quotation terms in which the price quoted by the exporter includes the costs of ocean transportation to the port of destination and complementary insurance coverage.

commercial and other government-sponsored cargoes – The total of non-governmental cargoes and those governmental cargoes other than the one originated by the Department of Defense, AID, and the Department of Agriculture under PL 480.

conferences – International organizations of maritime shipping firms which set standard rates and supervise other practices.

construction differential subsidy (CDS) – A direct subsidy to offset financial penalties of construction in American shipyards, and therefore of benefit to these shipyards alone. The subsidy is given to selected liner firms holding contracts with the government.

containers – Standard units of cargo packaging similar in size to truck trailers but lacking wheels. Their introduction has revolutionized ship design, port systems, and the economics of the transportation industry. *Cf.* breakbulk.

conversion – The refitting of a breakbulk ship or tanker to carry containers.

direct subsidies – Payments which are appropriated by Congress to maintain parity of cost between U.S.-flag ship construction and operating expenses and those of foreign-flag operators. The primary mechanisms are construction differential subsidy and operating differential subsidy.

DOD – Department of Defense.

dollar retention – The avoidance of dollar payments to foreign sources through the employment of U.S. products and services.

dry bulk – Cargoes that can be placed aboard ship unpackaged, such as agricultural grains and mineral ores; handled by highly automated loading equipment and usually carried in full shipload lots.

export freight receipts – Revenues received by ocean freight carriers for transporting exports.

FAS – Free alongside ship. Export quotation terms under which the price quoted by the exporter includes all costs incurred in delivering the merchandise to shipside ready for loading at the port of embarkation.

FIO – Free in and out. Export quotation terms under which the responsibility of the exporter includes the costs of loading the merchandise into the vessel at the port of embarkation and the costs of unloading it at the port of destination.

flags of convenience – Sometimes called flags of necessity; those nations whose vessel registration regulations and tax structures make them desirable places for foreign owners to register their vessels. See PANLIBHON.

flags of convenience fleets – Those vessels registered under the flags of convenience but whose beneficial owners are nationals of other countries.

foreign-flag shipping – Vessels owned, operated, and manned by nationals of countries other than the United States.

foreign-to-foreign revenue – Revenue earned for the carrying of freight loaded in one foreign port for delivery in another foreign port. *Cf.* third-flag fleets.

general agency agreements (GAA) and contract operations – Agreements between the U.S. government and U.S. shipping companies under which the shipping companies agree to man and operate vessels for the government. General agency agreements usually pertain to liner-type vessels of the Reserve Fleet; contract operations, to Navy Department tankers.

general cargo — Mark and count goods. See Appendix A for examples. *Cf.* breakbulk, dry bulk.

General Purpose Ship — A standard unit of measure for annual ship capacity developed for this study. See Appendix B for a full discussion of GPS.

high technology ships — LASH/SEABEE and container vessels. These ships apply new ship design and cargo handling concepts to international freight service. *Cf.* breakbulk.

impact — The sum of net foreign exchange receipts and net dollar retention.

import freight receipts — Revenues received by ocean freight carriers for transporting imports.

indirect subsidies — Subsidies which are not appropriated directly by Congress but which involve the provision of goods or services to U.S. operators. Included are rate preference, cargo preference, and ship exchange programs.

intermodalism — The concept of transportation as a door-to-door service rather than a point-to-point system. As the name implies, the movement of goods is coordinated among different modes to insure rapid and efficient transportation.

irregular service — Used interchangeably with tramp service; composed of vessels especially designed to carry dry bulk cargoes such as ores and grains as well as liner-type vessels operated without fixed itinerary or schedule.

LASH, SEABEE — Two types of vessels which carry barges. LASH is Prudential Lines' design; SEABEE is Lykes' entry. The ocean-going vessel acts as a shuttle between ports, taking on and discharging the barges, which navigate the port systems.

liner service — Composed of vessels carrying breakbulk cargo over fixed itineraries on regular schedules.

load factor — A measure of vessel utilization. The ratio of tons carried to annual ship capacity.

measurement ton — A unit of capacity related to cargo density. For purposes of this study general cargo is defined as two measurement tons to each long ton; defense cargo is also calculated at two to one; bulk at one to one.

Military Sea Transportation Service (MSTS) — An agency of the Department of the Navy charged with arranging the transportation of men and materiel on ocean-going vessels.

National Defense Reserve Fleet — Ships held by the Navy and put into service under GAA.

net charter fees — The difference between charter fees paid and charter fees received.

nonliner service — Composed of irregular service and tanker service. For purposes of this study only irregular service is included.

operating differential subsidy (ODS) — A direct subsidy designed to offset higher operating costs of U.S.-flag operators, primarily caused by requirements of the use of U.S. labor on U.S.-flag ships.

PANLIBHON — Acronym for the principal flags of convenience used by U.S. shipowners, which are those of Panama, Liberia, and Honduras. Through government agreements vessels beneficially owned by U.S. entities revert to U.S. control in times of national emergencies.

port charges — Amounts paid by the ship from its revenues for the services it purchases in port, such as cargo handling, wharfage, pilotage, fuel, loading, and taxes.

Public Law 480 cargoes — Cargoes carried under Public Law 480, the enabling act for the Food for Peace program.

rate preference — An indirect subsidy which reserves government-impelled cargoes for U.S.-flag ships at higher than world rates.

rebates — A practice of returning a percentage of shipping charges to steady customers. This is outlawed for U.S.-flag firms.

recapture — A provision of the Merchant Marine Act of 1936 that requires directly-subsidized lines to return to the government half of any profits in excess of 10% return on capital necessarily employed, up to the amount of subsidy.

RESPOND — A proposal for a planned schedule of availability of sealift capacity for various levels of DOD demand short of all-out war.

ship exchange — An indirect subsidy which permits U.S.-flag operators to exchange older or smaller vessels to the National Defense Reserve Fleet and purchase at a discount newer or larger vessels from this same fleet. This provision, which expires this year, has been an important mechanism in the replacement of ships in the indirectly-subsidized fleet.

shipping contract and berth term — Terms employed for the carrying of Department of Defense cargo; under berth term the cargo is treated much as ordinary commercial cargo; under shipping contract vessel space is contracted for a stated period of time at a negotiated rate.

tanker service — Composed of vessels designed principally for carrying liquid bulk cargoes; some vessels in tanker service are equally suitable for carrying dry bulk cargo as well. Only in the latter instance are they considered in this study.

third-flag fleets — Ocean carriers that participate in trade between trading partners other than the one whose flag they bear. Norway, Great Britain, and Greece are active in this trade. *Cf.* bilateralism.

time and voyage charters — The hiring of U.S.-flag vessels by the Department of Defense; time charters are for stated periods of time while voyage charters cover only a single voyage.

time series analysis — A statistical technique of projecting future performance based on past performance.

trade-in, trade-out — The exchange of vessels into and out of the Reserve Fleet by U.S.-flag operators under the terms of the Ship Exchange Program.

trade route concept — The requirement that directly-subsidized operators serve specified ports with some definite frequency. There are 29 trade routes at present, although several are combined operationally into trade areas.

tramp service — See irregular service.

transportation companies — Carriers that are components of an intermodal system on a cooperative basis.

turnaround — The round trip time of a vessel including loading and unloading.

vessel cost in port — Composed of port charges plus the portion of other ship costs such as wages, depreciation and consumption of stores incurred during stays in port.

vessel revenue — The portion of total ship revenue attributable to the ship and the services it provides; derived by subtracting port charges from total revenue.

About the Authors

James R. Barker, Vice President and Director of the Transportation Services Group at Harbridge House, Inc., during the period this study was conducted, is now Executive Vice President of Temple, Barker & Sloane, Inc. He is a graduate of Columbia University in economics with an MBA degree with distinction from Harvard School of Business Administration.

Robert Brandwein, project director for this study, is a Vice President of Harbridge House, Inc. He received a bachelor's degree in economics from Cornell University, received the master's degree in economics from Brooklyn College, and has completed course work toward a doctorate in economics at The American University.